The Morality of Defensive Force

Jonathan Quong is Professor of Philosophy and Law at the University of Southern California. He taught previously at the University of Manchester. He is an associate editor for *Philosophy & Public Affairs*, an associate editor for *Ethics*, and an area editor for *Pacific Philosophical Quarterly*.

T0355140

'Among its many virtues, *The Morality of Defensive Force* offers a sustained and powerful critique of the moral responsibility account.'

Michael Otsuka, *Criminal Law and Philosophy*

'*The Morality of Defensive Force* is packed with forceful, novel arguments. It will no doubt become a cornerstone of work on the justifications and limits of defensive harm. It strikes a great balance between being accessible to those who want to pick it up for a particular topic—for example, those interested only in the necessity condition, the bearing of evidence on rights, or the means principle— and at the same time being a rewarding, well-integrated read.'

Joseph Bowen, *Ethics*

The Morality of Defensive Force

JONATHAN QUONG

OXFORD
UNIVERSITY PRESS

Great Clarendon Street, Oxford, OX2 6DP,
United Kingdom

Oxford University Press is a department of the University of Oxford.
It furthers the University's objective of excellence in research, scholarship,
and education by publishing worldwide. Oxford is a registered trade mark of
Oxford University Press in the UK and in certain other countries

© Jonathan Quong 2020

The moral rights of the author have been asserted

First published 2020
First published in paperback 2022

Published in the United States of America by Oxford University Press
198 Madison Avenue, New York, NY 10016, United States of America

British Library Cataloguing in Publication Data
Data available

Library of Congress Cataloging in Publication Data
Data available

ISBN 978-0-19-885110-3 (Hbk.)
ISBN 978-0-19-288331-5 (Pbk.)

For Becca

Contents

Acknowledgements

I have been working on this book for a long time, and several institutions and a lot of people have generously helped me along the way.

I was lucky to have several periods of leave that allowed me to work on the manuscript. In 2010–11 I was a Laurance S. Rockefeller Visiting Faculty Fellow at Princeton's University Center for Human Values. In the summer of 2012 I was a Harsanyi Visiting Fellow at the Australian National University's Centre for Moral, Social and Political Theory. In 2012–13 I held a Leverhulme Trust Research Fellowship. And in the fall of 2016 I had a sabbatical from my home institution, USC, which I spent as a visiting scholar in the Philosophy Department at Harvard. I'm very grateful to all of these institutions for providing the support that helped make the work on this book possible.

I'm also very thankful to my editor at OUP: Peter Momtchiloff. Peter first approached me about this book in April 2014, and I think I told him at that time that it wasn't too far from being finished. He is, I am very sure, accustomed to philosophers who don't meet their own deadlines, but I'm nevertheless very appreciative of the patience he has shown me, and for his faith in the project.

I would also like to thank the amazingly talented Renée Jorgensen Bolinger for designing the wonderful cover art for the book.

For many useful comments and conversations I am very grateful to: Christian Barry, Saba Bazargan-Forward, Endre Begby, Selim Berker, Renée Jorgensen Bolinger, Luc Bovens, Kim Brownlee, Susanne Burri, Sarah Buss, Richard Child, Tom Christiano, Matthew Clayton, David Cummiskey, Louis deRosset, Tyler Doggett, Cécile Fabre, Kim Ferzan, Joanna Firth, Helen Frowe, Jerry Gaus, John Goldberg, Peter Graham, Elizabeth Harman, Marcus Hedahl, Deborah Hellman, Joe Horton, Thomas Hurka, Leora Katz, Nicola Kemp, Leslie Kendrick, Brian Kogelman, Niko Kolodny, Christine Korsgaard, Christopher Kutz, Seth Lazar, R. J. Leland, Christian List, Graham Long, Andrei Marmor, Dan McDermott, Jeff McMahan, David Miller, Chris Mills, Tim Mulgan, Liam Murphy, Kristi Olson, John O'Neill, Mike Otsuka, Jonathan Parry, Govind Persad, Ryan Pevnick, Michael Rabenberg, Ketan Ramakrishnan, Mark Reiff, Massimo Renzo, Arthur Ripstein, Jake Ross, Ben Saunders, Samuel Scheffler, Paul Schofield, Micah Schwartzman, Tom Sinclair, Nic Southwood, Hillel Steiner, Uwe Steinhoff, Zofia Stemplowska, Rebecca Stone, Victor Tadros, Patrick Tomlin, Chad Van Schoelandt, Alec Walen, Steve Wall, Gary Watson, Ralph Wedgwood, Steve de Wijze, Andrew Williams, Gideon Yaffe, and a number of anonymous reviewers.

Some people from this list deserve special thanks. Chris Mills organized a workshop at the University of Warwick on a draft of the manuscript in

February 2018. Susanne Burri, Cécile Fabre, Helen Frowe, Jeff McMahan, Mike Otsuka, and Victor Tadros agreed to participate, and each offered extremely perceptive comments on the manuscript. I'm so grateful to each of them, and to Chris, for investing so much time in helping me with the book.

I owe additional thanks to Victor and Jonathan Parry, who served as the two reviewers of the manuscript for OUP. Victor and Jonathan each provided immensely helpful comments that led, I hope, to many improvements at a relatively late stage.

I am also deeply indebted to Cécile, Jeff, and Mike. When I first started working on this topic more than ten years ago, they each provided me with the encouragement that I needed. Each of them has also provided extensive and penetrating comments on virtually everything that I have written on this topic, often suffering through several versions of the same material. That they have each been so extraordinarily generous will not be a surprise to anyone who knows them. I really can't thank them enough.

I also owe special debts of gratitude to Tom Sinclair and Zofia Stemplowska. It's hard to overstate how much they have each helped me during the time I've been working on this book. They have provided me with way more commentary, insight, and encouragement than I deserve. I'm amazingly lucky, and so happy, to count them as friends.

Finally, I can't express how much I owe to Becca. She is my best critic and my biggest supporter. She has endured thousands of conversations and dozens of drafts about defensive force, and has helped me work through every idea in the book. She makes me better than I am, and I dedicate the book to her.

Material from the following papers has been revised for inclusion in the book:

'Agent-Relative Prerogatives to Do Harm.' *Criminal Law and Philosophy*, Volume 10, Issue 4, 815–29, doi: 10.1007/s11572-014-9345-y. Reprinted by permission from Springer: Copyright © 2014, Springer Science+Business Media Dordrecht.

'Proportionality, Liability, and Defensive Harm.' *Philosophy & Public Affairs*, Volume 43, Issue 2, 144–73, doi: 10.1111/papa.12056. Copyright © 2015, Wiley Periodicals, Inc., reprinted with permission.

'Rights Against Harm.' *Proceedings of the Aristotelian Society, Supplementary Volume*, Volume 89, Issue 1, 249–66, doi: 10.1111/j.1467-8349.2015.00252.x. Reprinted by courtesy of the Editor of the Aristotelian Society: Copyright © 2015.

'Liability to Defensive Harm.' *Philosophy & Public Affairs*, Volume 40, Issue 1, 45–77, doi: 10.1111/j.1088-4963.2012.01217.x. Copyright © 2012, Wiley Periodicals, Inc., reprinted with permission.

'Killing in Self-Defense.' *Ethics*, Volume 119, Issue 3, 507–37, doi: doi.org/10.1086/597595. Copyright © 2009, the University of Chicago Press, reprinted with permission.

1
Introduction

Albert is angry because Betty has refused to go on a date with him. As an act of revenge, he is going to wrongfully assault her, an assault that will cause serious harm. There is no time to call the police, but Betty can avert Albert's wrongful assault by using defensive force. Under these conditions almost everyone, bar pacifists, agrees that it is permissible for Betty to use some defensive force, even if doing so causes Albert serious harm.

Although the moral permissibility of using defensive force, at least in cases like this one, is widely accepted, it raises a host of difficult questions. What is the moral basis for the permissible use of defensive force? Wrongful attackers like Albert, it seems, are liable to defensive force—that is, they have forfeited claims against the imposition of such force—but what are the necessary and sufficient conditions to render oneself liable to defensive force? Most of us believe that defensive force, even when used against an unjust aggressor, must be proportionate in order to be permissible, but what makes this true, and on what basis are judgements of proportionality determined? Most of us also believe it is wrong to use defensive force when doing so is unnecessary, but again, the justification for this constraint is not obvious, nor is it clear what it means for defensive force to be unnecessary.

This book aims to answer these questions, among others, and thus to provide an account of the main moral principles that govern the permissible use of defensive force by individuals.

1.1 Defensive Force in Context

There is a strong presumption that it's wrong to deliberately harm others, especially when doing so would normally infringe a person's moral rights. A powerful justification is required to overcome this presumption. In this respect defensive force resembles punishment—perhaps the only other case where it's widely believed to be permissible to deliberately inflict harm on others in ways that would normally infringe a person's moral rights.

But the analogy to punishment breaks down, at least with respect to the philosophical literature. A longstanding and well-developed debate regarding the justification of punishment includes consequentialist, retributivist, and communicative accounts, along with various hybrid theories. It's fair to say that

The Morality of Defensive Force. Jonathan Quong, Oxford University Press (2020). © Jonathan Quong.
DOI: 10.1093/oso/9780198851103.001.0001

philosophers have spent a lot of time developing normative principles or theories regarding the justification of punishment. The same is not true regarding the morality of defensive force. The reasons for this may be partly a path-dependent quirk of academic philosophy. But it may also be that there is no well-developed debate—with rival theories—about the justification of defensive force because the answer seems too obvious. When considering punishment part of what generates the puzzle is the way different theories seem to pull us in opposite directions. Consequentialists look at the harm caused by punishment and ask: What good, if any, will it do in the future? Retributivists look at the harm caused by punishment and ask: How could this be a fitting response to what the wrongdoer has done? Given the temporal structure of punishment—we punish someone after a crime has been committed—these rival moral perspectives seem destined to lead to sharply different views regarding the necessary and sufficient conditions for justified punishment.

But when contemplating the use of defensive force, consequentialist and non-consequentialist considerations might seem largely congruent. Defensive force is typically used to prevent a wrongful threat before it eventuates, or to minimize the severity of a wrongful threat in progress. Justified uses of defensive force will thus typically produce good outcomes, but they also protect individual moral rights, and seem a fitting response to attempted wrongdoing. Likewise, unjustified uses of defensive force—for example defensive force that is disproportionate or unnecessary—can be condemned both for failing to maximize the good, and also for violating individual moral rights. The main rival moral theories thus seem to converge, for the most part, regarding the use of defensive force, and this perhaps explains the lack of a well-established debate regarding the overall justification of defensive force.

What has emerged instead is an increasingly sophisticated debate about the more specific conditions that are widely accepted as regulating the permissible use of defensive force, in particular liability, proportionality, and necessity. There are complex rival views about the moral basis of liability to defensive harm, rival accounts of the necessity and proportionality constraints, and different positions regarding the appropriate relationship between the three constraints.

These debates are important. It's essential to understand what makes the imposition of defensive harm unnecessary, or why someone cannot be liable to disproportionate defensive force. The bulk of this book is concerned with developing answers to these types of questions. But I also think we can't fully answer the more specific questions without stepping back and considering some deeper questions:

- How do the principles regulating defensive force cohere with other parts of morality? For example, are the principles regulating defensive force derived from other, more general moral principles, or are they *sui generis*?

- What is the fundamental moral basis for the use of defensive force? Is it, for example, a means of equitably distributing harm or risk of harm? Is it a way to minimize the amount of unjust harm people suffer? Is it simply an extension of individuals' moral rights over their bodies and property?

One of my aims in this book is to show that we cannot develop an adequate account of the morality of defensive force without addressing these deeper questions.

Consider, for example, the following question: How much harm is it proportionate for a defensive agent to impose on a liable attacker? Although there is widespread agreement that defensive harm must be proportionate in order to be permissible, there are few explicit accounts (apart from appeals to intuition) of *why* defensive force must be proportionate, and similarly few attempts to explain exactly how judgements of proportionality are determined. Given the central role proportionality plays in the morality of defensive force, this lacuna is surprising.

It is less surprising, however, once we think about what would be needed to provide the requisite explanations. To know why defensive force must be proportionate and how judgements of proportionality are determined, we must take a substantive position on why people should be permitted to use defensive force at all. Suppose the explanation is this: defensive force is justified because it is one way of ensuring that people are made to bear the costs that arise from their voluntary decisions. On this view, the morality of defensive force is, at least in large part, a special case of distributive justice. We ought to allocate burdens and benefits in accordance with the correct principles of distributive justice, and cases where defensive harm might be deployed are merely instances where there are unavoidable harms to be distributed. As Jeff McMahan puts it, 'the determination of liability to defensive harm is a matter of justice in the ex ante distribution of unavoidable harm'.[1] If we accept this view about the morality of defensive force, we are then in a position to develop an explanation of proportionality. Defensive harm is proportionate, on this view, when the wrongful attacker is made to bear only those costs created by his voluntary choices—it would be disproportionate to impose harms on an attacker when he cannot be held morally responsible for the creation of those harms.

I think there are serious problems with this general view of defensive force and the implications of this view for proportionality, and I develop my concerns about proportionality in Chapter 4. But my point here is more limited. A full explanation of why defensive force must be proportionate, and how proportionality is determined, depends on one's deeper view regarding the justification of defensive force. If we abstain from tackling the deeper question, our ability to

---

[1] Jeff McMahan, 'Self-Defense Against Justified Threateners', in *How We Fight: Ethics in War*, ed. Helen Frowe and Gerald Lang (Oxford: Oxford University Press, 2014), 117.

make progress understanding the specific principles regulating defensive force will be significantly compromised.

Consider another issue on which there is general agreement: it is wrong to impose unnecessary defensive harm on an aggressor. Justified defensive force must meet the condition of being necessary. Why must justified defensive harm meet this condition and how do we know whether a given imposition of harm is necessary? I believe these questions cannot be adequately answered in isolation, that is, we cannot answer these questions simply by reflecting on the nature of 'necessity' as it appears to operate within the domain of defensive force. Instead, the necessity condition only makes sense as an instantiation of a more general moral right that individuals possess: the right to be rescued when others can fulfil the correlated duty at reasonable cost.

An important theme of the book is thus that we cannot understand the morality of defensive force until we ask and answer deeper questions about how the use of defensive force fits with a more general account of justice and moral rights. The principles that regulate the use of defensive force are not *sui generis* and cannot be understood in isolation. Instead, these principles need to be understood by reference to the role that defensive force plays in some broader picture.

1.2 An Overview

What, then, is the broader picture? As I see it, the morality of defensive force is one part of a theory of justice for nonideal conditions. Consider a world that is idealized in the following two senses: no one ever threatens anyone else's rights, and serious accidents—where someone faces a sudden threat to her body or property as a result of bad luck—never occur. In a world like this, defensive force would never be needed. Each person would have moral rights over everything to which she was rightfully entitled, and she would never need to use force to defend her body or property. Once we relax these assumptions—once we consider a world where some people threaten the moral rights of others, and where serious and sudden accidents do sometimes happen—the permissibility of defensive force becomes a practical question. Under what conditions, if any, can someone use force to defend what is rightfully hers? This is not a question about how to distribute or allocate rights over resources or other advantages and disadvantages (including the costs arising as a result of noncompliance). That is a distinct question that is answered by the appropriate principles of distributive justice, principles that can be applied to conditions of full compliance and conditions of partial compliance. Rather, the question is this: Given that the appropriate principles of distributive justice have told us what is rightfully yours and what is rightfully mine, what does justice permit you to do, as a private individual, to defend what is rightfully yours? This book is my attempt to answer this question.

Chapters 2 and 3 address the grounds of permissible defensive force. Most philosophers assume that any successful justification for the use of defensive force must appeal to the liability of the person on whom defensive harm is imposed. A person is liable to defensive harm when he forfeits his rights against the imposition of the harm, and thus is not wronged, or has no standing to complain, about the imposition of the harm. A good deal of the recent literature consists in debating the necessary and sufficient conditions for liability. In Chapter 2 I offer my own account. What matters for liability, I argue, is whether you treat others *as if* they lack rights against the harms that you might impose. When you act in this way, you treat others as if they are not entitled to the equal concern and respect all persons are normally owed, and so it's appropriate that you bear special liability for your actions when the people you harm do in fact have rights against the harmful acts you perform. I call this the *moral status account of liability*.

To illustrate, suppose that Albert is threatening to shoot and kill Betty. Absent special facts, this would typically be a grave violation of Betty's rights, and thus Albert's act is likely impermissible unless Betty has somehow lost or forfeited her right not to be killed. The permissibility of Albert's act thus depends on the assumption that Betty lacks the right not to be killed. This is the sense in which he treats her as if she lacks a right by shooting her. Since he treats her in this way, he can be liable to defensive harm when Betty retains her right not to be killed—for example, if she is an innocent victim of an attempted murder.

But not all instances where we threaten to harm others involve treating those others as if they lack rights against harm. For example, a careful and conscientious driver whose car unavoidably swerves out of control and threatens to hit a pedestrian does not, I believe, threaten to violate the pedestrian's rights. And the permissibility of the driver's behaviour does not depend on the assumption that any given pedestrian lacks a right not to be killed. It is permissible to drive carefully and conscientiously even though there is a very small risk that doing so may cause harm. We do not have general moral rights against being killed or harmed by others' behaviour. Rather, we only have moral rights that others refrain from performing harmful (or potentially harmful) acts when we can reasonably demand that they refrain from performing the act. It's not reasonable to demand that others refrain from careful and conscientious behaviour when the behaviour poses only an extremely low risk of harm, particularly when the behaviour forms an essential part of a pattern of life from which almost everyone substantially benefits. The careful and conscientious driver is thus not liable to defensive harm.

Two things are worth noting, at this stage, about this account of liability. First, it rejects the view that a person's liability to defensive force depends only on whether her act would be wrong if she knew all the facts. Liability is triggered by a failure to respect other people's moral rights, but moral rights are not determined by asking whether someone's act would be wrong if she knew all the facts (e.g., if the conscientious driver could know, in advance, that her car would swerve out of control later today). I defend this conclusion about moral rights in Chapter 6. Second, the moral status account ties liability directly to our broader judgements about justice and individual moral rights. Not all harmful acts violate individual moral rights, and thus we cannot make any sound judgements about liability to defensive harm in isolation—we need to know what a person can reasonably demand of another, since only then can we know what sorts of claim rights individuals possess against one another.

As noted above, some believe that liability provides the only basis for the permissible use of defensive force. But this view is mistaken. Liability, on its own, is incapable of providing a justification for the use of defensive force.[2] If Albert is liable to defensive force, this simply means he lacks a right, or has no standing to complain, if defensive force is imposed on him. But using defensive force typically harms the person on whom force is imposed, and without a positive moral reason to harm someone, imposing the harm would be gratuitous and unjustified. Liability can thus, at most, only ever provide one part of a justification for the use of defensive force. A full justification requires an account of the positive moral reason to impose the harm. This might seem like a trivial task: successful defensive force will avert harm to one or more innocent people, and this is all the justification we need. But things are not so simple for several reasons. First, not all justified defensive force averts harm. It is sometimes permissible, for example, to use defensive force to avert threats to our civil or political liberties, even when we will not be materially harmed if those liberties are violated. Preventing the violation of individual rights, even when harm will not be caused, can be a justification for imposing defensive harm on liable aggressors. Second, it is sometimes permissible to impose defensive harm on non-liable persons. There are, I argue, agent-relative prerogatives to use defensive force to protect what is rightfully yours, even when doing so will cause harm to a non-liable person. Chapter 3 develops and defends this conclusion.

My view about the justification of defensive force is thus unusual in several respects. Whereas most philosophers seek a single justification for the use of defensive force, I argue that there are several distinct justifications. Sometimes the justification is that using defensive force will avert a liable attacker's unjust aggression. Other times defensive force is permissibly imposed on non-liable persons because the defensive agent has an agent-relative prerogative to accord disproportionate weight (disproportionate when viewed impartially) to her own life.

That said, all justified cases of defence do have a common feature: the defensive agent must be defending what rightfully belongs to her or some other person. The common purpose of justified acts of defensive force is thus not necessarily to avert

---

[2] Cécile Fabre emphasizes this fact in 'Permissible Rescue Killings', *Proceedings of the Aristotelian Society* 109 (2009): 149–64.

harm, or wrongful harm. Rather, the common purpose of such acts is to defend people's rightful entitlements—to enable people to defend what is rightfully theirs as determined by the appropriate principles of social or distributive justice.

Perhaps surprisingly, this is an unorthodox position to take regarding the relationship between social justice and the morality of defensive force. On one influential view—developed in different ways by Jeff McMahan, Michael Otsuka, Kaila Draper, Saba Bazargan-Forward, and Kerah Gordon-Solmon, among others—defensive force is a mechanism by which harms can be allocated in accordance with the correct principles of distributive justice. On this view, persons sometimes find themselves in situations where someone will unavoidably suffer harm. But we can appeal directly to principles of distributive justice—for example a responsibility-sensitive conception of fairness—to determine how the harm should be allocated. On this picture, the morality of defensive force is not downstream from questions of social or distributive justice—it's not something we consider *after* we have worked out what belongs to whom. Defensive force is rather a constitutive part of distributive justice—another way in which burdens and benefits can be fairly allocated.

This view seems mistaken to me for several reasons. First, it's often impermissible to use defensive force even when doing so would bring about a fairer or more equitable distribution of harm or risk of harm. It's not permissible, for example, to toss a coin to decide whether to use an innocent bystander's body as a shield against a lethal projectile, even though this distributes the risk of death equally between the bystander and yourself.[3] Conversely, it's sometimes permissible to deploy defensive force even when doing so is inconsistent with a fair distribution of harm. For example, you may permissibly use proportionate force to repel a wrongful aggressor from taking your wallet, even if you can foresee that doing so will result in the wrongful aggressor taking someone else's wallet instead. You don't have to toss a coin before deciding to use proportionate defensive force in this case.

I've pointed to some cases where it seems counterintuitive to suppose that the use of defensive force is governed by the aim of bringing about a fair distribution of harm. But there is a more general reason to be sceptical of this approach. Principles of distributive justice are meant to ensure that the political, economic, and legal institutions of a society are structured to give each person a fair share of the benefits and burdens of that society over the course of their lives. The principles govern the whole scheme—they can't be directly applied in isolated instances without reference to the broader distributive scheme. Suppose, for example, that the correct principle regulating the distribution of burdens and

---

[3] To be clear, the philosophers mentioned in the preceding paragraph don't claim that it is permissible to do this. I'm rather pointing out that a view of defensive force as a special case of distributive justice struggles to explain why it is not permissible.

benefits in society is one that maximizes the position of the least advantaged members. It doesn't follow that an individual employer should make hiring decisions by asking herself who is the least advantaged applicant and give this person the job. This decentralized and direct application of the principle is very unlikely to promote a just distribution overall. Similarly, even if some version of responsibility-sensitive egalitarianism is the correct principle of distributive justice, it doesn't follow that individuals acting in a private capacity should always be governed by this principle when deciding whom to benefit or harm in particular cases. Suppose Albert bears the greatest local responsibility for a particular threat. Forcing Albert to bear the harm from this threat may not be consistent with achieving a responsibility-sensitive egalitarian distribution of burdens and benefits more generally—this will depend on a huge array of other facts about Albert's life and the lives of others.

To be clear, I'm not making the false claim that principles of distributive justice *never* directly apply to the choices of private persons—that they somehow only apply to institutions or persons acting in some institutional capacity. I'm only making the modest—and I think indisputable—point that we cannot assume principles of distributive justice apply directly to individual decisions concerning local distributions of burdens or benefits. More strongly, when we reflect on the role that principles of distributive justice play in securing an overall fair scheme, it's often the case that these principles do not directly govern the decisions of individuals.

Of course it's open to proponents of the distributive view of defensive force to explain why, with regard to defensive force, it makes sense for individuals to be directly governed by principles of distributive justice—why doing so will secure a meaningful form of justice. But such explanations are mostly absent from the literature. And I argue, particularly in Chapters 2 and 4, that there are in fact no good reasons to apply distributive principles directly in this way to the use of defensive force. The principles regulating defensive force do not direct agents to bring about particular distributions of harm. They set limits on what we can do— consistent with our other duties of justice—to protect what belongs to us.

Chapters 4 and 5 focus on the nature of these limits, in particular the limits set by the conditions of proportionality and necessity. In Chapter 4, I provide a new account of proportionality, that is, an account of the degree or amount of defensive force to which a wrongful attacker is liable. Contra the dominant view in the literature, I argue that an attacker's degree of moral responsibility for the threat he poses is irrelevant to determining how much defensive force is proportionate. It is irrelevant because an attacker's degree of moral responsibility has no bearing on the stringency of the right that an attacker threatens to violate. I argue that it is the stringency of the right that the attacker threatens to violate that determines how much defensive force it is proportionate to impose. The more stringent the right that is threatened, the greater the degree of defensive force that is proportionate. This is thus another way in which the morality of defensive force depends on our understanding of broader questions of justice—in this case, an account of what moral rights persons possess, and how the stringency of such rights is determined.

As I've noted, it is widely believed that the imposition of defensive force cannot be permissible unless doing so is *necessary* to avert a threat. Although widely accepted, the moral basis of the necessity condition remains poorly understood. It might seem easy to justify the necessity condition. It is always wrong to impose *gratuitous* harm—this is the imposition of harm for which there is no positive moral reason. Unnecessary harm is surely gratuitous, and thus unnecessary defensive harm is wrong. But this simple explanation is false. Suppose Albert is threatening to wrongfully assault Betty and she has two ways of averting his threat: she can shoot and kill him, ensuring she suffers no harm, or she can jump to safety, spraining her ankle, but ensuring Albert will suffer no harm. All plausible formulations of the necessity condition converge on the conclusion that shooting Albert is not necessary and thus impermissible. But shooting Albert would not be gratuitous since there is a positive moral reason to do so: it would save Betty from suffering a sprained ankle. Thus, unnecessary defensive harm is not wrong because it is gratuitous.

More recent formulations of the necessity condition instead present it as a type of consequentialist constraint on the permissible use of defensive harm. Defensive harm is unnecessary when the net moral value of imposing the harm is not as great as that of some other feasible course of action. I believe, however, that these formulations face serious problems, so in Chapter 5 I defend a revisionary account of the necessity condition. I argue that the condition is a particular instance of a more general moral right: the right to be rescued from serious harm when others can do so at reasonable cost. By grounding the necessity condition in the right to be rescued, we arrive at more plausible conclusions in certain cases. In particular, there are cases where the defensive agent correctly believes that if she exercises her liberties in a particular way—for example, going to a dangerous neighbourhood, or returning home to an angry spouse—another agent will threaten her with unjust harm such that she will need to impose defensive harm to avert the wrongful attack. I argue that only a rights-based conception of the necessity condition yields the correct conclusion that these defensive agents do not impose unnecessary harm. The analysis of the necessity condition thus contributes to the book's broader theme: the justification and application of the principles regulating defensive force depend on a more general account of individual rights within a just society, in this case, the assumption that individuals have a right to be rescued when others can do so at a reasonable cost, and that this right cannot be forfeited as a result of wrongdoing.

Chapters 6 and 7 consider the relevance of agents' evidence and intentions to the permissible use of defensive force. I defend three main ideas in these chapters.

First, I reject what I call the fact-relative view of moral rights against harm. On this account, a person's rights against harm depend only on facts about the world, and not on anyone's evidence or beliefs about those facts. On this view of moral rights, you can violate someone's rights by performing ordinary activities such as pressing a doorbell, despite having no evidence that the act is going to cause harm. There is, I argue in Chapter 6, no plausible version of the fact-relative view that can adequately explain the scope of our rights against harm.

Instead, I argue for a different view, one where moral rights against harm are determined by asking what we can reasonably demand of each other, where what we can reasonably demand of each other depends, in part, on the evidence that agents can reasonably be expected to have. This view of moral rights has dramatic implications for the morality of defensive force. We only render ourselves liable to defensive harm when we threaten to violate someone else's moral rights. If some version of the fact-relative view is correct, then we become liable to defensive harm whenever we perform acts that turn out to cause fact-relative unjustifiable harm to others, or at least whenever we can foresee that this might occur. This means that, in principle, ordinary voters who cast their ballots in good faith for political candidates, doctors who save patients, bus drivers who take people to work in factories, and countless others are all potentially liable to defensive force for performing these seemingly permissible, indeed often praiseworthy acts, since they can foresee some chance that performing the act will contribute to a fact-relative unjustified harm. Although this is a conclusion that McMahan and others defend, it has always struck me as unlikely to be true. Once we realize that moral rights against harm are not fact relative, we can reject these conclusions. People who perform activities that are permissible in light of the best evidence available to them, and which don't depend on the assumption that others lack moral rights, do not make themselves liable to defensive force when their acts unfortunately cause others to face threats. Once again, I argue that we cannot develop the best account of the morality of defensive force without delving more deeply into more general questions about the nature of justice and the nature of moral rights.

Finally, in Chapter 7 I turn to consider a further constraint on the permissible use of defensive force. Suppose Albert has wrongfully launched a lethal projectile toward Betty, and the only way she can save herself is to grab an innocent bystander's body and use it as a shield, which results in the bystander, rather than Betty, being killed by the projectile. It seems clear that Betty is not permitted to save herself in this way. But now consider a similar case. Albert has wrongfully launched a lethal projectile at Betty, and once again she only has one way to save herself: she can use her metal-reinforced umbrella as a shield, but this will result in the lethal projectile bouncing off her umbrella and killing a nearby innocent bystander. In this case I think it's clearly permissible for Betty to act. What, if anything, explains this difference?

The most influential answer appeals to the distinction between acts where the harm is intended, as opposed to acts where the harm is foreseen but not intended. Many people believe that, other things being equal, it is more difficult to justify acts where the harm is intended either as a means or as an end, as compared to acts where the harm is merely foreseen. The doctrine of double effect is one influential moral principle that incorporates this idea, and many philosophers use it to explain the intuitive difference between cases like the ones involving Betty and the lethal projectile.

I argue, however, that there is a better way to explain the difference between these sorts of cases. What makes it wrong for Betty to use the innocent bystander's body as a shield is that she cannot achieve the good outcome that is meant to justify her act (saving her life) without making use of someone else's body or rightful property in a way that also causes significant harm to that person. The purpose of having moral entitlements—distributing moral rights over bodies and the external world—is to create a fair framework within which each person can choose how to make use of what is rightfully theirs. If something is rightfully yours, it is not available to be used by others (without your consent) for their purposes, however laudable those purposes might be. Rightful ownership entails that it is up to you to decide for what purposes your body and other property will be deployed. The fact that the bystander's body would be useful to Betty, in our first case above, cannot serve to justify her use of it since it doesn't belong to her.

I thus defend a particular version of the *means principle*: it is wrong to use a person's body or property without that person's consent unless the person is duty bound to allow such use. I argue that this principle can explain a wide range of judgements about the permissible use of defensive force. Indeed, with this principle in hand, we never need to appeal to the intentions with which an agent acts to explain pairs of cases like the one involving Betty and the lethal projectile. The wrongness of violating the means principle is explained not by reference to an agent's aims or state of mind, but rather by whether she acts as if the person who is harmed is under a duty to use his body or other entitlements in service of the objective that might otherwise justify the act. If the person is under no such duty, the agent's act is unjustified. What matters, on this account, is not whether the agent aims at evil, or whether she intends harm. Instead, what matters is that the only available justification for harming the victim depends on an assumption— that the victim is duty bound to allow her body or property to be used for some purpose—that is false, and so the victim is wrongfully exploited when the means principle is violated.

The means principle is in this way closely connected to another widely accepted moral idea: the doctrine of doing and allowing. The doctrine of doing and allowing tells us, among other things, that when it is justifiable to allow someone to be harmed, part of what makes it justifiable is the fact that the victim can avoid suffering the harm only by making use of things that rightfully belong to you and that you are not duty bound to provide. The means principle tells us that when you can perform a harmful act that brings about good consequences, it is wrong to do so when the benefit can only be realized by making use of things that rightfully belong to others when those others are not duty bound to use their resources in this way. Both principles derive from a more fundamental idea: rights to control bodies and resources can create a fair framework within which persons can be independent and decide how to make use of their fair share of the world. This returns us, once again, to one of the book's central themes: we cannot understand the principles regulating the use of defensive force in isolation from wider questions about the just distribution of rights over persons and property. Defensive force is not a means of bringing about just distributions of harm. But the principles regulating defensive force are justified, in large part, because they reflect deeper ideas embodied in our best account of justice, for example, the idea that persons are morally independent, and as such people's rightful entitlements cannot be appropriated whenever doing so would be sufficiently useful for others.

1.3 Scope and Method

Before moving on, I should say something about the book's scope and method. My aim is to provide an account of the central principles regulating the permissible use of defensive force, but the book does not provide a complete or comprehensive theory of the morality of defensive force. The book does not, for example, have much to say about how the morality of defensive force should inform our legal and political institutions, including institutions that govern the laws of war. I hope that the arguments in this book will prove useful to those who work in the philosophy of criminal law, the ethics of war, and other related areas, but I don't focus on the implications for these other areas of inquiry, though I do occasionally make use of examples from the ethics of war.

I will, however, make one cautionary remark here. What is true about the permissible use of defensive force by private individuals may not apply in any straightforward sense to the morality of defensive force as exercised by agents of a legitimate political institution, or exercised against agents of such an institution. Legitimate political institutions have functions that individuals do not, and as a result, they may have justifications for the use of force, and claims against the use of force, that private individuals may lack. This doesn't entail that the principles regulating defensive force as deployed by private individuals have no implications for how state officials may act, or how we may act with regard to state officials— that would be very surprising given that one of a legitimate state's central purposes is to protect individual rights. It entails only that we should be cautious in considering how the principles of private defensive force apply, or fail to apply, to institutional actors.

A related way in which the scope of the book is limited is that it doesn't address some of the problems that arise under nonideal conditions. Of course in one way the book is entirely concerned with nonideal circumstances: cases where people use defensive force to protect what is rightfully theirs. But the arguments nevertheless do involve a fair bit of idealization. I mostly assume that we know what belongs to whom, and that rights over persons and property have been justly allocated.

The real world looks nothing like this. We often don't know what people's just entitlements are, and even when we do know, or are reasonably confident about it, the existing legal regime does not allocate to people what they are entitled to as a matter of justice. How the moral principles of defensive force apply under these conditions is a very difficult question, one that has often been ignored in the existing literature. I hope this is a question that will receive much more attention in the future, but I set this question aside in my discussion.[4]

Throughout the book I make some assumptions about moral rights, and it might be helpful to make those assumptions explicit now. I assume that we each have a set of moral rights. These rights *reflect our status* as free and equal persons. We are free in the sense that no person is naturally subject to any other person's authority. We are each free to develop and pursue our plans and projects, provided we can do so without violating the rights of others. We are equal because we all have this same status as free persons, and our lives also have equal importance or value from an impersonal standpoint. Moral rights also *protect our interests*, for example, our interest in not suffering harm or our interest in controlling resources that enable us to pursue our projects.

Some moral rights are *claim* rights whereas others are *liberty* rights. If Betty has a claim right, then at least one other person owes a duty to Betty. For example, Betty's claim right against being assaulted correlates with Albert's duty to refrain from assaulting her. On the other hand, if Betty has a liberty right to φ, this entails that Betty is not under a duty to refrain from φ-ing.

In paradigmatic cases of permissible defensive force, a wrongful attacker—this will often be Albert in the chapters to follow—threatens to violate the moral rights of a victim—usually Betty—but the victim has the opportunity to use defensive force to avert the threat. In these paradigmatic cases, most agree that Albert forfeits some of his moral rights, and so Betty gains a liberty to impose defensive force on Albert, while retaining her own claims against being attacked or inter-fered with. A good deal of the book will be concerned with developing a detailed understanding of what happens in cases that have this structure.

But although rights are an important part of the morality of defensive force, they are not the whole story. On my view, we have pro tanto reasons to fulfil the duties that we owe to right-holders, but these reasons can sometimes be

---

[4] Rebecca Stone takes up this challenge in 'Private Liability without Wrongdoing' (unpublished manuscript).

outweighed by other considerations. Claim rights cannot be permissibly overridden whenever the marginal benefits of doing so outweigh the costs, but sometimes the beneficial consequences of contravening a duty are sufficiently great that it becomes morally permissible to do so. Thus, like most philosophers who work on the ethics of defensive force, I believe there are *lesser evil* justifications for contravening a person's moral rights. I believe, for example, it is permissible to redirect a lethal projectile away from five innocent people and toward one innocent person, even though in doing so we contravene the one person's right not to be killed. Unlike most philosophers working on defensive force, I also believe *agent-relative* reasons can provide a justification for contravening a person's moral rights, and Chapter 3 makes the case for this view. When we have a sufficient justification for imposing harm on innocent people, our act is *widely proportionate*. When we lack an adequate justification for imposing harm on innocent people, our act is *widely disproportionate*.

When we contravene a person's moral rights and we lack an adequate justification for doing so, I will say that we *violate* the victim's rights. When we possess a sufficient justification, I will say that we *infringe* the victim's rights. When I wish to remain neutral between these possibilities, I will say we *contravene* the victim's rights. When we infringe a person's rights, we do not act wrongly or impermissibly (I'll use those terms interchangeably), but we do *wrong* the victim. We fail to fulfil a duty that we owe to the victim, and this may have important implications regarding secondary duties to apologize or compensate the victim.

I'll conclude this chapter by saying a few things about methodology. Like many others working on this topic, I rely on thinly described examples involving threats and the imposition of harm. Sometimes these examples are used to illustrate the moral implications of a particular principle or view, sometimes they are used to draw readers' attention to the role or function a moral concept plays within a given theory, and sometimes the examples are presented as provisional moral data that stands in need of a deeper explanation. Some philosophers decry the use of such examples. The complaints about these examples take many different forms. Some argue that the thinness of such examples deprives them of relevant ethical information about the agents involved.[5] Some object that many moral judgements about particular cases are vulnerable to evolutionary debunking.[6] And others complain that our reactions to these examples are vulnerable to various biases, including framing effects.[7]

---

[5] See for example Kwame Anthony Appiah, *Experiments in Ethics* (Cambridge, MA: Harvard University Press, 2008), 195–97.

[6] See for example Joshua D. Green, 'The Secret Joke of Kant's Soul', in *Moral Psychology*, vol. 3, *The Neuroscience of Morality: Emotion, Brain Disorders, and Development*, ed. Walter Sinnott-Armstrong (Cambridge, MA: MIT Press, 2008), 35–79; and Peter Singer, 'Ethics and Intuitions', *Journal of Ethics* 9, no. 3–4 (2005): 331–52.

[7] See for example Walter Sinnott-Armstrong, 'Framing Moral Intuitions', in *Moral Psychology*, vol. 2, *The Cognitive Science of Morality: Intuition and Diversity*, ed. Walter Sinnott-Armstrong, (Cambridge, MA: MIT Press, 2008), 47–76.

Considering all the objections to stylized examples in moral philosophy would be a monograph-length project of its own, so I can't pursue that project here.[8] Instead I will make three brief points. First, like many others, the more general method I rely upon is that of reflective equilibrium: going back and forth between particular judgements and more general principles, along with more general theories, with the aspiration of reaching a position where particular judgements cohere with more general principles and theories. Thus, even when examples are presented as moral data that stand in need of explanation, these judgements are never taken as beyond revision. If, after due reflection, the more general principles and theories that seem correct conflict with our judgement in a particular case, the judgement may have to be abandoned. Second, and relatedly, since I believe there is no credible alternative to the method of reflective equilibrium, anyone who hopes to say anything about moral rightness and wrongness must rely on considered convictions about particular cases at some stage. The alternative is to implausibly insist that we can be given sufficient reason to accept theories or moral principles without considering how those principles apply in particular cases. Third, as I've already mentioned, some of the examples in the book are presented not to elicit moral intuitions that must then be explained, but rather to illustrate the implications of a view, or to make clear what role a moral concept plays in some wider theory. Sometimes, the best way to understand a more abstract principle or theory is to see how its different components work in particular cases. Objections concerning the reliability of moral judgements about particular cases are irrelevant when examples are used in this way.

Finally, consider a different sort of methodological objection. Some believe that any specific domain of moral inquiry, such as the morality of defensive force, must be approached via some general ethical theory such as act consequentialism, rule consequentialism, or contractualism. Those general ethical theories each purport to represent the truth about all of morality, or at least the part of morality that concerns what we owe to each other. To know what is true about the morality of defensive force, some will say that we must first decide which of these general ethical theories is true, and then apply that theory to our topic.

This book doesn't proceed in that way. I assume that people have moral rights, and those rights cannot be permissibly infringed whenever the marginal benefits of doing so outweigh the costs. In that sense the book is premised on the assumption that certain versions of consequentialism are false. But I make no attempt to directly derive the principles regulating the permissible use of defensive force from a more general ethical theory, such as contractualism. There are several reasons for this.

---

[8] For very helpful discussions regarding the use of examples and intuitions in moral and political philosophy, see Kimberley Brownlee and Zofia Stemplowska, 'Thought Experiments', in *Methods in Analytical Political Theory,* ed. Adrian Blau (Cambridge: Cambridge University Press, 2017), 21–45; and Jeff McMahan, 'Moral Intuition', in *The Blackwell Guide to Ethical Theory*, 2nd ed., ed. Hugh LaFollette and Ingmar Persson (Oxford: Wiley-Blackwell, 2013): 103–22.

First, most versions of contractualism depend, at least in large part, on comparing the strength of the complaints that different individuals would have under different candidate moral principles, and selecting the principle where the person who is most disadvantaged by the principle has the weakest complaint compared to those most disadvantaged by other principles.[9] This method, however, is not well suited to many of the problems that arise concerning the use of defensive force.[10] Consider, for example, what contractualism could tell us regarding the question of how much force is proportionate for a defensive agent to impose on a wrongful attacker. It seems that we should weigh the complaints of the wrongful attacker against those of the innocent victim when evaluating different proposals. But I doubt this will be very helpful. The strength of the attacker's complaints against suffering defensive harm should not be weighed equally against the strength of a victim's complaints against suffering unjust harm since the attacker is the one who has unjustly brought about the situation that calls for defensive force. The attacker's complaints would thus have to be discounted somehow, perhaps by appeal to the fact that he could have reasonably avoided posing an unjust threat. But determining how much the attacker's complaints against defensive force should be discounted doesn't itself seem amenable to contractualist reasoning. Moreover, as I argue in Chapter 4, the best way to conceptualize the proportionality constraint is not by discounting the strength of an attacker's complaint against suffering unjust harm. Rather, we need a way of measuring the value of the right that the attacker threatens to violate, a means of measurement that will also give us a sense of what it would be permissible to do in defence of the right. Put differently, we cannot make non-moralized comparisons of the strength of attackers' and defenders' complaints against suffering harm: the strength of their complaints is dependent on prior judgements regarding whether the harm a person might suffer is one to which he is liable. I am thus sceptical that there is a noncircular way for contractualism to compare the strength of an attacker's and defender's complaints as a means of arriving at a plausible principle of proportionality.

Second, contractualism is ill suited to address the permissibility of using defensive force when doing so imposes serious or fatal harms on innocent people. Suppose, for example, Albert is wrongfully threatening to kill five innocent victims. The victims can avert Albert's attack only by throwing a grenade in his direction, killing him, but this will also foreseeably kill a bystander. Is it permissible for the victims to throw the grenade? The leading forms of contractualism do not permit the aggregation of individual claims or complaints, and so contractualists must

---

[9] T. M. Scanlon offers the most influential formulation of this view in *What We Owe to Each Other* (Cambridge, MA: Harvard University Press, 1998).

[10] This is not to deny that the contractualist method may be helpful with regard to some questions within the morality of defensive force. See, for example, Renée Jorgensen Bolinger, 'The Moral Grounds of Mistaken Self-Defense' (unpublished manuscript).

answer this question only by comparing individual complaints. We may grant that contractualism can satisfactorily resolve cases where we must choose between saving a larger or smaller number of people.[11] Yet I cannot see how contractualism, without radical revisions, can explain what seems true in this case, namely, that it is permissible for the victims to throw their grenade and kill the bystander. The more general problem is that the permissibility of using defensive force sometimes depends on the aggregation of individual claims in a way that contractualism standardly prohibits. Contractualism, at least its most influential formulations, identifies principles or rules that no individual person can reasonably reject. But the fact that a principle or rule cannot be reasonably rejected is neither a necessary nor sufficient condition for determining when it is permissible to impose serious harm on others.[12] Sometimes, as in the example with the grenade we've just considered, it seems clear that it is permissible to act on a principle that some people can reasonably reject. Other times, even though fairly situated contractors might all accept a principle permitting harm *ex ante*, it is not permissible to act on that principle *ex post*.

Although I have focused on contractualism, I believe any attempt to apply some general theory of act or rule consequentialism to the morality of defensive force is even less likely to produce plausible results. Rather than trying to develop principles for defensive force from a general ethical theory, I seek to bring my judgements about particular cases into coherence with more general principles that, on reflection, seem to capture what is important about the permissible use of defensive force. These more general principles, moreover, draw on wider judgements concerning justice—in particular, the shape and function of individual moral rights in a just society. By closely studying the morality of defensive force, I believe we also reach a deeper understanding of the way moral rights work, and what role rights play in establishing just relations between persons.

---

[11] Michael Otsuka persuasively argues that contractualism cannot satisfactorily resolve these cases. See Otsuka, 'Saving Lives, Moral Theory, and the Claims of Individuals', *Philosophy & Public Affairs* 34, no. 2 (2006): 109–35.

[12] I make this point in 'Contractualism', in *Methods in Analytical Political Theory*, ed. Adrian Blau (Cambridge: Cambridge University Press, 2017): 83–84. Joe Horton also makes a compelling case that contractualism—understood to require an individualist restriction—cannot adequately resolve various questions concerning the permissibility of imposing risks of harm. See Horton, 'Aggregation, Complaints, and Risk', *Philosophy & Public Affairs* 45, no. 1 (2017): 54–81.

2
Liability

Let's go back to the beginning. Albert is angry because Betty has refused to go on a date with him. As an act of revenge, he is going to wrongfully assault her—an assault that will cause serious harm. There is no time to call the police, but Betty can avert Albert's wrongful assault by using defensive force. In a case like this everyone, bar pacifists, agrees that it is morally permissible for Betty to use some degree of defensive force. In this case, and many others, an important part of what makes the imposition of defensive harm morally permissible is the fact that the person on whom the harm is imposed is *liable* to defensive harm. For now, we can say that an attacker is liable to defensive harm when he forfeits some of the moral rights that he would normally possess against being harmed, and thus he is not wronged, and has no standing to complain, when some defensive harm is imposed on him.[1]

Understanding when a person is liable to defensive harm is of central importance to the morality of defensive force. First, because imposing harm on those who are liable to bear the harm does not wrong those people, it's much easier to justify imposing harm on liable persons than it is to justify imposing harm on non-liable persons. If Albert maliciously threatens Betty with lethal force, it's easy to see why it may be permissible for Betty to harm or even kill Albert in self-defence. It's much more difficult to understand how Betty could permissibly kill an innocent bystander if this were the only way to save herself from Albert's attack; the innocent bystander has done nothing to make himself liable, and so Betty would be contravening an innocent person's rights to save herself. Second, whether a person is liable to defensive force is crucial in determining whether that person may permissibly engage in counter-defence. If Albert makes himself liable to defensive harm by maliciously attacking Betty, then he is, other things being equal, not entitled to engage in counter-defence when Betty uses necessary and proportionate force to defend herself from his initial attack. Third, determining who is liable to defensive harm has important implications regarding when third parties may intervene in a violent conflict. Third parties may intervene to prevent one liable person from harming a non-liable person, but typically may not intervene to protect a person from having harm imposed to which that person

---

[1] This initial description of moral liability to defensive harm follows Jeff McMahan's account, though I have made some modifications. See McMahan, 'The Basis of Moral Liability to Defensive Killing', *Philosophical Issues* 15, no. 1 (2005): 386.

The Morality of Defensive Force. Jonathan Quong, Oxford University Press (2020). © Jonathan Quong.
DOI: 10.1093/oso/9780198851103.001.0001

is liable. Finally, questions of liability often bear on issues of compensation. If a person is not liable to suffer some harm, but that harm is imposed, then that person has at least a prima facie claim to compensation since the harm imposed was wrongful. Harms imposed on people who are liable to bear them do not have the same capacity to ground claims of compensation.

What *makes* a person morally liable to defensive harm? In this chapter I canvass three answers to this question, but I argue that all three answers are flawed.[2] After some conceptual preliminaries in section 2.1, section 2.2 considers the *culpability account*. On this view, a person only becomes liable to defensive harm when he is culpable for an unjust threat of harm to others. The culpability account suffers from two main problems. First, whatever interpretation we adopt, it yields coun-terintuitive results. Second, it's unclear why culpability should be the grounds for liability to defensive harm given that culpability does not play a central role in other judgements about liability and rights forfeiture. In section 2.3, I assess the *moral responsibility account*. This view holds that a person can be liable if he acts in a way that results in a threat of impermissible harm to others, so long as the threat of impermissible harm was a foreseeable consequence of his act. This account, however, yields counterintuitive results in certain cases in which a person acts in a way that seems permissible but through brute bad luck ends up posing a threat of harm to innocent others. Worries about this problem for the moral responsibility view might lead us to embrace an *evidence-relative account*, whereby a person can only become liable when she performs an act that is wrong in light of the evidence available to her. In section 2.4, however, I argue that this view is also suspect because it yields counterintuitive results in certain cases where a person makes a reasonable mistake and attacks an innocent person.

Having considered and rejected three candidate conceptions of liability, sections 2.5 through 2.7 develop and defend an alternative view: the *moral status account*. What matters for liability, I argue, is whether you behave *as if* others do not have the sort of moral claims against harm that each person normally possesses. When you act in this way, you treat others as if they lack the standard

---

[2] I do not discuss two other answers: the *causal account*, and the *duty view*. The causal account is implicitly advanced by Judith Jarvis Thomson in 'Self-Defense', *Philosophy & Public Affairs* 20, no. 4 (1991): 283–310. It has also been adopted by Suzanne Uniacke, *Permissible Killing: The Self-Defence Justification of Homicide* (Cambridge: Cambridge University Press, 1994); and Fiona Leverick, *Killing in Self-Defence* (Oxford: Oxford University Press, 2006), chap. 3. I omit discussion of this view since others have subjected it to decisive criticism. See, for example, Jeff McMahan, 'Self-Defense and the Problem of the Innocent Attacker', *Ethics* 104, no. 2 (1994): 276–7; and Michael Otsuka, 'Killing the Innocent in Self-Defense', *Philosophy & Public Affairs* 23, no. 1 (1994): 74–94. For a more general critique of causal accounts of liability in law and morality, see Arthur Ripstein, *Equality, Responsibility, and the Law* (Cambridge: Cambridge University Press, 1999), 32–42. The duty view of liability is advanced by Victor Tadros. See for example Tadros, 'Duty and Liability', *Utilitas* 24, no. 2 (2012): 259–77. I omit discussion of the duty view since I don't believe it competes with the views considered in this chapter; it is better understood as an account of what liability *is* rather than as an account of the moral basis of liability.

moral claims necessary to protect them from the harms you might impose, and so you cannot reasonably demand that any innocent people whom you threaten refrain from using necessary and proportionate defensive force against you. But when you do not treat others as if they lack rights against harm—when the justification for your act accords the appropriate weight to the moral claims each person has—then it would be unreasonable to hold you liable for the harms that result from your act.

Before proceeding to the main arguments, one important clarification will be helpful. I make use of Derek Parfit's distinction between three different standards of moral evaluation.[3] An act is wrong in the *fact-relative* sense when it would be wrong if we knew all the relevant facts. An act is wrong in the *belief-relative* sense if it would be wrong if our beliefs about the facts were true. Finally, an act is wrong in the *evidence-relative* sense when our act would be wrong if the relevant facts were what the available evidence gives us sufficient (or apparently sufficient) reason to believe they are. I use the term *justified beliefs* to indicate that a person's beliefs are rational in light of the available evidence—that is, she believes what she has sufficient (or apparently sufficient) reason to believe.

To illustrate, suppose Betty believes that Albert is going to murder her in order to inherit her fortune, and the only way to save her life is by killing Albert. If Betty acts on the basis of these beliefs, then we can say that her act is permissible in the belief-relative sense. If Betty's beliefs are also justified, then her act is also permissible in the evidence-relative sense. Her act is wrong in the evidence-relative sense if her beliefs are not justified. If Betty's beliefs are true, then her act of self-defence is also permissible in the fact-relative sense. Her act would be wrong in the fact-relative sense if it turned out she was mistaken and Albert posed no threat to her. Only in those cases where the different standards diverge will we need to make use of these different standards. Otherwise we can assume that the three standards converge.

2.1 Some Preliminaries

Consider the following general definition of liability. A person, A, is liable to have a cost, C, imposed on him by another person, B, when A lacks a claim right against B's imposition of C. This general definition, however, is at odds with ordinary usage. For example, I lack a claim right against your imposition of heartbreak on me when the girl I would like to date chooses you over me. But it would be bizarre to say that I am liable to this heartbreak. In this case, and others with a similar structure, using the term liability seems inapt because the cost being imposed is

---

[3] Derek Parfit, *On What Matters,* vol. 1 (Oxford: Oxford University Press, 2011), 150–1.

one against which persons don't typically possess claim rights, except perhaps in very unusual circumstances. The term liability is normally used in a more limited range of cases: cases where A lacks a right against the imposition of C, but where persons typically, or at least in many contexts, do possess rights against the imposition of C. Persons typically have rights not to have their property damaged, rights not to be imprisoned, rights not to be assaulted, and rights not to have their wealth taken from them. When someone lacks rights against one of these costs being imposed, we say the person is liable to suffer this burden. So a better general definition of liability is:

> *Liability*: A person, A, is liable to have a cost, C, imposed on him by another person, B, when A lacks a claim right against B's imposition of C, where persons typically, or in many contexts, do have claim rights against the imposition of C.

Our focus, of course, is on a more specific type of liability, that is, liability to defensive harm:

> *Defensive Liability*: A is liable to have some harm, H, imposed on him by B when he forfeits at least one of the claim rights he possesses against B's imposition of H, and where the imposition of H is part of defending some person from a wrongful threat.[4]

This is only a thin description of the concept, one that remains to be filled in by some more substantive account of the basis of forfeiture.[5]

Some worry that the notion of rights forfeiture is too open ended. For example, some worry that rights forfeiture is permanent, whereas intuitively it is impermissible, perhaps even incoherent, to impose 'defensive' harm on an attacker after the attack has occurred. Others worry that forfeiture places no restrictions on the reasons why a liable person can be harmed. If Albert wrongfully threatens Betty and thus forfeits his right against the imposition of some harm, can the harm be imposed for reasons that have nothing to do with averting his threat to Betty? For example, can we impose the harm on Albert because doing so will create new

---

[4] You are *fully* liable to some defensive harm when: (a) you forfeit at least one right against the harm being imposed, and (b) you retain no other rights against the imposition of the harm, and thus (c) you are not wronged if the harm is imposed on you. You are *partially* liable to some defensive harm when: (d) you forfeit at least one right against the harm being imposed, (e) you retain at least one right against the imposition of the harm, and thus (f) you are wronged if the harm is imposed on you, but not to the same extent as you would be had you not forfeited some rights. In this chapter we focus, for simplicity, on cases of full liability, but we return to discuss cases of partial liability in Chapter 5.

[5] Victor Tadros rejects even this thin account because it makes forfeiture a necessary condition of defensive liability. See Tadros, 'Orwell's Battle with Britain: Vicarious Liability for Unjust Aggression', *Philosophy & Public Affairs* 42, no. 1 (2014): 48, and 'Causation, Culpability, and Liability', in *The Ethics of Self-Defense*, ed. Christian Coons and Michael Weber (New York: Oxford University Press, 2016), 113–15.

employment opportunities for Carl? Intuitively this seems clearly wrong, yet sceptics worry that the appeal to rights forfeiture cannot explain why.

These worries are misplaced.[6] There is no principled reason why forfeiture must be permanent, nor any reason why it cannot be restricted in other ways. On my view, the basis of forfeiture is the attacker's wrongful treatment of the victim, in particular, behaving as if the victim lacks moral rights that she in fact possesses. This basis explains why the wrongful attacker only forfeits rights against acts that defend the victim from the wrongful attack.[7] A wrongful attacker does not become liable to harms imposed for any purpose—the harms must be caused by acts that avert or mitigate the wrongful threat, or else the harms must be caused by acts that the defensive agent justifiably believes stand some chance of averting or mitigating the wrongful threat. The harms imposed must meet one of these conditions to qualify as harms to which the wrongful attacker might be liable.[8]

Three final points are worth noting. First, the mere fact that an attacker is liable to defensive harm does not suffice to establish that it is morally permissible to impose the harm. Even when someone lacks a right against the imposition of some harm, there must be a sufficient justification to impose the harm. Of course in standard cases of self-defence there is a positive reason to impose the harm: doing so can avert or mitigate a wrongful threat. But it's important not to lose sight of the fact that liability can only ever be part of a justification for imposing defensive harm. Second, a person is never liable to defensive harm *simpliciter*—a person is always liable to a particular *proportionate* level of defensive harm. How the issue of proportionality is determined is an important and difficult question, one that we will postpone until Chapter 4. In this chapter I focus only on the question of what a person must do in order to be liable to *any* degree of defensive harm. Third, some philosophers argue that an attacker cannot be liable to defensive harm whenever the imposition of that harm is unnecessary, for example, because a less harmful method of defence is available. In Chapter 5 I will argue that things are more complex, but nothing in this chapter will turn on this question.

---

[6] For a more comprehensive defence of rights forfeiture against a variety of worries, see Gerald Lang, 'Why Not Forfeiture?' in *How We Fight: Ethics in War*, ed. Helen Frowe and Gerald Lang (Oxford: Oxford University Press, 2014), 38–61.

[7] In this respect I endorse what is known as the *narrow*, as opposed to the *broad*, account of liability. On the broad account, a wrongful attacker can be liable to proportionate harms that might avert or mitigate any wrongful threat, not merely the wrongful threat posed by the attacker. On the narrow view, an attacker is only liable to defensive force that serves to avert his own wrongful threats.

[8] For a somewhat different view, see Helen Frowe, *Defensive Killing* (Oxford: Oxford University Press, 2014), 99–101. For the subjective condition, Frowe focuses only on the defensive agent's beliefs (beliefs about whether there is a threat and whether the act can avert or mitigate it), not whether the beliefs are justifiable. This seems a mistake to me. Suppose Albert has wrongfully broken Betty's legs. Betty is a deluded fan of the *Back to the Future* movies, and she unjustifiably believes that if she runs over Albert with her car (a replica of the DeLorean), she can travel back in time to avert Albert's attack. Betty believes running over Albert with her car is necessary to avert his attack, but this unjustified belief does not seem sufficient to render her act a genuinely defensive act to which Albert might be liable.

2.2 The Culpability Account

The culpability account declares that only those persons who are culpable for posing a wrongful threat of harm have forfeited rights against defensive harm.[9] I assume that an agent is *fully culpable* for a threat of harm when the following conditions are met:[10]

(1) The agent acts in a way that results in a threat of impermissible harm to an innocent person or persons.

(2) The agent intends or foresees this harm, or else is acting recklessly or negligently.[11]

(3) There are no relevant excusing conditions (e.g., blameless ignorance, duress, or diminished mental capacity).

If Albert's threat meets these conditions, then Albert is fully culpable for the harm he is threatening, and the culpability account declares him to be liable to defensive harm. When one or more excusing conditions are present, the agent isn't fully culpable for the threat, though he may be *partially* culpable depending on the nature and extent of the excusing conditions.[12]

The culpability account can be developed in different ways.[13] But I believe all versions of the culpability view face two decisive objections. First, any version of the culpability account yields counterintuitive results in certain cases. Consider:

Mistaken Attacker: The identical twin brother of a notorious serial killer is driving during a stormy night in a remote area when his car breaks down. Unaware that his brother has recently escaped from prison and is known to be hiding in this same area, he knocks on the door of the nearest house, seeking to phone for help. On opening the door, Resident justifiably believes the harmless twin is the killer. Resident has been warned by the authorities that the killer will

---

[9] For a defence of the culpability account, see Kimberly Kessler Ferzan, 'Justifying Self-Defense', *Law and Philosophy* 24, no. 6 (2005): 733–9, and 'Culpable Aggression: The Basis for Moral Liability to Defensive Killing', *Ohio State Journal of Criminal Law* 9 (2012): 669–97. At one time Jeff McMahan endorsed a version of the culpability account. See McMahan, 'Self-Defense and the Problem of the Innocent Attacker', 259–63. He has since rejected this view. See McMahan, 'The Basis of Moral Liability', 389–93.

[10] See McMahan, *Killing in War* (Oxford: Clarendon Press, 2009), 159. For a more comprehensive discussion of culpability, see Larry Alexander and Kimberly Kessler Ferzan with Stephen Morse, *Crime and Culpability: A Theory of Criminal Law* (Cambridge: Cambridge University Press, 2009).

[11] Alexander and Ferzan deny that negligence can render a person culpable. See *Crime and Culpability*, chap. 3.

[12] For detailed discussions of excusing conditions see McMahan, *Killing in War*, chap. 3; and Alexander and Ferzan, *Crime and Culpability*, chap. 4.

[13] I assess some of the different options in Jonathan Quong, 'Liability to Defensive Harm', *Philosophy & Public Affairs* 40, no. 1 (2012): 50–3.

certainly attack anyone he meets on sight, and so Resident lunges at him with a knife.[14]

Because Resident acts on the basis of justified beliefs, his act of 'self-defence' is permissible in the evidence-relative sense. He thus cannot be culpable—he has a full epistemic excuse—and so the culpability account declares that he is not liable to any defensive harm the identical twin might impose. This conclusion, however, doesn't seem right. After all, the identical twin is the victim of an unprovoked and intentional attack by Resident. Surely the person who intentionally initiates the fact-relative wrongful attack—Resident—is liable to defensive harm. Surely Resident lacks the standing to complain if the twin must break Resident's arms to prevent himself from being killed.[15]

Consider another case:

Coerced Assassin: Terrorists have captured Albert's child. They truthfully tell Albert that he must assassinate ten innocent government officials or else the terrorists will torture and murder Albert's child. Albert would normally never wrongly hurt anyone, but to protect his child he proceeds with the assassination attempt.

In this case I believe Albert is fully excused on account of duress: it would be a mistake to blame Albert for giving in to the terrorist's demand. But it remains wrong for Albert to carry out the assassination, and he is liable to defensive harm if imposing such harm can prevent his assassination of the innocent government officials. This is another case where the culpability account seems to yield the wrong result.

Of course it is open to the proponent of the culpability account to bite the respective bullets in the face of each objection—to insist that whether or not the result is counterintuitive, it is a result we ought to accept because the culpability account is the best account of liability to defensive harm. The plausibility of such a move depends on culpability otherwise serving as a plausible basis for determining liability. But it does not. The problem is that culpability is closely tied to, if not synonymous with, being blameworthy. Blame and moral rights, however, come apart in many contexts. Individuals can be blameworthy for acting on bad motives, but so long as they don't violate anyone's rights, their own moral rights

<hr>

[14] I take this example (with slight modifications) from McMahan, 'The Basis of Moral Liability', 387. McMahan presents this example as part of his critique of the culpability account.

[15] Notice that holding Resident liable to some defensive force need not imply that he is equivalent in every respect to someone who culpably attempts a murder. Resident is not culpable for his mistake and so there are powerful reasons for the innocent twin at the door to regret having to impose defensive harm on Resident—reasons not present, or not present to the same extent, when defensive force is imposed on fully culpable attackers.

are unaffected. And conversely, people can act in ways that are not blameworthy (because their acts are justified or excused) but nonetheless be held responsible—that is, they can be required at the bar of justice to pay costs or suffer damages—for the consequences of those blameless actions. Given the lack of a clear rationale for tying liability to defensive harm so closely to being blameworthy, and given the counterintuitive results that the culpability account generates, I believe that we ought to look elsewhere for the basis of liability to defensive harm.

2.3 The Moral Responsibility Account

According to the moral responsibility account, a person is liable to defensive harm if that person is morally responsible for a wrongful threat of harm to others.[16] More precisely, if: (a) a person performs an act that foreseeably might result in a threat of harm to innocent persons, and (b) the foreseeable threat to others eventuates and is fact-relative impermissible, then (c) the person is liable to defensive harm.[17] Moral responsibility is thus a fairly thin concept. It does not entail being an appropriate subject of praise, blame, or other reactive attitudes. Rather, the term is used to describe all those situations where the consequences of a decision can be traced to a person's voluntary agency because those consequences were foreseeable to the agent who made the choice.

The moral responsibility account has a number of further features. First, it allows that excusing conditions such as blameless ignorance, duress, or diminished mental capacity can diminish a person's moral responsibility.[18] Thus, on some versions of the account, the degree of liability will vary in accordance with the degree of moral responsibility.[19]

---

[16] See McMahan, 'The Basis of Moral Liability', 394–404, *Killing in War*, 157–8, 175–7, and 'Who Is Morally Liable to Be Killed in War', *Analysis* 71 (2011): 548. A version of this account was first proposed by Kaila Draper in 'Fairness and Self-Defense', *Social Theory and Practice* 19 (1993): 73–92, esp. 84. Draper continues to endorse the account, with some modifications. See Draper, *War and Individual Rights* (Oxford: Oxford University Press, 2016), chap. 4. It is also developed by Otsuka, 'Killing the Innocent in Self-Defense' and 'The Moral Responsibility Account of Liability to Defensive Killing', in *The Ethics of Self-Defense*, ed. Coons and Weber (New York: Oxford University Press, 2016). More recently, a modified version of this view has been developed by Kerah Gordon-Solmon, 'What Makes a Person Liable to Defensive Harm?' *Philosophy and Phenomenological Research* 97, no. 3 (2018): 543–67.

[17] The person need not directly pose the threat—moral responsibility for the threat is sufficient (e.g., a mob boss who indicates to his subordinates that an innocent person should be harmed can be liable to defensive harm even if he doesn't pose the direct threat).

[18] McMahan, *Killing in War*, 155–8. Note that on McMahan's view liability can also be affected by the degree of a person's causal contribution to the threat, and also by how many, if any, other people bear moral responsibility for the threat. See McMahan, 'Who is Morally Liable to be Killed in War', 548. I set these further complicating conditions aside here since they are not relevant for my critique of his view.

[19] This proposal will be the subject of sustained analysis in Chapter 4.

Second, the moral responsibility account can deem individuals liable to defensive harm even when they are not culpable. For example, the moral responsibility account can explain why Resident in Mistaken Attacker is liable to defensive harm. Even though Resident has an epistemic excuse that is sufficient to render him entirely non-culpable, he still made the choice to attack another person, and a foreseeable consequence of attacking another person whom one believes to be liable is that one might be mistaken. But when we cannot foresee that our acts pose any real risk of harm to innocent people, then we cannot be liable should any harm result from our acts. If, for example, Albert's flipping of a light switch in his home starts a chain of unforeseeable events that causes Betty (in another house) to suffer a severe electric shock, the harm Betty suffers cannot be attributed to Albert's voluntary agency, and thus he cannot be liable to any defensive harm.[20]

At the heart of the moral responsibility account is an appeal to a notion of *distributive fairness*. If Albert engages in some activity that he can foresee might result in harm to innocent others, and if that risk of harm eventuates and there is now harm to be distributed, it is only *fair* that Albert should be the person who bears that harm. After all, why should anyone other than Albert have to bear the harm that Albert's own decisions have created? Here we find the familiar and powerful luck egalitarian intuition that individuals ought to bear the costs for their own choices, but should not be held liable for the costs of brute luck, or the responsible choices of others.[21]

As I indicated in Chapter 1, I deny that principles of distributive justice directly inform the morality of defensive force. But below I set this general disagreement aside and present two other objections to the moral responsibility account of liability.

2.3.1 Counterintuitive Results

First, the moral responsibility account produces some counterintuitive results. Consider the following cases:[22]

Conscientious Driver: Driver, who always keeps his car well maintained and always drives carefully and alertly, decides to drive to the movies. On the way a

---

[20] This example is borrowed with slight modifications from Judith Jarvis Thomson, *The Realm of Rights* (Cambridge, MA: Harvard University Press, 1990), 229.
[21] Both Otsuka and Gordon-Solmon make the connection explicit between luck egalitarianism and the moral responsibility account. See Otsuka, 'The Moral Responsibility Account of Liability to Defensive Killing'; and Gordon-Solmon, 'What Makes a Person Liable to Defensive Harm?'
[22] I take both cases from McMahan, *Killing in War*, 165. Seth Lazar argues that some of the cases considered in this section illustrate that there is no meaningful difference in moral responsibility between the person posing the threat and the person subject to the threat. See Lazar, 'Responsibility, Risk, and Killing in Self-Defense', *Ethics* 119, no. 4 (2009): 699–728.

freak accident occurs that causes his car to veer out of control in the direction of a pedestrian. The out-of-control car will now kill the pedestrian unless the pedestrian destroys the car with a grenade, thereby killing Driver.

Driver is liable to defensive harm on McMahan's view because Driver can foresee that there is a very small risk of one's car veering out of control when one chooses to drive carefully and conscientiously. Driver is thus morally responsible when bad luck strikes and his car veers towards the pedestrian. In Ronald Dworkin's terms, Driver suffers bad option luck, not bad brute luck.[23] If the only way for the pedestrian to save her life is to destroy the car with a grenade and thereby kill Driver, Driver is liable to this harm since Driver is morally responsible for the unjust threat of harm to the pedestrian. But this conclusion—that Driver forfeits his rights against the imposition of defensive harm—strikes me as counterintuitive.

The moral responsibility account produces an even more counterintuitive result in the following case:

Ambulance Driver: An emergency medical technician (EMT) is driving an ambulance to the site of an accident to take one of the victims to the hospital. She is driving conscientiously and alertly but a freak event occurs that causes the ambulance to veer uncontrollably towards a pedestrian. The out-of-control ambulance will now kill the pedestrian unless the pedestrian destroys it with a grenade, thereby killing the EMT (the victim whom the EMT was going to pick up will be fine).

Here the EMT is not merely engaged in an evidence-relative permitted activity; she has a positive and powerful moral reason to be driving. I assume that many readers will find the conclusion that the EMT is nevertheless liable to defensive harm to be deeply counterintuitive. Moreover, if Driver and EMT are liable to defensive harm, then it's also impermissible for them to defend themselves against being killed by the pedestrians. This also strikes me as false.

McMahan is aware that many people may find these conclusions hard to accept, yet he seems to believe that this is a price worth paying—that the alternative solutions to these cases are even more problematic.[24] In particular, McMahan points out that it seems intuitively permissible for the pedestrians in these examples to defend themselves. McMahan believes this intuition is sound,

---

[23] Ronald Dworkin, *Sovereign Virtue: The Theory and Practice of Equality* (Cambridge: Harvard University Press, 2000), 73. Renée Jorgensen Bolinger, however, offers a compelling argument that proponents of the moral responsibility account cannot help themselves to Dworkin's distinction between brute and option luck in life or death cases like this one. See Bolinger, 'Mistaken Defense and Normative Conventions', PhD Dissertation, University of Southern California, 2017. 12–13.

[24] McMahan, *Killing in War*, 178–82.

and that it indicates that Driver and the EMT are liable to defensive harm. This argument can be stated as follows:

P1   In both Conscientious Driver and Ambulance Driver, it is permissible for the pedestrians to impose harm on Driver or the EMT in self-defence.

P2   It is not permissible to save one innocent person from harm if doing so will impose harm of equal or greater magnitude on another innocent (i.e., non-liable) person.

Therefore

C1   Driver and the EMT must be liable to the defensive harm the pedestrians can permissibly impose.

The second premise in this argument seems supported by the widely accepted moral principle that, other things being equal, it is worse to do harm than to merely allow harm. If we accept this premise, and the further intuitive premise that the innocent pedestrians in these examples are permitted to impose harm in self-defence if necessary, then it seems hard to avoid McMahan's conclusion that Driver and the EMT are liable to defensive harm. After all, if Driver and the EMT are not liable, then how can the pedestrians be justified in doing harm in order to avert suffering harm?

We should resist the conclusion of the argument by rejecting (or rather modifying) the second premise. Most people do not believe it is *always* impermissible to impose harm on one innocent person to avoid an equivalent level of harm befalling another innocent person. Most people believe, for example, that it is permissible to kill an innocent person who has been unexpectedly thrown by a gust of wind towards the bottom of a well where you are trapped if this is the only way to save yourself from being killed by the innocent person's falling body. Similarly, I believe that it would be permissible to redirect a runaway trolley away from one's child or spouse onto a side track, even if this will foreseeably kill an innocent person trapped on that side track.

These judgements indicate the existence of an *agent-relative prerogative* that permits us, under certain conditions, to override the general presumption against doing harm in order to avoid allowing harm. Although I postpone a full defence of this idea until Chapter 3, it is plausible and coheres with many people's intuitive judgements in a range of cases. If such prerogatives exist, then we do not need to believe that Driver or the EMT must be liable in order to believe that the pedestrians are morally permitted to impose defensive harm on them. It's more plausible to see these cases as instances of symmetrical defensive harm, where two innocent people are tragically locked in a lethal conflict, and where each one has an agent-relative permission of self-defence. If the pedestrians in these cases impose harm in self-defence, this is morally permissible, but does *infringe* the rights possessed by both Driver and the EMT. Harming or killing Driver or the EMT ought to be seen as entirely different (not merely different in degree) to harming or killing a murderer, yet the moral responsibility account has difficulty drawing this obvious moral distinction.[25] Drawing this distinction has further implications, since it determines what third parties might permissibly do in such cases. On McMahan's view, a third party who observes the events in Conscientious Driver may permissibly intervene and kill Driver (who is liable on McMahan's view) to save the non-liable pedestrian, but cannot permissibly kill the pedestrian in order to save Driver. I believe, however, that because Driver is not liable it would not be permissible for a third party (with no special relationship to either person) to intervene in the conflict: there is no reason for the third party to treat Driver any differently than the pedestrian; both are non-liable.

In sum, it is not plausible to suppose that Driver or the EMT has forfeited their rights against defensive harm and may be liable to be killed if necessary. Moreover, we don't need to accept the moral responsibility account in order to believe that the pedestrians in these examples are permitted to defend themselves—we only need to believe that sometimes individuals have an agent-relative permission to infringe or override the rights of innocent people in order to save themselves from severe harm or death.

2.3.2 A Dilemma

The moral responsibility account holds that an agent's decision to φ only renders the agent liable if it is *foreseeable* that φ-ing might result in a threat of impermissible harm to others. If the harm is unforeseeable to the agent, then the agent is not liable. But this reliance on the notion of foreseeability exposes the moral responsibility account to a serious dilemma.[26]

We need to know what it means for a threat of harm to be foreseeable to an agent. First, consider a belief-relative account. On this view, a threat of harm as a result of φ-ing is foreseeable to an agent only if the agent's current beliefs give her sufficient reason to believe there is some chance that a threat may eventuate. When we combine this account of foreseeability with the moral responsibility account, however, we get absurd results. Suppose Albert is a father who is culpably ignorant of the fact that giving alcohol to an infant poses any risk of harm. On the belief-relative account of foreseeability, Albert is not morally responsible when he

---

[25] Although Gordon-Solmon's revisionary version of the moral responsibility account may do better in drawing this distinction. See Gordon-Solmon, 'What Makes a Person Liable'.

[26] Bolinger raises a similar worry, though she develops the objection somewhat differently. See Bolinger, 'Mistaken Defense and Normative Conventions', 13–15.

threatens to poison his child with alcohol, and thus he cannot be liable to any defensive force if doing so is needed to save the child from death. This conclusion seems unacceptable.

To avoid results like this, we might adopt an evidence-relative view of foreseeability. On this view, a threat of harm as a result of φ-ing is foreseeable to an agent only if the agent's evidence gives her sufficient reason to believe that there is some chance a threat may eventuate. On this account, although Albert may not believe giving alcohol to an infant poses any risk of harm, the risk of harm is foreseeable to Albert since he has access to the relevant evidence, and thus he can be liable to defensive force. But the evidence-relative view, as stated, is incomplete. Suppose Albert is deciding whether to press a button on his phone. Albert does not believe that doing so poses a risk of harm to others, but if he possessed an advanced degree in electronics, he would be able to see that there's a chance his phone has been tampered with and turned into a detonator for a bomb. Does Albert's evidence give him sufficient reason to believe pushing the button on his phone poses a risk of harm to others? Some people exposed to this evidence (those with advanced degrees in electronics) would conclude that there's a risk of harm to others. But, since he lacks the requisite expertise, the risk of harm seems not to be foreseeable to Albert in the evidence-relative sense.

We need a way to explain why the risk of harm is not evidence-relative foreseeable to Albert in this case without reverting to a belief-relative standard. What we should presumably say is that a threat of harm as a result of φ-ing is foreseeable to an agent only if it is *reasonable* to expect the agent to have performed whatever acts are necessary to gather the relevant evidence and understand its significance. In other words, we need to appeal to a *moralized* version of the notion of evidence-relative foreseeability. It is not reasonable to expect agents to perform acts that are unduly costly or that involve violating the rights of others. It is typically not reasonable to expect someone who is not an electrical engineer to possess an advanced degree in electronics, and this explains why it is not foreseeable to Albert that pushing the button on his phone will pose a risk of harm to others.

This moralized conception of foreseeability yields intuitively plausible results in the cases considered so far, but it generates a puzzle for the moral responsibility account. Why are costs to the agent relevant to determining whether the agent can foresee that an act poses a risk of harm to others but irrelevant to determining whether the agent is liable to defensive harm for knowingly performing a risk-imposing activity? Compare the following cases:

Russian Roulette: A villain hands Albert a gun with a million chambers and makes the following sincere threat: 'I have put a bullet in one of these chambers. You must point the gun at innocent Betty and pull the trigger, or else I will murder you.' Albert reluctantly points the gun at Betty and prepares to pull the trigger. Although he does not know it, the one bullet is in the chamber that is about to fire.

Cell Phone: Albert is about to press a button on his cell phone. He currently has no evidence that doing so poses any risk of harm to anyone else. But a fanciful thought suddenly occurs to him: What if someone has tampered with my phone and turned it into a detonator for a bomb? He realizes that he could drive to the nearest technically equipped police station to have his phone examined, but this would take several hours and Albert has calls to make. Albert decides to press the button on his phone. Although he does not know it, *ex ante* there was a one-in-a-million chance that his phone had been turned into a detonator, and unfortunately that chance has eventuated and his pressing the button detonated a bomb that kills an innocent person, Betty.

The moral responsibility account deems Albert liable, in principle, to defensive harm in the first case, but if we adopt the moralized view of foreseeability, not in the second case. Whether a risk of harm is foreseeable depends on the costs an agent can be expected to bear in obtaining available evidence, but once we've deemed that an act involves a foreseeable risk of harm, costs to the agent—in the Russian roulette case, the fact that Albert will be killed by the villain if he doesn't shoot the gun—become irrelevant to whether the agent is liable for performing the act. But this asymmetry seems very difficult to justify. If being inconvenienced for several hours is costly enough so that Albert cannot reasonably be expected to bear this cost to discover whether his act poses a risk to others, and thus Albert remains non-liable when he presses the button in Cell Phone, why is Albert liable to defensive force in Russian Roulette when the alternative to acting is death? I don't see any plausible way of answering this question. I do not see why our responsibility for acquiring information about whether activities are risky should be sensitive to how costly it is to acquire the information, but our responsibility for engaging in risk-imposing activities should be completely insensitive to how costly it is to refrain from engaging in those activities. Responsibility should either be sensitive to costs in both cases or neither, but there is no good reason to sharply distinguish between them.

Suppose the proponent of the moral responsibility account were to concede this point, and agree that whether people should be liable to defensive force for knowingly engaging in risk-imposing activities should depend on whether they can be reasonably required to refrain from those activities, or whether this requirement would be too costly. This concession would rob the moral responsibility account of its distinctive feature, namely, that we can use a relatively thin notion of moral responsibility—are the potential consequences of the act foreseeable to the agent?—to determine when agents are, at least in principle, liable to defensive force. We would need a much richer moral theory to tell us when it is fair or reasonable to require agents to refrain from performing a given act. We could still use the language of moral responsibility, but it would be playing a very different role. To say that an agent is morally responsible would simply be one way of stating the conclusion that an agent is appropriately liable to defensive force; moral responsibility would no longer be doing explanatory work.

The moral responsibility account is thus impaled on the horns of a dilemma. It can rely on a nonmoralized conception of foreseeability, but this leads to clearly absurd results regarding liability to defensive harm. Alternatively, it can rely on a moralized conception of foreseeability, but this undercuts the justification for holding conscientious drivers and certain other risk-imposing agents liable to defensive force.[27]

2.4 The Evidence-Relative Account

To avoid the objections presented against the moral responsibility approach, we might instead endorse an evidence-relative account.[28] On this view, a person can only become liable to defensive harm when he acts in a way that: (a) meets the minimum conditions of voluntariness (or moral responsibility in McMahan's sense), (b) is evidence-relative impermissible, and (c) results in a threat of harm that is fact-relative impermissible.

The evidence-relative account differs from the culpability account because it is insensitive to excusing conditions other than full epistemic excuses. That is, even if Albert is excused for his attack on Betty for reasons of duress or diminished responsibility, so long as his attack meets the three conditions above, he is liable to defensive harm. What matters is voluntarily performing an evidence-relative impermissible act, not one's culpability for that act. In this way the evidence-relative account avoids some of the objections that plagued the culpability view. It also avoids the counterintuitive implications of the moral responsibility view. Neither of the two drivers in Conscientious Driver and Ambulance Driver is liable on the evidence-relative account since both act in ways that are morally permissible given the evidence available to them. And it avoids the dilemma I pressed against the moral responsibility account, since acts must be wrong in the evidence-relative sense (rather than foreseeably wrong in the fact-relative sense) to potentially generate liability. Furthermore, it reflects the common-sense intuition that it

---

[27] A different problem for McMahan's moral responsibility account—one that focuses on an alleged dilemma it generates regarding killing in war—is pressed by Seth Lazar in 'The Responsibility Dilemma for *Killing in War*: A Review Essay', *Philosophy & Public Affairs* 38, no. 2 (2010): 180–213. For McMahan's response see McMahan, 'Who is Morally Liable to be Killed in War'.

[28] For evidence-relative accounts, see Bradley Jay Strawser, 'Walking the Tightrope of Just War', *Analysis* 71, no. 3 (2011): 537–8; and Bas van der Vossen, 'Uncertain Rights against Defense', *Social Philosophy & Policy* 32, no. 2 (2016): 129–45.

seems somehow wrong or unfair to hold people liable when they did exactly what any rational person would have believed was permissible given the available evidence.

However, the evidence-relative view still faces one of the same key difficulties as the culpability account. Consider a slightly different version of Mistaken Attacker:

Police Intervention: The identical twin brother of a notorious serial killer is driving during a stormy night in a remote area when his car breaks down. Unaware that his brother has recently escaped from prison and is known to be hiding in this same area, he knocks on the door of the nearest house, seeking to phone for help. The authorities have warned Resident that the killer is certain to attack anyone he meets on sight. On opening the door, Resident justifiably believes the harmless twin is the killer and lunges at him with a knife. Just at that moment, a police officer arrives on the scene who *knows* the person being attacked by Resident is the killer's innocent twin. The police officer realizes the mistake that Resident has made, and now sees that the only way to save the twin from being killed is to shoot and kill Resident first. Alternatively, the police officer could let Resident kill the twin.

I believe it is clear that the police officer is morally permitted to shoot Resident in order to save the twin. If this judgement is correct, then Resident must be liable to *some* level of defensive harm; if he was not liable to any defensive harm, the officer would not have sufficient grounds to shoot him (morality does not typically permit killing one non-liable stranger to save another).

My intuition about this case is firm, but suppose that proponents of the evidence-relative account are unmoved: they insist that Resident is not liable to defensive harm, and so the police officer is not permitted to intervene. Maybe this bullet biting gains some plausibility from the fact that the police officer must either kill Resident or allow Resident to kill the twin. But suppose the police officer has the following two choices, either of which will end the conflict: impose a moderate level of harm on the twin, *or* impose a slightly more serious (but nonfatal) level of harm on Resident. I think it's clear that the police officer ought to impose the slightly more serious harm on Resident, but this judgement cannot be correct unless Resident bears some liability—otherwise the officer ought to impose the lesser harm.

Now consider the following case:

Duped Soldiers: A group of young soldiers is successfully fooled by a totalitarian regime into believing that the regime is good and just and is under repeated attacks from their evil neighbours, the Gloops. The regime's misinformation campaign is subtle and convincing—the soldiers are justified in believing what they are told by the regime. Once the misinformation campaign is complete, these soldiers are given orders to attack and destroy a Gloop village on the border which, they are told, is really a Gloop terrorist camp plotting a major attack. In fact, everything the regime has said is a lie, and the Gloop village contains only innocent civilians. The soldiers prepare to shell the village and are about to (unknowingly) kill all the innocent civilians in it. A peacekeeping force from a neutral third country patrols the border and could avert the attack, but only by killing the soldiers.

It is deeply implausible to hold, as the evidence-relative account must do, that both the soldiers and the Gloops are equally non-liable to attack, and so the neutral peacekeeping force has no reason to treat an attack on the soldiers any differently than the attack on the Gloops. If, for example, the number of soldiers and Gloops is equivalent, then the evidence-relative view of liability requires that the peacekeepers allow the soldiers to kill the Gloops, since it is not permissible to kill non-liable strangers in order to save an equivalent number of non-liable strangers. The evidence-relative account gets the wrong answer in this case, and I think this provides us with a strong reason to reject it.

The two examples in this section suggest that individuals who are not culpable on grounds of blameless ignorance can nevertheless sometimes be liable to defensive harm, but this is inconsistent with the evidence-relative account.

2.5 The Moral Status Account

In paradigmatic cases where A is liable to defensive force—for example, where A wrongfully attempts to murder B—A treats B as if B lacks important moral rights. Put differently, A fails to treat B in accordance with the moral status that she in fact possesses. Since A treats B as having this diminished moral status, A cannot reasonably demand that B (or some third party) refrain from imposing proportionate and necessary defensive harm. Such a demand would conflict with ideals of equality and reciprocity. A would be saying, in effect, 'I demand that you respect my moral rights, even though I am not extending the same treatment to you.' This is objectionably inegalitarian: the demand implies that A is not bound by the same moral requirements as others. The demand is also objectionable because of its nonreciprocal content: A demands that B treat A in ways that A is unwilling to treat B. I think the unreasonable character of A's imagined demand explains why A is liable to defensive force. We cannot treat others as having diminished moral status while insisting that others respect our moral status even at the cost of suffering serious harm or death.[29]

---

[29] This doesn't entail that moral demands must always satisfy conditions of equality and reciprocity to be reasonable. Sometimes there are good reasons to disregard these conditions, but these reasons are

In cases like Conscientious Driver and Ambulance Driver, however, things are different. Driver and the EMT do not treat anyone as having a lesser moral status than they in fact possess, and this is why they are not liable to defensive force. There are two different ways we might explain why this is so. First, we might argue that agents like Driver and the EMT do not violate anyone's moral rights, and thus cannot be liable to defensive force. This argument, however, depends on a controversial thesis about moral rights. On this view, whether B has a claim right that A refrain from φ-ing depends in part on A's evidence. When A does not have sufficient evidence that his φ-ing poses undue risk of harm to B, then he does not violate any duty he owes to B by φ-ing, even if B turns out to be harmed by A's φ-ing, and thus would have been duty bound to refrain from φ-ing had he been aware of all the facts. Put differently, moral rights are not fact relative. This explains why agents like Driver and the EMT are not liable: they don't violate anyone's moral rights.

Although I endorse this view of moral rights, and will defend it in Chapter 6, we can also explain why agents like Driver and the EMT are not liable without taking a position on whether moral rights are fact relative. Even if moral rights are fact relative, it remains the case that Driver and the EMT do not treat anyone as having a lesser moral status than they in fact possess, and this is what matters for liability to defensive force, or so I will argue in the remainder of this chapter. So even if moral rights are fact relative, how we treat others in the evidence-relative sense provides the appropriate standard for determining who is liable to defensive force.

Consider the decision to engage in prudent driving (i.e., driving in accordance with the fairly designed rules of the road). It is foreseeable that, even if everyone observes the rules, a certain number of accidental fatalities will occur every year. But even though we know that the activity will result in a certain number of innocent people being killed each year, it's widely believed that the practice of prudent driving is morally permissible. Let's assume that this moral judgement is correct—let's assume that the general practice of prudent driving is morally permissible because the risk of harm arising from accidents does not fall disproportionately on any particular person or group, the risk of harm is acceptable in light of the benefits everyone derives, and the harms are not instrumental in achieving the benefits. Moreover, in industrialized societies almost everyone benefits from the social practice of prudent driving, and it's difficult to say that any given person benefits much more (or less) than others. Even those people who don't own cars derive significant benefits from the practice of prudent driving: they rely on others (family, friends, and bus drivers) to drive them places, they receive goods and services that are delivered by trucks, and they derive major

not present in paradigmatic instances of defensive force where a wrongful aggressor threatens an innocent victim.

benefits from local and global economies that are heavily reliant on the practice of driving.[30]

If these claims are true, then when any particular instance of prudent driving results in unintended harm to innocent people, this cost has already been counted in the evidence-relative justification of that particular instance of driving. If the best moral theory has already determined that permitting the practice of prudent driving is permissible *despite* the harms that will predictably result to innocent people, then I believe it is unreasonable to hold individual prudent drivers liable to defensive harm for the particular harms that result from their driving.[31]

Paradigmatic cases of liability to defensive harm, however, are different. In these cases, the person who is liable to defensive harm, A, acts in a way that foreseeably might result in harm to some other person (or group), B, and the risk-imposing act that A performs would not be evidence-relative permissible unless those who might be harmed lack rights against the imposition of the harm. Consider a simple case: A intends to kill B and attacks B with lethal force. A's act is (absent some other justification) evidence-relative impermissible *unless* B is liable to bear the lethal harm that A is about to impose. If this is not the case—if B is not liable to lethal harm—then A is liable to defensive harm. Or consider a case where A recklessly drives too fast in order to get to the movies, thereby imposing a risk of harm on pedestrian B. Reckless driving is evidence-relative impermissible precisely because it imposes an unacceptable risk of harm on people who are not liable to bear harm. Because A's act of reckless driving could only be evidence-relative permissible if B was liable to the harm, A ought to be liable to defensive harm if his reckless driving turns out to pose a threat to non-liable B.

These cases involve one person (the agent who imposes harm) treating another (the person on whom harm is imposed) either *as if* the latter lacks certain rights, or else as if those rights do not have the stringency or moral weight that they do in fact possess. My proposal is that when one person, A, behaves in this way with regard to another person, B, A assumes a special kind of responsibility for harms that B might suffer. By that I mean that A acts in a way that she ought to know would impose impermissible harm *unless* B lacks claims against the harm, and this means that A ought to be liable to defensive harm unless B lacks such claims.[32]

---

[30] It's true that there are a small number of people—perhaps the Amish are an appropriate example—who eschew driving and live in a way that is largely isolated from the benefits of the practice (though even the Amish engage in trade with outsiders), but I set these unusual cases aside here. It's also important to stress that I only make this claim about benefits for the practice of *prudent* driving, that is, driving that conforms to well-designed rules aimed at ensuring a reasonable degree of safety.

[31] I also believe that such prudent drivers cannot be singled out as morally liable to compensate people who are harmed by their nonnegligent conduct.

[32] An important exception may be cases where a person is tasked with an institutional role, like that of a prison guard, which requires the person in question to treat others as if they lack important rights. I address this topic in section 2.7.4.

There is an important moral difference between engaging in some activity that carries some risk of harm to innocent others but that the correct moral theory declares to be evidence-relative permissible given the balance of costs and benefits, and acting in a way that would not be evidence-relative permissible unless we assume that certain others lack rights that people normally possess. In the case of prudent driving, we could say that the risk-imposing agent accords each person the concern and respect they are owed. The fact that he imposes a certain risk of harm on others is consistent with everyone's moral status, since the risk of harm is (we are assuming) justifiable to all persons in light of the balance of costs and benefits of the practice of prudent driving. But in paradigmatic cases of liability to defensive harm things are different. The risk-imposing agent does not treat everyone with the concern and respect they are normally due: she acts as if some people have fewer rights (or less stringent rights) or moral claims relative to others. Since the risk-imposing agent has made this choice, it seems reasonable that she be liable to some defensive harm should those others turn out not to be liable to the harm she ends up imposing. This rationale appeals to an idea of *reciprocity*: that our standing to press claims against others depends in part on how we treat those others.[33] If I treat you with the concern and respect that you are owed, as determined by the correct moral theory, then you owe me nothing less. However, if I treat you as if you lack some rights, then I forfeit some of the claims I would otherwise have against you should you turn out to have those rights.

Some might object that this proposal is unfair in certain cases like Mistaken Attacker. After all, if Resident does what he justifiably believes to be permissible given his epistemic situation, why should he be liable to defensive harm when the facts turn out to be different than the evidence gave him reason to believe? Surely this imposes an unfairly demanding standard of conduct on Resident.

Although this objection might seem tempting, I think it should be resisted. It would indeed be unfair to blame someone, or criticize her, if her actions are evidence-relative permissible. Such negative reactive attitudes are only appropriate when someone has acted in a way that she had adequate reason to suspect might be wrongful. But liability to defensive harm is not a reactive attitude. A person can be liable for the consequences of her actions even when she is not blameworthy or subject to criticism. Even when we do not act wrongly in the evidence-relative sense, we sometimes gamble with the moral rights of others in the sense described above: we act in ways that we ought to know would be wrong

---

[33] In this respect my proposal overlaps with David Miller's recent, more wide-ranging discussion of the moral basis of human rights. See Miller, 'Are Human Rights Conditional?' in *Human Rights and Global Justice: The 10th Kobe Lectures*, ed. Tetsu Sakurai and Makoto Usami (Stuttgart: Franz Steiner Verlag, 2014), 17–35. For another recent defence of a reciprocity condition regarding the possession of moral rights, see David Rodin, 'The Reciprocity Theory of Rights', *Law and Philosophy* 33, no. 3 (2014): 281–308. Rodin's view is more ambitious than Miller's or mine, since he claims reciprocity is one of the *grounds* of moral rights, and not merely a condition for possession.

but for the assumption that certain others lack rights. Though it does not make sense to blame us when we act in these ways, it does make sense to say that we may forfeit some of our rights when we take these sorts of risks.[34]

The critic who insists that what matters for liability is only whether the agent acted permissibly in the evidence-relative sense fails to notice that not all evidence-relative permissible acts are alike. Some actions are evidence-relative permissible because the correct moral theory tells us that the action is permissible even though it imposes a risk of harm on innocent people. In these cases, each person's claims or interests have been taken fairly into account in determining that the action is evidence-relative permissible, and so performing the action is consistent with showing appropriate regard for each person's moral status. Other actions are evidence-relative permissible, however, only because the evidence gives us reason (or apparent reason) to believe that some person has lost his standing to press claims against us, or at least that his claims have less weight. In these cases, if we proceed with the risk-imposing activity, we treat those whom we might harm differently than we do in the former cases: those individuals are not accorded the same status that innocent persons are normally accorded.[35] I believe this difference in treatment makes an important moral difference for liability.

I therefore propose the *moral status account* of liability to defensive harm:

A is liable to defensive harm for ϕ-ing when: (a) the evidence-relative permissibility of ϕ-ing depends on the assumption that at least one person, B, lacks a moral right, but (b) B in fact possesses the relevant moral right, and thus (c) B faces a threat, or apparent threat, to her rights.

Three points require clarification. First, this account provides a set of conditions for a person to be liable to proportionate defensive harm, but what constitutes proportionate harm will be determined by the stringency of the right that the attacker threatens.[36] Second, this formulation allows that harmful *omissions* may also be covered by the moral status account. For example, if A chooses not to throw B a life preserver when this omission is both evidence- and fact-relative

---

[34] Note that in other contexts we can accrue moral duties to bear costs as a result of our actions even when, *as a matter of fact*, there is no other reasonable action open to us, and thus our actions are blameless. For example, in the well-worn case where I need to break into your empty cabin to survive an unexpected storm, I may still be required to compensate you for the damage caused and any resources I used, even though there was no other reasonable course of action open to me.

[35] On my view, you accord someone diminished moral status whenever the evidence-relative permissibility of your act depends on assuming the person in question lacks a right that they in fact possess. This might strike some readers as overly dramatic—if I make a mistake about your ownership of a pencil, do I really treat you as having diminished moral status? My answer is yes, though obviously the diminishment is relatively minimal. The more serious the error about someone's moral rights, the more serious the failure with regard to moral status.

[36] I will explain and defend this view of proportionality in Chapter 4.

impermissible, A may be liable to defensive harm.[37] Third, the threat to B must be a reasonably foreseeable consequence of A's φ-ing.[38] Finally, the account can explain why attackers who will not in fact harm innocent persons can sometimes be liable to defensive force. I will have more to say about this last issue below.

2.6 Advantages

There are four main reasons to accept the moral status account of liability to defensive harm. First, it does not yield any obviously counterintuitive results in the relevant range of examples. It gets the correct results in Mistaken Attacker and Duped Soldiers. Resident and the soldiers may be blameless in making their respective mistakes, but they are nonetheless liable to defensive harm because they perform acts whose evidence-relative permissibility they ought to know depends on the assumption that the people whom they attack lack important or stringent rights. But unlike the moral responsibility view, the moral status account does not implausibly declare that Driver and the EMT are liable to defensive harm. In these cases, the evidence-relative permissibility of getting behind the wheel of a vehicle and imposing a tiny risk of harm on others does not depend on treating those others as if they lack any rights against harm.

Second, the idea underpinning the moral status account is independently plausible. To treat others as if they lack moral rights against having harm imposed is a grave matter, and so it's plausible to suppose that, when we act in this way, we must accept a certain substantive responsibility for our actions. When we act in this way, we go out on a moral limb: we knowingly take the risk of treating others as if they lack moral rights, and we also ought to know that the permissibility of our actions depends on this judgement about the moral status of others. When we take such a risk, it is only reasonable that we—as opposed to the innocent person who now faces a threat of harm—may be liable to defensive harm when our judgement about the moral status of others turns out to be mistaken.

Third, the moral status account can explain why, as McMahan plausibly claims, moral justification ought to defeat otherwise valid instances of liability to defensive harm.[39] Consider the following case:

---

[37] In this sense, I am in agreement with much of what Cécile Fabre says about wars of subsistence in *Cosmopolitan War* (Oxford: Oxford University Press, 2014), chap. 3.

[38] Something like the proximate cause standard in tort law is what I have in mind here. For an illuminating discussion of this standard see Arthur Ripstein, *Private Wrongs* (Cambridge, MA: Harvard University Press, 2016), 91–3.

[39] McMahan, 'The Basis of Moral Liability', 399–400, and *Killing in War*, 42–5. By 'justification' McMahan means acts that are not only fact-relative permissible, but also are such that there is a positive moral reason to perform the act. This distinction will not be relevant to the discussion that follows since any fact-relative permissible act that causes harm to innocent people will necessarily also be a justified act in McMahan's sense.

Justified Bomber: Bomber acting in a just war is about to drop a bomb on an enemy target. The bombing is fully justified according to the correct principles of *jus in bello*, but it will kill a certain (proportionate) number of innocent civilians as a side effect. The civilians have an antiaircraft gun that they could use to shoot down and kill Bomber before he is able to drop the bomb.

In this case, although Bomber's act is justified all things considered, it involves the imposition of unjust harm on the civilians—that is, it infringes the rights of the civilians.[40] Thus, it looks like the moral responsibility account must declare that Bomber is liable to the defensive harm that the civilians might impose since Bomber is morally responsible for threatening the rights of the innocent civilians. To resist this conclusion McMahan argues that Bomber's justification defeats or nullifies what would otherwise seem (on his account) to be a valid instance of liability to defensive harm. But it's difficult to understand how this argument coheres with the moral responsibility account. Why should liability track moral responsibility for an *impermissible* imposition of harm on innocent people, rather than simply moral responsibility for the imposition of harm on innocent people regardless of whether it is permissible all things considered? The claim that we must adopt the former position looks ad hoc or stipulative if we adopt the moral responsibility view of liability.[41]

The moral status conception, however, can explain *why* justification defeats liability. Although Bomber threatens to kill the civilians below, in acting in accordance with the correct principles of just war that are themselves justified by whatever turns out to be the correct moral theory, he treats those civilians in a way that is consistent with their moral status—that is, he acts in accordance with moral principles that are justified (we assume) in a manner consistent with according appropriate concern and respect to all persons. Thus, Bomber remains non-liable. The conflict between Bomber and the civilians thus represents another case of symmetrical self-defence, like Conscientious Driver, where both parties are not liable to defensive harm, but each party has, on my view, an agent-relative permission to infringe the rights of the other in self-defence if necessary.

The moral status account also yields a more plausible explanation of *when* justification defeats liability. On one view, justification defeats liability whenever

---

[40] Unjust harm is thus different than impermissible harm. The former refers to whether the harm is imposed on non-liable individuals, whereas the latter refers to whether the action of harm imposition is morally justified all things considered. There can be cases, like Justified Bomber, where unjust harm is imposed in the course of a permissible action.
[41] For criticism of McMahan on this point see Uwe Steinhoff, 'Debate: Jeff McMahan on the Moral Inequality of Combatants', *Journal of Political Philosophy* 16, no. 2 (2008): 222–3. For McMahan's reply see McMahan, 'Debate: Justification and Liability in War', *Journal of Political Philosophy* 16, no. 2 (2008); 227–44; and *Killing in War*, sect. 2.1.

the person who is otherwise liable to defensive harm acts in a manner that is permissible in the fact-relative sense.[42] But this seems incorrect. Consider:

Accidentally Permissible Killing: Albert intends to kill Betty because he falsely believes Betty is culpably threatening his life—as a matter of fact Betty poses no threat to Albert. Moreover, Albert's beliefs about Betty's threat are not justified given the evidence, and so his action is evidence-relative impermissible. Albert points his gun and prepares to fire at Betty in 'self-defence' but unbeknownst to Albert, killing Betty is the only way to save five thousand innocent others from being killed (Betty is about to unwittingly and non-culpably release a lethal toxin that will kill the five thousand). Albert's killing of Betty is thus, in the fact-relative sense, morally permitted: it is an instance of an all-things-considered permissible killing of an innocent person to avert a great harm, though there is no way for either Albert or Betty to be aware of this fact. Just as Albert is about to shoot, Betty sees that Albert is about to shoot her (for no reason as far as she can see), and she has the chance to shoot Albert in self-defence.

In this example, Albert is mistaken about why he may permissibly shoot Betty, but he acts with fact-relative permission. If we believe that a person cannot be liable to defensive harm when his imposition of harm on others is fact-relative permissible, then we ought to believe that Albert is not liable to defensive harm. But this is implausible. Betty would not, I believe, *wrong* Albert—she would not threaten any of Albert's rights—if she were to shoot him in self-defence. The moral status conception of liability can explain this conclusion, since on this view what matters is whether the evidence-relative permissibility of Albert's act depends on the assumption that Betty is liable to the harm that Albert intends to impose. Because Albert acts *as if* Betty lacks rights against the harm he threatens to impose, Albert cannot avoid liability to defensive harm when, despite the fact that Betty is not liable to his attack, it fortuitously turns out that his act is permissible in the fact-relative sense. But, unlike the evidence-relative account of liability, the moral status view does not implausibly declare that a person who acts with evidence-relative permission can *never* be liable to defensive harm. Instead, the moral status conception declares that what matters is whether a person, judged from the evidence-relative standpoint, acts as if others lack rights against harm. When, and only when, our actions have this particular feature—treating others with something less than the concern and respect they are due—we make ourselves liable to defensive harm.

---

[42] See McMahan, 'The Basis of Moral Liability', 399–400, and *Killing in War*, 43. It's not clear whether McMahan would in fact endorse the view described above, since he says only that fact-relative permissibility is *necessary* to defeat liability, while remaining neutral on whether it is *sufficient* to do so.

Finally, another important advantage of the moral status account is its capacity to reach intuitively plausible judgements in a range of cases where a defensive agent justifiably, but mistakenly, believes that she faces a genuine threat of harm. Consider the following case:[43]

> *Albert's Bluff.* Albert maliciously decides to scare Betty. He points what he knows to be an unloaded gun at Betty's head and says, 'I'm going to blow your brains out.' Betty, believing Albert's threat to be real, pulls out her own gun and kills Albert in 'self-defence'.

Intuitively, Betty does not wrong Albert. The moral status account explains why. It declares that Albert is liable to defensive force, since the evidence-relative permissibility of his act depends on the assumption that Betty lacks certain rights (we have moral rights against being threatened in this way), and this causes Betty to justifiably believe that she faces a threat to her moral rights. Thus, when she uses defensive force against Albert, she does not infringe his rights and so does not become liable to defensive force herself.

This is the correct result. Albert should not be permitted to defend himself against Betty as if he were an innocent person being wrongly attacked. And Betty doesn't seem to wrong Albert, since he gives her every reason to believe that he is about to murder her.[44] The moral status account correctly distinguishes cases like Albert's Bluff from Mistaken Attacker. In the latter case, the twin at the door has done nothing to make himself liable to defensive force, and so when Resident attacks the twin, Resident becomes liable to defensive force. In both cases the defensive agent has a justified belief that defensive force is permitted, but only Albert is liable to defensive force.[45]

You might worry, however, that the moral status account's resolution of such cases is ad hoc. Albert does not threaten any fact-relative wrongful harm in Albert's Bluff. What is the basis for holding him liable in the same way as someone who poses an actual lethal threat?

The moral status account, however, is well positioned to answer this worry. Regardless of whether you in fact pull the trigger, it is impermissible to pull out a gun, point it at someone's head, and issue a threat. To threaten someone in this

---

[43] I borrow the basic details of this case from Kimberly Kessler Ferzan, 'The Bluff: The Power of Insincere Actions', *Legal Theory* 23, no. 3 (2017): 169.

[44] This is confirmed when we consider what it would be permissible for a third party, someone with full information, to do. A third party could not permissibly kill or seriously harm Betty to save Albert even though Albert poses no actual threat of harm to Betty. This is best explained by the fact that Albert is liable to the harm Betty imposes, and Betty remains non-liable.

[45] The moral status account thus does not eliminate the possibility of defensive agents suffering bad moral luck with regard to their liability, but that is not a compelling objection to the account. To eliminate the possibility of defensive agents suffering bad moral luck, we would have to endorse the evidence-relative account considered earlier, and that account is vulnerable to decisive objections.

way is a violation of that person's moral rights. We have claim rights against being *threatened* with harm, not merely rights against being actually harmed. Moreover, whether your act is a threat does not depend on whether you are sincere when you issue the threat. A mugger who tells his victim, 'Hand over your wallet or I'll shoot' has violated his victim's rights even if he has no intention of shooting, and even if he has no intention of keeping the wallet. Whether A violates a duty he owes to B is generally not a matter of what A believes or even intends, but rather whether A's behaviour conforms to a certain objective, publicly verifiable standard of conduct.[46] Thus, in one important sense, cases like Albert's Bluff are no different than standard cases of wrongful aggression. Albert violates Betty's rights by threatening her, and in doing so, he gives her sufficient reason to believe that he will violate further rights unless she takes defensive action.

But even if you accept the premise that Albert violates Betty's rights merely by making the threat, and thus makes himself liable to some defensive harm, you might balk at the idea that Albert is liable to be killed. After all, there's a difference between the right Betty has not to be threatened with death, and the right she has not to be murdered. The latter right is much more stringent, and this surely bears on the extent of Albert's liability.[47] But if Albert is only liable to something much less serious than being killed, we haven't found a satisfactory solution to Albert's Bluff: intuitively, Betty does not wrong Albert *at all* if she kills him.

To explain this result, we need to recognize that liability to defensive force is a relationship that identifies conditions under which one person lacks the standing to complain about another person imposing defensive force, where the purpose of the defensive force is to avert some *prospective* injustice. Its primary practical import is at the point in time prior to the injustice being committed, or at least prior to the unjust act being completed. Consider a paradigmatic case of liability to defensive force: Albert is about to murder Betty to gain an inheritance, and she can only save herself by killing him. Virtually everyone agrees that, in this case, Albert is liable to be killed by Betty. Now suppose that Betty kills Albert in self-defence before he can harm her. What explains the fact that Albert was liable to lethal defensive force? It cannot be that Albert killed Betty since this isn't what happened: Betty killed Albert. Instead, liability is a matter of what we justifiably believe will occur at t2 in light of what the aggressor did at t1. If, in the case we've just been considering, Albert is liable to lethal defensive force when Betty must decide whether to kill him, this is explained by things that Albert has already done. Albert has made choices and taken action that give Betty sufficient reason to believe that he is wrongfully attacking her with lethal force. In virtue of having given Betty that evidence, he forfeits the standing to complain if she imposes

---

[46] I offer a limited argument for this claim in Chapter 7.
[47] Chapter 4 defends the thesis that the amount of defensive force to which an attacker renders himself liable depends on the stringency of the right he threatens.

defensive harm on him. He cannot reasonably say to Betty, 'You have to wait to see whether I really kill you before you can know whether I'm liable to lethal defensive force. If you try to use defensive force against me before knowing what will happen, you are gambling with my moral rights, and you yourself will be liable should it turn out that, for any reason, I'm unable or unwilling to kill you.' This speech is clearly absurd. Albert cannot put the burden of being mistaken on Betty in this way. By performing sufficiently threatening actions, Albert forfeits his rights: there's no sense in which his forfeiture is contingent on how things might later turn out.

With this analysis of the paradigmatic case in hand, it's now easy to explain Albert's Bluff. At the point at which Betty must decide whether to impose defensive harm in Albert's Bluff, the facts might be identical to the facts in the paradigmatic case in which Albert intends to murder Betty. The very same considerations that ground Albert's liability in the paradigmatic case also ground Albert's liability in the case where he is bluffing. The fact that Albert does not sincerely intend to murder Betty is irrelevant in the same way it is irrelevant when someone makes an insincere promise to perform an act. Just as insincere promises result in a change of moral rights and duties, so do insincere threats.[48]

You might worry that this explanation, whatever its virtues, is inadequate. For example, suppose that Betty learns that Albert's threat is not genuine in Albert's Bluff—that he is only maliciously joking. Surely it's impermissible for Betty to shoot Albert, and this is most plausibly explained by the fact that Albert is not liable to defensive force. Once Betty knows that the harm will not eventuate, she also surely learns that Albert is not really liable to defensive force. Doesn't this show that liability does depend, at least in part, on what will occur in the future?

I don't think so. In this variant of Albert's Bluff, it would be wrong for Betty to harm Albert because doing so is *unnecessary*. She can easily avoid imposing harm on Albert without suffering any serious cost herself, and thus shooting Albert violates the necessity condition on the permissible use of defensive force. In Chapter 5 I will argue that an attacker can be at least partly liable to defensive force even when harming the attacker violates the necessity condition. If that argument succeeds, then there's nothing puzzling about concluding that Albert can be liable to defensive force in Albert's Bluff, but it may be unnecessary and wrong for Betty to use force against him when she can avoid doing so without incurring undue costs.

In sum, although it's common to assume that an attacker's liability to defensive force depends entirely or primarily on what he is going to do in the future, this assumption is false. An attacker's liability instead depends on what acts he has

---

[48]   In this respect, I agree with the conclusions reached by Ferzan and Bolinger, though they arrive at this conclusion via different arguments than the one I've offered. See Ferzan, 'The Bluff'; and Bolinger, 'Mistaken Defense and Normative Conventions'.

already performed. By performing various threatening acts, an attacker gives a defensive agent sufficient reason to believe that she is being wrongfully attacked. This is why the attacker forfeits his rights against defensive force. You cannot complain about the imposition of defensive force when you give another person justifiable reason to believe that you are a wrongful aggressor.

2.7 Objections

The moral status conception of liability, recall, can be stated as follows:

> A is liable to defensive harm for ϕ-ing when: (a) the evidence-relative permissibility of ϕ-ing depends on the assumption that at least one person, B, lacks a moral right that persons normally possess, but (b) B in fact possesses the relevant moral right, and thus (c) B faces a threat, or apparent threat, to her rights.

In this section I confront further objections that might be pressed against this view.

2.7.1 Culpable versus Responsible Threats

The moral status account holds that people—like Resident in Mistaken Attacker— who are merely responsible but not culpable can be liable to defensive harm. But this, a critic might object, means that the moral status account fails to correctly distinguish between culpable and merely responsible threats. The view assumes that Resident is analogous to a culpable attacker, but this seems false. Surely Resident retains some rights that a culpable attacker loses. After all, Resident does not seem to act as *wrongfully* as a culpable attacker.[49]

To answer this objection we must distinguish claims about proportionality from claims about whether agents are liable to any defensive force. The claim that, other things being equal, culpable attackers are liable to *more* defensive force than non-culpable attackers doesn't conflict with the moral status account. The moral status account identifies the necessary and sufficient conditions for liability to any degree of defensive force, but doesn't provide an account of how proportionality is determined. In Chapter 4, I will argue that culpability is not, in fact, one of the direct bases for determining proportionality, but one could reject the arguments in Chapter 4 while accepting the moral status account of liability.

---

[49] Saba Bazargan offers a response to this objection on behalf of a version of the moral responsibility account. See Bazargan, 'Defensive Liability Without Culpability', in *The Ethics of Self-Defense*, ed. Christian Coons and Michael Weber (New York: Oxford University Press, 2016), 69–85.

Second, we must distinguish non-comparative and comparative claims about liability. The proponent of the objection might be making the following non-comparative claim: non-culpable persons cannot be liable to any defensive force, and thus the moral status account must be mistaken. This claim seems clearly false. It is counterintuitive to suppose that Resident cannot be liable to any defensive force, and we also have independent reasons to be sceptical that culpability is the main basis for liability to defensive force. Alternatively, the proponent of the objection might be making the following comparative claim: if a defensive agent has a choice whether to impose defensive harm on a culpable or non-culpable attacker then, other things being equal, it would be wrong to impose defensive harm on the non-culpable attacker, suggesting, at a minimum, that culpability can determine liability in cases where the defensive agent faces culpable and non-culpable attackers.

But we can account for the intuitive difference between culpable and non-culpable attackers without directly invoking a culpability-based view of liability. First, in many cases other things are not equal—culpable attackers are often culpable partly because they threaten to violate more stringent rights than non-culpable attackers. A murderer threatens to commit a more serious injustice than a negligent driver, even if both are threatening to kill an innocent person. Thus, in many cases I believe culpability merely correlates with what really matters for determining the degree of liability, namely, the stringency of the right that is threatened.[50] But what about cases where things really are equal? In these cases we can explain the difference between culpable and non-culpable attackers by appeal to moral desert.[51] Here is how the argument goes:

P3   There are impersonal reasons (i.e., reasons unconnected to individual rights) to avoid imposing harm, or allowing harm to be imposed, on people who do not deserve to suffer harm.

P4   People who are not blameworthy for any serious wrongdoing do not deserve to suffer harm, but the same is not true of people who are blameworthy for serious wrongdoing.

Therefore

C2   There are impersonal reasons (i.e., apart from considerations of liability) to avoid imposing harm on responsible but non-culpable threats that do not apply in the case of culpable threats.

---

[50] I defend this idea in Chapter 4.

[51] This line of response can also be deployed in defence of the moral responsibility account. But this argument cannot help the responsibility account avoid the objection to which I claim it is vulnerable, namely, its failure to distinguish between cases like Conscientious Driver as opposed to cases like Duped Soldiers.

This argument can explain the intuitive judgement that, other things being equal, it is wrong to impose harm on a non-culpable attacker when one could have imposed harm on a culpable attacker instead. Both attackers can be, as the moral status view insists, liable to defensive harm. But we have additional impersonal reasons to avoid imposing harms on the non-culpable threat because he is innocent of any blame, reasons not present in the case of culpable threats.

Some might resist this appeal to moral desert. Some deny that people can ever deserve to suffer harm. But people who hold this view are unlikely to believe it is intuitively obvious that one must impose harm on culpable rather than non-culpable attackers, other things being equal. If culpable attackers do not deserve to suffer harm, and everything else is in fact equal, then there is no reason to prefer that culpable rather than non-culpable attackers should be selected when a choice is possible.

2.7.2 Resident and Driver

Some may object that the moral status account cannot coherently treat Resident in Mistaken Attacker differently from Driver. They may argue that Resident has an evidence-relative justification for his act that is analogous to the justification for Driver's act. The act of careful and conscientious driving is justified, we have been assuming, in large part because the probability of harming an innocent person is extremely low, but the benefits of permitting the practice are very large. But the same justification is apparently available for Resident's act. A rule permitting people to use necessary and proportionate force when they have compelling evidence that they are faced with a liable attacker can be justified by appeal to the fact that the probability of innocent people being harmed by this practice is extremely low (cases like Mistaken Resident are going to be very rare), but the benefits of permitting the practice are very large (many innocent people may be able to avert unjust harm). But if Resident has the same justification as Driver then the moral status account declares him non-liable, despite what I have claimed.

I don't think this objection succeeds. I have a preliminary reply and a main reply to the objection. The preliminary reply is that I suspect a rule permitting defensive force under the conditions described is either *more likely* to result in harm to innocent persons that the objection assumes, or else *less likely* to deliver benefits than the objection assumes. In most contexts where people believe that they must exercise defensive force, they have had little time to carefully assess the evidence and deliberate over possible courses of action—time is typically tight and a decision must be made very quickly. If the standard of evidence required for defensive force to be evidence-relative permissible is indexed to the time agents have to make a decision, then we cannot require agents to have too much evidence regarding the liability of the attacker, but this means the probability of mistaken uses of force will increase to the point where it's no longer the case that we can say the rule permitting defensive force is extremely unlikely to result in harm to an innocent person in any given instance. This problem could be evaded by requiring a very high standard of evidence to be met before it is permissible for agents to use defensive force, but since defensive agents rarely have time to gather much evidence, this high standard will mean most agents will not be permitted to use defensive force against wrongful aggressors, thus diminishing the benefits the rule delivers. Of course it's open to proponents of this objection to propose a Goldilocks solution to the dilemma: identify a standard of evidence low enough to permit the vast majority of fact-relative permissible uses of defensive force but high enough to prohibit the vast majority of fact-relative impermissible uses. Whether this can be done depends on the epistemic conditions in which most agents will find themselves, and so I don't claim that such a solution isn't possible, though I strongly doubt any plausible rule can yield anything close to the same balance of costs and benefits that we are assuming is delivered by the rule permitting careful and conscientious driving.

But even if the preceding preliminary reply to the objection is not successful, there is a more compelling reply available. The objection assumes that Resident and Driver can rely on the same justification for their respective acts, but they cannot. *Ex ante*, Driver has no reason to believe that his act is likely to cause any harm. But *ex ante* Resident is virtually certain that his act will cause serious harm. Because Resident is virtually certain that his act will cause serious harm, his act cannot be evidence-relative justified by appeal to the fact that it's very unlikely to harm anyone. It must instead be justified in part by appeal to the fact that the person who is harmed is liable to be harmed or at least very likely liable to be harmed. Driver need make no such assumption to justify his act of careful and conscientious driving. If Resident did not have sufficient evidence that the person at the door was a liable attacker, he would not be permitted to act on the rule permitting defensive force against apparently liable attackers. The justification for Resident's act thus must assume the liability or likely liability of the person whom Resident harms, whereas the justification for Driver's act involves no similar assumption. That's the crucial difference to which the moral status account of liability draws attention. It is the only account of liability of which I'm aware that draws this distinction between cases like Mistaken Attacker and Conscientious Driver.

2.7.3 Permissibility and Liability

The moral status account holds that if performing some act, ϕ, is permissible in the evidence-relative sense, and the justification for its permissibility does not involve assuming anyone who might be harmed by ϕ-ing is liable to the harm or lacks any rights that persons normally possess, then an agent who φ's is not liable to any harm that may be caused by his φ-ing.

Some may object that we cannot separate the question of whether φ-ing is evidence-relative permissible from the question of whether agents who φ will be held liable for harm that may eventuate. In some cases, the objection goes, an activity may only be permissible *if* those who perform the activity are held strictly liable for any harm or damage that occurs. For example, perhaps keeping tigers as pets, or owning various kinds of automatic weapons, are only permissible if those who own the tigers or the automatic weapons are held strictly liable for any harm that occurs as a result. In US tort law, for example, agents who engage in activities that involve excessive or abnormal levels of risk are held to a strict liability standard, whereas more ordinary risk-imposing activities are subject to a negligence standard.[52] If some activities are only permissible if the agents who perform them are held strictly liable for any harm caused, then the moral status account cannot be correct.

I have several responses to this objection. First, the objection tries to draw support by appeal to the way some jurisdictions handle compensatory liability. But the norms and principles governing compensatory liability may differ sharply from those that govern liability to defensive force depending on the primary purpose of compensatory liability. Many theorists, for example, hold that the primary function of tort law is to instantiate a fair distribution of the harms and benefits that arise from various activities. But a recurring theme of this book is the rejection of the idea that principles of distributive fairness play a direct role in regulating the morality of defensive force. If compensatory liability is governed by principles of distributive justice, then I deny that we can infer conclusions about defensive force by appeal to facts about tort law.[53]

Second, the objection assumes that some activities have the following structure: the benefits to Albert in φ-ing are not sufficient to permit him to φ given the risks imposed on Betty *unless* we use a regime of strict liability *ex post* to ensure that any costs Betty might suffer are transferred to Albert. A key assumption in generating the conclusion that φ-ing is permissible is that private law will be an effective means, *ex post*, of ensuring that Albert, and not Betty, suffers any costs arising from Albert's φ-ing. Imagine, however, that private law is not a reliable mechanism of allocating costs *ex post*—suppose that for some reason only some people have access to the tools of private law. Thus, when a victim suffers harm as a result of an agent nonnegligently φ-ing, the victim is only able to secure compensation 40 per cent of the time. If, by hypothesis, shifting the costs from victims onto the

---

[52] See Restatement (Second) of Torts § 519 (1977).

[53] Of course not everyone shares this particular picture of the role of tort law. Rebecca Stone suggests an alternative picture, where tort law is grounded in the morality of defensive force. See Stone, 'Private Liability without Wrongdoing'.

agents who φ is necessary for φ-ing to be permissible, then φ-ing is impermissible under conditions where compensation cannot be reliably secured. But now consider defensive force. Making risk-imposing agents liable to defensive force does not ensure victims will be able to successfully deploy defensive force and avert the threat—many victims will be unable to successfully use defensive force to avert a threat. Because the prospects of success in using defensive force are so uncertain— and not equitably distributed across the population—it makes no sense to suppose that holding agents liable to defensive force is an effective way of distributing the costs of activities in a way that can render otherwise impermissibly risky activities permissible.

Third, to constitute an objection to the moral status account, the objection needs to show that some risky activities are permissible *only* if the agents performing the activities are held strictly liable. But the fact that tort law recognizes a class of activities that are abnormally risky and subject to a strict liability standard does not necessarily support the conclusion that activities are only permissible if a strict liability standard is applied. There might be a plurality of different ways to regulate these activities, all of which would render performing the activities permissible. For example, rather than subjecting agents to a strict liability standard, we might have a regime where everyone who participates in or benefits from the abnormally risky activity is required to pay a tax, and these funds are used to compensate any victims who suffer harm from nonnegligent agents.

In sum, I deny that we should conceptualize liability to defensive force in distributive terms. Making agents liable to defensive force is not a reliable mechanism by which the costs of risky activities can be fairly allocated. If an agent has met all the standards of due care and precaution that others can reasonably demand of him in performing some risk-imposing activity, then the agent has treated any potential victims of the act with the concern and respect they are due. The moral status account thus correctly holds that such an agent is not liable to defensive force.

2.7.4 Too Broad?

I have suggested that one of the virtues of the moral status account—when compared to the moral responsibility account—is that it has more limited and plausible implications regarding the range of actors who are liable to defensive force. Agents, like Driver, are not liable merely in virtue of being responsible for a fact-relative wrongful threat of harm. Agents must treat others as if they lack rights that they in fact possess in order to be liable to defensive force on my view. But a critic might protest that my view in fact has much more wide-reaching, and implausible, implications concerning the scope of liability than I have admitted. This objection might be developed in several ways.

Some may object that the moral status account implausibly entails that state officials, such as judges and prison guards, render themselves liable to defensive force when they sentence and imprison innocent people who have been found guilty of crimes via a fair criminal procedure. By convicting and imprisoning such people, state officials mistakenly treat these people as having fewer moral rights than they in fact possess, and thus the moral status account apparently entails that these state officials are liable to defensive force. But this, says the critic, cannot be true.

This objection can be rejected because it relies on a false premise. The evidence-relative justification for state officials enforcing the criminal law in these cases need not depend on the assumption that the people who are convicted and imprisoned are *morally* liable to imprisonment. What justifies the acts of state officials in these cases is the fact that victims have been tried and convicted via a fair legal process, and thus are *legally* liable to punishment. Consider a case where a defendant is found guilty by a scrupulously fair legal procedure. The judge, however, correctly believes that the defendant is innocent because she has also seen additional evidence that was obtained illegally and thus excluded from the trial. I believe that the judge is permitted, indeed required, to sentence the defendant according to standard procedures despite what she believes. So long as there are powerful reasons to adhere to the rules of the criminal justice system—not to make exceptions to these rules *whenever* we believe we are in possession of the moral truth[54]—then the assumption of a defendant's moral liability is not required to make the act of punishment evidence-relative permissible.[55]

But perhaps the objection can be developed in cases that don't involve public officials. Suppose that, for example, you fire your cleaner because she has been convicted of petty theft, but the conviction was a mistake: the cleaner is not guilty of anything.[56] In firing the cleaner, it seems that you have treated her as if she lacks rights that she in fact possesses, but surely this doesn't render you liable to defensive force. This would show the moral status account to be implausibly broad in assigning liability.

I think this version of the objection can be safely dismissed. Even if the evidence-relative permissibility of firing the cleaner does rely on assuming the cleaner lacks moral rights that she in fact possesses, this is insufficient to render

---

[54] David Estlund, for example, argues that these reasons derive from the epistemic value of certain procedures. See Estlund, 'On Following Orders in an Unjust War', *Journal of Political Philosophy* 15, no. 2 (2007): 213–34. For a different explanation, see Daniel Viehoff, 'Legitimately Arresting the Innocent, and Other Puzzles about Officially Inflicted Harm' (unpublished manuscript). I am not here endorsing Estlund's or Viehoff's proposals—only pointing out that we might have a variety of reasons to adhere to rules that make it permissible to punish people who have been convicted of crimes according to a fair procedure.

[55] This is, of course, compatible with the further idea that some exceptions to the legal rule may be permissible or indeed obligatory in extraordinary cases (e.g., to save someone from being mistakenly executed).

[56] I owe this example to Victor Tadros.

you liable to defensive force. To be liable to defensive force you must also be threatening to violate some right that the cleaner has against you, and in countries like the United States and Great Britain, people who clean private homes typically do not have moral rights against being terminated without cause. You have the moral right to discontinue using the services of a cleaner for almost any reason. The cleaner has a right (I would argue) against being fired for certain discriminatory reasons (e.g., racism or sexism) but beyond that, you don't violate any right of the cleaner by terminating her services for any reason (e.g., you are now happy to have a messier house, or you'd rather spend the money on luxury avocados, or whatever). So the moral status account doesn't imply any liability in this case.

We could amend the case such that the employer and employee have a contract that stipulates that the employee can only be fired for a very limited set of reasons, one of which is conviction of a crime. But this won't support the objection. Once we describe the case in this way, it should be clear that what makes it evidence-relative permissible for the employer to fire the employee is an assumption about the *legal status* of the employee, and not the employee's moral status. And since the contract states that the employee can be fired when duly convicted of a crime, the employer would not be threatening to violate any right of the employee's in terminating the contract. I think something similar will be true about almost all other examples we might construct in an attempt to illustrate that the moral status account is overly broad in assigning liability to defensive force.

2.7.5 Evidence-Relative Duty

Consider the following variant of Mistaken Attacker:

> *Mistaken Attacker's Children*: The identical twin brother of a notorious serial killer is driving during a stormy night in a remote area when his car breaks down. Unaware that his brother has recently escaped from prison and is known to be hiding in this same area, he knocks on the door of the nearest house, seeking to phone for help. On opening the door, Resident justifiably believes the harmless twin is the killer. Resident has been warned by the authorities that the killer will certainly attack anyone he meets on sight, and so Resident lunges at him with a knife in order to protect her two children, whom she believes are about to be murdered by the person at the door.

Let's stipulate that Resident is morally required to use necessary and proportionate defensive force to protect her children from wrongful harm. Thus, in this case Resident is evidence-relative required to use defensive force against the person at the door, although this is wrong in the fact-relative sense.

The moral status account does not distinguish between acts that are evidence-relative permissible and acts that are evidence-relative required. It holds that Resident is liable even when she justifiably believes she is required to act for the sake of her children. She is liable because she acts as if the person at the door lacks important moral rights, and this assumption is mistaken. Some, however, might object that when an agent is evidence-relative required to perform an act, the agent cannot be liable to defensive force if the act unfortunately threatens harm to innocent persons. They will thus object that the moral status account gets the wrong result in cases like Mistaken Attacker's Children.

To assess this objection, we need to understand the rationale for the proposal that persons should be immune from liability to defensive force when they are evidence-relative required to perform a harmful act. Tadros makes the following suggestion:[57] if an agent is evidence-relative required to φ, then φ-ing is 'morally unavoidable'. The agent who finds herself in this position has, given her evidence, no way to avoid φ-ing while acting in the morally required way. But how exactly does this support the conclusion that the agent should be exempted from liability for φ-ing?

In many cases where a person is evidence-relative required to φ, where φ-ing involves some risk of harm to others, φ-ing also imposes risk on the person who performs the act.[58] In Mistaken Attacker's Children, for example, Resident exposes herself to significant risk by attacking the person at the door—that person is likely to fight back. This fact might be thought to bear on the matter of liability in the following way. If someone is morally required to bear significant risks for the sake of others, it would be unfair to also hold that person liable to defensive harm should the required act threaten fact-relative wrongful harm. Making such agents liable to defensive force would constitute an unfair distribution of harm and risk of harm among persons.

We should reject this proposal. Contra McMahan, liability to defensive harm is not a matter of justice in the distribution of unavoidable harm.[59] Suppose a lethal projectile is headed towards you and you can only save yourself by using a bystander's body as a shield. If liability were purely a matter of justice in the distribution of unavoidable harm then you could render yourself immune from liability to defensive harm by flipping a coin to decide whether to use the bystander's body as a shield. In doing so you would have given each of you a 50 per cent chance of survival, and since you are both innocent, this seems the fair

---

[57] Tadros, *The Ends of Harm: The Moral Foundations of Criminal Law* (Oxford: Oxford University Press, 2011), 232–4. To be clear: Tadros does not explicitly endorse the general thesis that a person who is evidence-relative required to φ is always immune to defensive force for any harm that results form φ-ing. He only advances the more modest thesis that a person's being evidence-relative required to φ can explain why, in some cases, it would be wrong to impose defensive force on that person.

[58] Tadros presents a case with this structure in developing his argument. See ibid., 233.

[59] McMahan, 'Self-Defense against Justified Threateners', 117.

distribution of risk. But I'm not aware of anyone who argues that it would be permissible to do this, or that you would not be liable to defensive harm if you did so and the bystander lost the coin toss.[60] We can be liable to defensive force even when this means we are exposed to greater risks of harm than others.[61]

Here is one further reason to doubt that an agent being morally required, in the evidence-relative sense, does not immunize the agent from liability to defensive force.[62] Sometimes an agent cannot be required to perform some beneficial act for the sake of others because the costs to the agent of doing so are too high. But if the costs to the agent are not too high, the agent may be duty bound to perform the act. Those who argue that being evidence-relative morally required to act immunizes an agent from liability are thus committed to the following odd conclusions. A third party who performs a supererogatory rescue of a victim at great personal cost can be liable to defensive force if the third party mistakenly threatens harm to a non-liable person, but in an otherwise identical case where the third party is required to perform the rescue because the costs are negligible, the third party cannot be liable to defensive force. I find it difficult to believe that a heroic act of self-sacrifice does not defeat liability, but doing what morality requires when it isn't costly to do so does defeat liability.

The moral status account, I think, delivers the more plausible and consistent results. Neither heroism nor moral requirement can defeat liability in cases when an agent treats another person as lacking moral rights that she in fact possesses.

2.7.6 Different Kinds of Mistakes

Consider the following case:[63]

Grenade Blast: Murderer approaches Victim with the intention of killing him. But Victim has been warned about Murderer's attack and prepares to throw a grenade at him (his only means of defence). Victim's evidence is that there is no one else about but, unbeknownst to him, two homeless men are sleeping nearby but completely obscured from Victim's view. If he throws his grenade, the blast will kill Murderer and the two homeless men.

In this case, the moral status account apparently implies that Victim is not liable to defensive force since the evidence-relative permissibility of Victim's act depends

---

[60] Otsuka makes this point in 'Killing the Innocent', 76-7.
[61] Of course, even if we do not think being evidence-relative required to φ *immunizes* the agent from liability, we might still believe that it affects the *degree* of defensive harm to which the agent is liable. We will return to this issue when we consider proportionality in Chapter 4.
[62] I am very grateful to an anonymous reviewer for suggesting this line of argument.
[63] Jonathan Parry offered this type of case as a possible counterexample.

only on the assumption that Murderer is liable to attack, and this assumption is correct. Since Victim has no evidence that two people are nearby, assumptions about their liability play no role in the evidence-relative permissibility of his act. To some, this conclusion will be counterintuitive. Surely Victim ought to be liable to defensive force on behalf of the two homeless people given that Victim intentionally throws a grenade, and doing so will kill two innocent people, which (let's stipulate) renders the act fact-relative impermissible.

I have two replies to this purported counterexample. First, I think reactions to the case may conflate distinct questions. One question is whether Victim is liable to any defensive force. Another question is whether the homeless men or third parties are permitted to use defensive force against Victim. The answer to the latter question can be yes, but we don't need to believe Victim is liable to reach this conclusion. In the next chapter I will defend the view that we each possess agent-relative prerogatives to defend ourselves from people who threaten us, even when the threats are not liable to defensive force. The homeless men, on my view, can thus permissibly defend themselves. Whether third parties can use force to defend the homeless men depends on whether doing so can be justified as a lesser evil. Some philosophers believe that killing one non-liable person can only be justified as a lesser evil when doing so saves the lives of at least five non-liable people, and the number might even be higher when the killing is intended as opposed to merely foreseen. I don't want to take a stand on these issues of proportionality here. Instead I will grant that there is no lesser evil justification for third parties to kill Victim in this case. If we assume that Victim is not liable to any defensive force, then I don't find this conclusion counterintuitive, though others may disagree. But I doubt there is going to be much consensus about whether it is permissible for third parties to kill Victim in this case, and so I don't think an appeal to intuition about this issue is a very compelling objection to the moral status account.

The preceding reply grants the assumption that Victim is not liable to defensive force on the moral status account. But I now want to query this assumption. Grenades are very dangerous and imprecise weapons. As a result, if you throw a grenade in a populated area, you ought to know that there's a very real chance someone may be seriously injured or killed by the blast, even when you don't see anyone around. Because of the risk of harm to others, the evidence-relative permissibility of throwing a grenade in a populated area depends on an assumption that anyone harmed by the blast is either liable to be so harmed, or else that there is some other justification (e.g., a lesser evil justification) for imposing such substantial risks on others. Put differently, exploding a live grenade in an ordinary, populated area is so dangerous that we each have a right against others exposing us to this kind of risk. The objection being considered is thus based on a false premise: I think Victim is liable to defensive force because the risks of exploding a grenade (at least in certain areas) are so great that others have claims he refrain from doing so even if he cannot immediately see anyone else around.

The proponent of the objection might protest as follows. Of course under *typical* circumstances, the benefits of detonating a grenade or firing a gun in a populated area are trivial, whereas the risks to others are great, and this is why others *typically* have claims against such acts. But the circumstances Victim faces are not typical. Victim correctly believes he will be wrongfully killed unless he throws the grenade, and since the costs to him of refraining from using the grenade are so great, it's no longer the case that others have claims against the risk he imposes by throwing the grenade.

I deny, however, that rights work in this way. The claim rights we possess against others must be determined by considering typical rather than atypical conditions. One of the reasons for this is that rights are meant to regulate our conduct with regard to each other in ways that are reasonably predictable. Right-holders need to be reasonably confident about most of the rights that they possess, and this isn't possible if the possession of the right is contingent on highly unusual circumstances being faced by the duty bearer. Before I enter a department store, for example, I need to know whether I have claims against people firing guns or throwing grenades in the store and potentially harming me. If I'm told 'It all depends on what precise circumstances any would-be duty bearer faces' then the rights I possess will be mostly opaque to me, thus depriving them of much of their value.

There could certainly be variations of the case where the homeless men lack claim rights against Victim throwing the grenade. Perhaps, for example, if they broke into Victim's home and were hiding in a closet, they would lack claims against Victim throwing the grenade since homeowners cannot reasonably be expected to assume that strangers might be hiding in their home when they engage in otherwise justified acts of self-defence. Once we construct a case where Victim cannot reasonably expect that his act poses any substantial risk to non-liable persons, then I don't think it's counterintuitive to suppose that the homeless men lack any claim rights against Victim. This is because claim rights have to be determined by considering what alleged right-holders can reasonably demand of alleged duty bearers. I say more in defence of this view of rights in Chapter 6.

But let's set aside the variations of Grenade Blast and confront the deeper worry that the example is meant to illuminate. The deeper worry is that the moral status account draws an arbitrary distinction between different kinds of justifiable mistakes that defensive agents make. When a defensive agent makes a mistake about a person's rights, as Resident does in Mistaken Attacker, this renders him liable to defensive force. But when a defensive agent makes a justifiable mistake about the consequences of his act, for example, whether his act has any significant chance of harming non-liable people (as Victim does in at least some versions of Grenade Blast) then the moral status account declares the defensive agent to be non-liable. In both cases, the agent who imposes the harm has justified beliefs that turn out to be mistaken. One is a mistake about rights and the other is a mistake about the empirical consequences of an act. But, the critic protests, why should this difference matter? Why should mistakes about the moral rights of others carry special significance?

In answer to this question I can only repeat what I've already said in defence of the moral status view. To make a justified mistake about whether one's actions will result in harm to anyone, or to a disproportionate number of people, need not involve treating others with anything less than the concern and respect they are due—it need not involve treating others as if they lack important rights against harm. But to make a mistake about other people's liability to harm is different. When you assume that others are liable to bear the harm that your actions will impose, you treat those others as entitled to less than the level of concern and respect they are due, and as a result you must accept a special responsibility if you turn out to be mistaken. To treat others as if they lack rights is a grave matter, and this is why mistakes about other people's rights are different from other kinds of mistakes we might make.

2.8 Conclusion

This chapter has defended a series of claims regarding liability to defensive harm. First, I argued that we should reject some of the leading conceptions of liability in the literature: the culpability account, the moral responsibility account, and the evidence-relative account. Second, I advanced and defended the moral status account of liability. On this view, you become liable to defensive harm when you incorrectly treat others as if they lack moral rights that persons normally possess. We do this, I argued, when the evidence-relative permission for our act depends on the assumption that those who might be harmed by our act lack rights that persons normally possess, but the potential victims do, as a matter of fact, retain these rights. This view of liability has various advantages compared to the other views in the literature. Perhaps most importantly, it correctly distinguishes cases like Mistaken Attacker from cases like Conscientious Driver. It correctly deems Resident liable to defensive harm, while holding Driver non-liable. Resident, unlike Driver, treats the person who might be harmed by his act as lacking important moral rights, but Driver does not.

How we treat others—in particular, whether we treat others as if they lack a certain moral status—is thus central to my account of liability, and the morality of defensive force more generally. Our treatment of others is determined by the reasons that do (or could) justify the acts we perform in light of our evidence, and this will have significant implications when we turn to consider matters of proportionality, the scope of rights against harm, and the question of what it is to harm someone as a means.

3

Agent-Relative Prerogatives

Any successful justification for using defensive force must answer at least two questions: What is the positive moral reason for using force? And who is the permissible target of the force?

Some believe that each question has only a single answer. In answer to the first question they say, 'averting wrongful harm'. And in answer to the second question they say, 'only those who are liable to defensive force'. Let's call this the *standard justification* of defensive force. There are several cases, however, that the standard justification struggles to explain. In particular, there is deep and sharp disagreement about cases involving *justified attackers* and *non-responsible threats*. Justified attackers threaten to infringe an innocent person's moral rights, but possess an all-things-considered justification for doing so. Non-responsible threats pose a threat of harm to an innocent person, but are not morally responsible for the threat that they pose.

Recall the following case:

> *Justified Bomber*: Bomber acting in a just war is about to drop a bomb on an enemy target. The bombing is fully justified according to the correct principles of *jus in bello*, but it will kill a certain (proportionate) number of innocent civilians as a side effect. The civilians have an antiaircraft gun that they could use to shoot down and kill Bomber before he is able to drop the bomb.

Some people, including me, believe that Bomber is not liable to defensive force because he acts with an appropriate moral justification, but that it is nevertheless permissible for the civilians to shoot and kill Bomber in self-defence.[1] If this is true, there must be a justification for killing Bomber that departs from the standard justification. Killing Bomber will not avert wrongful harm, and Bomber is not liable to defensive force.

---

[1] Jeff McMahan used to agree that the civilians could shoot down Bomber's plane, but has now changed his view. See McMahan, 'Self-Defense Against Justified Threateners', 104–37. Some may believe that whether the civilians are permitted to shoot down Bomber depends on whether Bomber is morally required or merely permitted to drop the bomb. In the previous chapter I argued that this does not make a difference to Bomber's liability and thus I do not think it makes a difference to what the civilians are permitted to do.

The Morality of Defensive Force. Jonathan Quong, Oxford University Press (2020). © Jonathan Quong.
DOI: 10.1093/oso/9780198851103.001.0001

Here is another familiar case, this time involving a non-responsible threat:

Well: Albert has been thrown by an unforeseeable gust of wind from the top of a well towards the bottom of the well. At the bottom of the well stands Betty who will be killed by Albert's falling body unless she shoots him with her trusty ray gun first. If she doesn't shoot, Albert will survive the fall unharmed due to his unusual bone structure.

Most people, including me, believe that it is permissible for Betty to shoot and kill Albert to save her own life. It is even clearer that Albert is not liable to defensive force because he exercises no agency at all. This is therefore another case that poses a serious challenge for the standard justification.

In response to these sorts of examples, there seem to be three main options. First, we might revise our conception of liability, developing a more expansive conception that will deem justified attackers and non-responsible threats liable to defensive force.[2] Second, we might revise our judgements regarding the permissible use of defensive force. Perhaps it isn't permissible for the civilians or Betty to use defensive force in these examples.[3] Third, we might take these examples as an indication that the standard justification isn't the only justification for the use of defensive force.[4]

I believe the first option is doomed to failure. There is no plausible conception of liability under which non-responsible threats are liable to defensive force. And although a number of philosophers have recently endorsed the second option, this also seems to me to be a serious mistake—one that I think is driven by the mistaken belief that the standard justification is the only justification for the use of defensive force, setting aside lesser evil justifications.

[2] Those who argue non-responsible threats are liable to defensive force include Thomson, 'Self-Defense', 283–310; Uniacke, *Permissible Killing*; and Leverick, *Killing in Self-Defence*, chap. 3. Others argue that non-responsible threats can be liable to at least some amount of defensive harm, and this fact can then be combined with a lesser evil justification to explain the permissibility of killing lethal non-responsible threats. See Tadros, *The Ends of Harm*, 251–5; Frowe, *Defensive Killing*, 67–70. David Rodin argues that justified attackers can be liable to defensive harm. See Rodin, 'Justifying Harm', *Ethics* 122, no. 1 (2011): 86–7.
[3] Those who deny it is permissible to kill non-responsible threats include McMahan, 'Self-Defense and the Problem of the Innocent Attacker', *The Ethics of Killing: Problems at the Margins of Life* (New York: Oxford University Press, 2002), 398–411, 'The Basis of Moral Liability', and *Killing in War*, 167–73; and Otsuka, 'Killing the Innocent in Self-Defense'. For similar views, see Ferzan, 'Justifying Self-Defense'; David Rodin, *War and Self-Defense* (Oxford: Clarendon Press, 2002), 79–89; and Noam Zohar, 'Collective War and Individualistic Ethics: Against the Conscription of "Self-Defense"', *Political Theory* 21, no. 4 (1993): 606–22.
[4] Those who pursue this option include Susanne Burri, 'The Toss-Up Between a Profiting, Innocent Threat and His Victim', *Journal of Political Philosophy* 23, no. 2 (2015): 146–65; Nancy Davis, 'Abortion and Self-Defense', *Philosophy & Public Affairs* 13, no. 3 (1984): 175–207; Tyler Doggett, 'Killing Innocent People', *Nous* 52, no. 3 (2018): 645–66; Fabre, 'Permissible Rescue Killings'; Gerald Lang, 'What Follows from Non-Liability?' *Proceedings of the Aristotelian Society* 117, no. 3 (2017): 231–52; and Susan Levine, 'The Moral Permissibility of Killing a "Material Aggressor" in Self-Defense', *Philosophical Studies* 45, no. 1 (1984): 69–78.

In this chapter I develop and defend an alternative to the standard justification, and thus endorse the third option. I argue that there are sometimes agent-relative prerogatives to impose harm on non-liable persons when doing so is required to protect what is rightfully yours. This justification differs from the standard justification in two respects. First, the positive moral reason to use defensive force is not to avert wrongful harm, but rather to protect what is rightfully yours. It's easy to conflate these reasons for action since protecting what is rightfully yours often serves to avert wrongful harm. But these reasons come apart in certain contexts, including cases involving justified attackers and non-responsible threats. Second, agent-relative prerogatives depart from the standard justification since they justify imposing harm on non-liable, as opposed to liable, targets.

Some have expressed deep scepticism about the appeal to agent-relative prerogatives.[5] And there is certainly something puzzling about this idea. I cannot appeal to agent-relative considerations as a sufficient justification for stealing your vital organs, even if I will die without them. I cannot push you in front of a lethal projectile in order to save myself from it. I cannot throw your body onto a grenade that is about to explode to save myself from the shrapnel. All of these acts seem clearly impermissible. A challenge, then, is to explain why an agent-relative justification does not have an implausibly expansive scope—permitting the use of force in a range of cases where it seems clearly wrong.

In response to this challenge, I argue that the agent-relative prerogative is constrained by the *means principle*. I argue that you may permissibly impose force on a non-liable person to protect what is rightfully yours provided that, in doing so, you do not use that person's body or other rightful property to obtain a benefit that you could not obtain without that person's body or property. This feature of the justification is unusual since it does not identify the permissible target of defensive force by reference to something that the target has done or failed to do. Instead, it simply prohibits targeting people whenever doing so would use that person as a means.

The agent-relative prerogative to impose defensive harm can successfully explain cases like Justified Bomber and Well without implausibly declaring that Bomber or Albert are liable to defensive force, and I think this is a powerful reason to endorse the view. The view also has further advantages. It provides a more plausible analysis of why neutral third parties seem to be in a different moral position with regard to the permissible use of defensive force in these cases, in particular why those who are threatened with harm sometimes can use force to defend themselves in contexts where it would be wrong for a third party to intervene.

---

[5] McMahan, 'Self-Defense Against Justified Threateners'; Tadros, *The Ends of Harm*, 202–8. For an earlier expression of scepticism about the appeal to agent-relative consideration in self-defence cases, see Thomson, 'Self-Defense', 307–8.

The chapter proceeds as follows. Sections 3.1 and 3. 2 consider and reject the alternative ways of responding to cases like Justified Bomber and Well briefly canvassed above: changing our conception of liability or revising our judgements regarding what is permissible in these cases. Section 3.3 introduces the notion of an agent-relative prerogative. Sections 3.4 and 3.5 provide an argument in support of an agent-relative prerogative to do harm. The argument begins with a famous case where most people intuitively agree it is permissible to perform an act that results in an innocent person's death. I show that this case is relevantly analogous to a case involving defence against a non-responsible threat. Having argued for the existence of an agent-relative prerogative, in section 3.6 I explain how such a prerogative applies to a range of cases involving non-responsible threats. Section 3.7 considers and responds to several objections. Section 3.8 concludes.

3.1 Expanding Liability

Our problem, recall, is that the standard justification of defensive force cannot explain why it is sometimes permissible to impose defensive force on justified attackers and non-responsible threats. Since these people are not liable to defensive harm, the standard view apparently prohibits using defensive force against them. But this clashes with what most of us believe.

One response is to deny that the standard justification has the stated implication. That is, one might defend a conception of liability that is sufficiently expansive such that either or both justified attackers and non-responsible threats are liable to defensive force, or at least lack rights against such force. Below I consider and reject three ways this might be done.

3.1.1 Thomson's Argument

Thomson defends the following argument for the permissibility of killing non-responsible lethal threats like Albert in Well (my reconstruction):[6]

P1   If X's killing you will violate your right not to be killed, then X loses his right not to be killed by you, and so you may permissibly kill X in self-defence.

P2   In Well, Albert is threatening to violate Betty's right not to be killed. Therefore,

C1   It is permissible for Betty to kill Albert in self-defence.

---

[6] Thomson, 'Self-Defense.'

This argument fails because P2 is false. As Otsuka and McMahan, among others, rightly point out, it is not plausible to suppose, as Thomson does, that non-responsible threats are guilty of threatening to *violate* anyone's rights.[7] This is because, in order for one person to violate another's rights, there must be responsible agency. For example, although it would make sense to say that you were killed by a boulder that fell from the top of a cliff as the result of an earthquake, it would not make sense to say that the boulder violated your right not to be killed. The boulder has no agency, thus cannot be subject to any moral duties, and so cannot violate (or even infringe) your rights. The same is surely true of a large baby falling from a cliff.[8] Since the large falling baby is a non-responsible threat, this seems to show, contra Thomson, that it is not permissible to kill non-responsible lethal threats in self-defence since such threats do not exercise responsible agency, and thus do not threaten to violate someone's rights.[9]

3.1.2 The Hybrid Justification

Tadros and Frowe each defend a hybrid justification for the permissibility of killing non-responsible threats, one that combines claims about enforceable duties and claims about lesser evil.[10] They argue that we each bear special responsibility for the harms that our bodies may cause. This means that if our body threatens to harm an innocent person, we are duty bound to bear certain costs to avert this harm, duties that exceed those of a regular bystander. This is true even when we are not morally responsible for the fact that our body threatens to harm someone else. If Albert could avoid landing on and killing Betty by bearing some significant costs, Tadros and Frowe suggest he would be duty bound to do so. They also claim that Albert is duty bound to bear such costs even if he cannot avoid landing on

---

[7] Otsuka, 'Killing the Innocent in Self-Defense', 79–84; McMahan, 'Self-Defense and the Problem of the Innocent Attacker', 276.

[8] The example of a falling stone or boulder is used both in Otsuka, 'Killing the Innocent in Self-Defense', 80; and McMahan, 'Self-Defense and the Problem of the Innocent Attacker', 276.

[9] The same problem holds true for Uniacke's account of the right to act in self-defence against 'unjust' threats, since this notion also relies on the idea that an unjust threat is someone who is going to violate your rights. For a version of this critique applied to Uniacke see Tziporah Kasachkoff, 'Killing in Self-Defense: An Unquestionable or Problematic Defense?' *Law and Philosophy* 17 (1998): 509–31, 518–19. For a debate between Uniacke and Kasachkoff on this and related issues, see Uniacke, 'In Defense of Permissible Killing: A Response to Two Critics', *Law and Philosophy* 19, no. 5 (2000): 627–33; and Kasachkoff, 'Comment and Reply to Suzanne Uniacke's "A Response to Two Critics,"' *Law and Philosophy* 19, no. 5 (2000): 635–9.

[10] See Tadros, *The Ends of Harm*, 248–56; Frowe, *Defensive Killing*, 67–70. Whether this is, strictly speaking, an argument that appeals to the liability of non-responsible threats depends on whether one accepts Tadros's view of the relationship between enforceable duties and liability. I believe F. M. Kamm is the first person to suggest a version of this argument, though her view differs in certain respects from the one sketched here. See Kamm, *Creation and Abortion: A Study in Moral and Legal Philosophy* (New York: Oxford University Press, 1992), 47–54.

Betty himself, and thus he lacks a right against having this cost imposed on him if doing so can save Betty's life.

But Tadros and Frowe do not claim that Albert is duty bound to suffer the cost of death in cases like Well. They only argue that non-responsible threats like Albert are duty bound to bear costs that exceed those of a bystander but fall short of death. How, then, do we arrive at the conclusion that it is permissible for Betty to kill Albert in Well?

They argue that Betty has a hybrid justification. The harm that Albert is duty bound to suffer does not weigh against Betty's act, since he is duty bound to suffer this harm. The question is then whether Betty has a sufficient justification for imposing the remaining harm on Albert, that is, the amount of harm that remains once we subtract the harm that Albert is duty bound to suffer from the total harm of death. Tadros and Frowe suggest that Betty has a lesser evil justification for imposing this remaining harm: the amount of harm she averts (her own death) is sufficiently great compared to Albert's remaining harm that it is widely proportionate to impose this harm.[11]

I think there are a number of problems with this proposal. First, I do not believe that we bear special duties to avert the harm that our bodies might cause when we aren't morally responsible for the threat and have exercised no agency. Suppose Albert amputates Carl's leg and uses the leg as a club to attack Betty. On Tadros's and Frowe's view, other things being equal, Carl has special duties to avert the threat to Betty, duties that go beyond those of an ordinary bystander, simply because it's his leg.[12] This is implausible.[13]

Second, the hybrid justification can only succeed if we suppose that non-responsible threats are duty bound to bear very significant costs to avert the harm that their bodies may pose. If the costs non-responsible threats must bear are not very great, then there will be too much harm that remains to be justified, and the lesser evil justification will not succeed. Suppose that Albert would be duty bound to bear the cost of two broken arms to avoid killing Betty in Well if this were a feasible option. Can it be the case that Betty has a lesser evil justification for killing Albert merely because he has an enforceable duty to suffer two broken arms? The answer is obviously no. If the answer was yes, then Betty would also have a lesser evil justification for killing an innocent bystander (if doing so could avert the threat) who was going to live exactly the same life as Albert but was going to fall and break both his arms at some point in the near future, since Betty would

---

[11] Tadros does not use the language of lesser evil or wide proportionality, but I think it's clear this is what he has in mind since he explicitly rejects any appeal to agent-relative prerogatives.

[12] You might think Tadros and Frowe can avoid this implication by insisting that once Carl's leg has been amputated it's no longer 'his' leg, and so the special responsibility assumption no longer holds. But we can imagine that Albert will reattach Carl's leg once he's done using it as a weapon. This just illustrates the more fundamental problem: whether or not Albert will reattach Carl's leg seems irrelevant. What matters is that Carl exercises no agency or control over what his leg is doing.

[13] Burri presses the same worry. See Burri, 'The Toss-Up', 152.

be imposing the same degree of non-liable harm on that bystander as she would be imposing on Albert. It is not credible to suppose that subtracting such a small degree of harm from the calculus could give Betty a lesser evil justification to kill a bystander.

The hybrid justification thus faces a dilemma. Either we assume non-responsible threats cannot be duty bound to bear very serious costs to avert the threats that their bodies pose, in which case there is no successful lesser evil justification for imposing the remaining harm. Or else we make very implausible assumptions regarding how much harm non-responsible threats are duty bound to bear. Frowe, for example, suggests a non-responsible threat like Albert would be duty bound to suffer paralysis in order to avert the threat that his body poses to Betty in Well.[14]

But even if this were a plausible assumption about the extent of Albert's duty, it has the extraordinarily counterintuitive implication that Betty has a lesser evil justification for killing a bystander who is, for independent reasons, about to become a paraplegic, if doing so is necessary to save her life. This implication is too far at odds with our considered moral judgements to be acceptable. Thus, the hybrid justification does not succeed.

3.1.3 Justification and Liability

Perhaps part of the solution lies in a more modest conception of liability, one that makes justified attackers liable to defensive force but not non-responsible threats. David Rodin defends a version of such a view.[15] His account of liability is roughly as follows:

Rodin's Liability: X is liable to defensive force when X is morally responsible for threatening to violate or infringe the rights of others.

Although Bomber has a lesser evil justification for dropping the bomb on the enemy target, he will infringe the rights of the innocent civilians below in doing so.[16] Thus on Rodin's account, Bomber becomes liable to defensive force despite being justified in dropping the bomb. Rodin thus rejects the view that justification defeats liability.[17]

---

[14] Frowe, *Defensive Killing*, 69.   [15] See Rodin, 'Justifying Harm', 86–7.

[16] Recall that X infringes Y's right when he acts contrary to the duty that correlates with the right, but has an all-things-considered justification for doing so.

[17] In Chapter 2, recall, I claimed that a justification of a particular sort does defeat liability—namely, a justification that doesn't depend on treating anyone as if they lack moral rights. When X acts with such a justification, then X acts in a way that is consistent with according each person the concern and respect that they are due, and so X shouldn't be liable for harms that others may suffer as a result. X, in

Rodin offers two arguments in support of his view. First, he claims that interpersonal reciprocity underpins many of our moral rights. As he puts it, 'I have the right that you not kill me in part because (and to the extent that I do) respect your reciprocal right I not kill you.'[18] If this is true, then liability cannot be defeated by broader justifications (e.g., lesser evil justifications) that have nothing to do with the reciprocal nature of the rights and duties we have with regard to one another. Rights infringements breach the reciprocity condition regardless of whether they are justified by wider considerations. Second, Rodin points out that benefits to third parties do not affect a person's liability to defensive harm in many cases. For example, if Albert is going to wrongfully murder Betty, but doing so will have some unintended benefits for Carl, this doesn't render Albert any less liable to defensive force. Rodin suggests that this is further evidence that moral reasons that stand apart from the reciprocal relationship between the right-holder and the duty bearer should have no effect on liability even when the harm-imposing agent is justified in acting.[19]

I don't find either of these arguments persuasive. As for the first, it's not true that I have the right that you not kill me *because* I respect your reciprocal right that I not kill you, at least insofar as 'because' identifies the justificatory ground for the right.[20] We typically have reciprocal duties to respect one another's rights not to be killed, but these duties are typically reciprocal only because most adults possess the same moral status and because we each have similar interests. But we have duties to refrain from killing small children, for example, even though they are not under a reciprocal duty. The inability to fulfil or violate a potential duty owed to others need not undermine the claims we can make on others.

As for Rodin's second argument, the inference on which it depends is dubious. Although it's true that, when we act wrongly, the foreseen benefits of our wrongful acts cannot 'count' in our favour by diminishing our liability, this does not necessarily support a similar conclusion when we act with adequate justification. When we act wrongly, without justification, and threaten another person's moral rights, there is an obvious reason why any benefits our act might have for third parties do not work to offset our liability: those benefits are, by hypothesis, insufficient to justify our action. If some reason is insufficient to render an act permissible, it would be strange to nevertheless count that reason as somehow offsetting one's substantive responsibility for the wrongful act. But when some reason does provide a sufficient justification for action, there's nothing puzzling

---

other words, should not be liable for the fact that, in the conditions in which he acts, the morally justified act unavoidably harms innocent people.

[18] Rodin, 'Justifying Harm', 87.   [19] Ibid., 100–1.
[20] Rodin clearly endorses the view that reciprocity is a justificatory ground for the right in 'The Reciprocity Theory of Rights'.

about supposing that it might insulate you from liability for the consequences of the act.

There is also a more general problem with the view that justification cannot defeat liability. Consider the following case:

Trapped Miners: A group of twenty miners are trapped in a mineshaft that is flooding. The miners will all be dead soon unless the floodwaters can be redirected. Albert can redirect the floodwaters into a different mineshaft by pressing an emergency button. Pressing the button, however, has a second effect: it permanently closes the doors in yet a different mineshaft. This will trap the single miner, Betty, in that shaft. Albert presses the button, saving the twenty miners and trapping Betty. Betty will now die of dehydration unless she uses her grenade to blast through the wall, creating an escape route. Blasting through the wall, however, will kill Albert, who is standing on the other side of the wall.

In this story, Albert has a sufficient moral justification for performing an act that causes an innocent person to face a lethal threat. He differs from Bomber in that he does not currently pose a threat to Betty: his act of pushing the emergency button is in the past and there's nothing that can be done now to avert his act. But like Bomber, he is morally responsible for his act.

If justification cannot defeat liability, Albert is liable to be killed by Betty in this example. This seems counterintuitive. By that I don't mean that it is counter-intuitive to suppose that Betty can permissibly kill Albert. Rather, I mean that it is counterintuitive to suppose that Albert forfeits his right not to be killed in the same way as a murderer does. To sharpen the point, consider a variant of the example in which Betty can choose between blasting two different parts of the wall with her grenade. If she chooses the west side of the wall, she will kill Albert. If she chooses the east side, she will break an uninvolved bystander's legs. It is not permissible to break a non-liable person's legs to avoid killing someone who is liable to be killed. Thus, if justification does not defeat liability, it is obvious that if Betty chooses to save her life, she must kill Albert rather than break the bystander's legs. But this seems clearly incorrect. Albert didn't act impermissibly in pushing the emergency button, and so he doesn't have a weaker claim not to be harmed by Betty than the bystander. If Betty is permitted to harm anyone in order to save herself, it is the bystander and not Albert.

In sum, I believe that we should reject the claim that justification cannot defeat liability. The positive arguments that Rodin advances in its favour do not seem persuasive, and the view also has counterintuitive implications in cases such as Trapped Miners. Of course, if justification does defeat liability, then justified attackers are not liable to defensive force, and this leaves us with only two options: either revise our judgement that it is sometimes permissible to use defensive force against justified attackers, or else find a non-liability-based justification for defensive force in these cases. The next section considers the former option.

3.2 Revising Our Judgements About Permissibility

In Chapter 2 we considered the moral responsibility account of liability. On this view, a person cannot be liable to defensive force unless he is morally responsible for posing an impermissible threat of harm to others. Most proponents of this conception of liability thus conclude that, just as it is morally impermissible to use defensive force against an innocent bystander, it is morally impermissible to use defensive force against non-responsible attackers or threats (at least, absent a lesser evil justification). I will call this the *moral responsibility argument*.

I take Michael Otsuka's initial version of the argument as representative.[21] Otsuka's argument focuses on killing non-responsible threats, but the scope of the argument can easily be broadened to include impositions of harm generally, and also to include justified attackers:

P3   It is impermissible to kill a bystander to prevent oneself from being killed (*Inviolability of a Bystander thesis*).

P4   The killing of a non-responsible threat and the killing of a bystander are, other things being equal, on a par as far as permissibility is concerned (*Moral Equivalence thesis*).

Therefore,

C2   It is impermissible to kill such a threat to prevent oneself from being killed.

I think both premises of this argument are false. The second premise is false because it fails to be sufficiently sensitive to the fact that killing non-responsible threats rarely violates the means principle, whereas the killing of bystanders often does.[22] I will elaborate on this claim in sections 3.3 and 3.4. Here I focus on the first premise.

The most plausible justification of the first premise is that it is entailed by a particular version of the doctrine of doing and allowing:

DDA Prohibition: It is always impermissible to kill or harm some non-liable person(s) to save an equivalent number of non-liable person(s) from roughly equivalent harms.

---

[21] Otsuka, 'Killing the Innocent', 76. Note that Otsuka offers a somewhat different argument in 'The Moral-Responsibility Account', which focuses on so-called innocent obstructors. I address this argument later in the chapter.

[22] Strictly speaking, this may not show that the second premise is false, but rather that the 'other things being equal' clause is so important that the scope of the argument is drastically reduced.

If DDA Prohibition is true, then so is the conclusion of the moral responsibility argument. Indeed, DDA Prohibition makes the second premise redundant—it establishes the conclusion in a single step. But notice what this means: DDA Prohibition establishes the truth of the view that it is impermissible to kill non-responsible threats in self-defence, but it does so by stipulating the very point that is disputed, namely, whether or not it is always impermissible to kill one innocent person to save another person.

DDA Prohibition has prima facie plausibility because it reflects the widely accepted view that doing harm is worse than allowing harm. But even if doing harm is worse than allowing harm, this does not entail that DDA Prohibition is true. There might be other considerations that sometimes override or nullify the fact that doing harm is worse than allowing harm, even when the number of lives at stake is equivalent.[23] Indeed, there seem to be examples where this is exactly what happens. Consider the following pair of cases:

Man on the Track: There is a runaway trolley whose brakes have failed headed down a track where your child is trapped and will be killed by the trolley. Fortunately there is a side track onto which the trolley can be diverted, but there is one man trapped on this side track, and he will be killed if you divert the trolley.

Man on the Overpass: There is a runaway trolley whose brakes have failed headed down a track where your child is trapped and will be killed by the trolley. Fortunately you are standing on an overpass under which the trolley must pass before it reaches your child. Next to you stands a large man. This large man's weight (but not your own) would be sufficient to stop the trolley. If you pushed him off the overpass, he would land on the tracks and stop the trolley before it reaches your child, though he will be killed if you do so.

I assume that many people believe that considerations of partiality make it permissible to act in the first case, but that considerations of partiality do not suffice to make it permissible to act in the second case. If the first half of this judgement is correct, then DDA Prohibition is false. But even those who do not share this view regarding the permissibility of acting in Man on the Track may still believe the reasons not to act in Man on the Track are not as weighty as they are in Man on the Overpass. This difference, even if one does not believe it changes what is permissible, is presumably explained by the fact that you would be using or intending the death of the large man in a way you do not use or intend the death of the man in Man on the Track. Provided that it is more clearly impermissible to act in Man on the Overpass than it is in Man on the Track, this should cast some doubt on the claim that DDA Prohibition is obviously or unproblematically true.

---

[23] For this reason, most philosophers who defend some version of the doctrine of doing and allowing defend a view that is significantly weaker than DDA Prohibition—they typically claim only that, other things being equal, doing harm is worse than allowing harm.

DDA Prohibition implies that there can never be countervailing considerations in one-versus-one cases that trump the prohibition on killing an innocent person. But there seems to be a clear difference between Man on the Track and Man on the Overpass—indeed I suspect many may believe there is a decisive difference regarding what is permissible. This gives us a reason to doubt whether DDA Prohibition is really true. Perhaps there are ways for proponents of DDA Prohibition to explain away the intuitive difference between these cases—they might argue, for example, that the intuitive difference only tracks a difference in excuse rather than justification, though I doubt this explanation is plausible. My claim is simply that, absent some compelling explanation, the difference between these cases gives us good reason to doubt whether DDA Prohibition is true.

Of course, after careful reflection we may decide that there is no sound reason for treating bystanders differently from non-responsible threats, but it seems right to say that we must consider the various arguments that might support this asymmetric treatment *before* we can confidently endorse DDA Prohibition. What we cannot do is assert the truth of DDA Prohibition as a way of denying that any method for distinguishing bystanders from non-responsible threats is possible. If this is correct, then the moral responsibility argument cannot establish the conclusion that it is impermissible to kill non-responsible threats in self-defence. The most the argument does is remind us—if we needed reminding—that there is a strong presumption against killing innocent people, and that any claim that it is permissible to kill an innocent person must be supported by a justification that either outweighs, nullifies, or undercuts this presumption. The rest of this chapter is devoted to developing and defending such an argument.

3.3 An Agent-Relative Prerogative

Recall the puzzle that we confront. The standard justification for the use of defensive force tells us that the positive reason to impose defensive force is to avert wrongful harm, and thus the permissible targets of defensive force are only those who threaten to impose wrongful harm. Although this standard justification does well in explaining many paradigmatic uses of defensive force, it cannot explain the permissibility of using defensive force against justified attackers and non-responsible threats. The solution, I believe, is that the standard justification is not the only justification of defensive force. Defensive force is sometimes justified not as a way of averting wrongful aggression, but rather as the exercise of an agent-relative prerogative to impose harm on innocent people to protect what is rightfully yours. X has an agent-relative prerogative to impose harm on Y when:

(i) X may permissibly impose the harm on Y;

(ii) Y retains a right against X acting in a way that imposes the harm;

(iii) It is impermissible for a morally motivated stranger to impose the same harm on Y;

(iv) X's permission to act is explained, at least in part, by appeal to the disproportionate (when viewed impartially) weight we may each attach to our own lives.

If there are such agent-relative prerogatives, it explains why it can sometimes be permissible to harm or even kill people when there is no liability-based or lesser evil justification for doing so.

Why can we attach disproportionate weight to our own lives and interests? Because we don't act from an austerely impersonal perspective, one where each person's life and projects has the same importance. Instead we each inhabit a particular perspective—our own—and as a result, some considerations have greater significance for us than for others. *Your* life is of particular importance to *you*. As a result, you have stronger reasons to perform various acts and to care about various outcomes than others do. For example, you have much stronger reasons to care for your child than others, and much stronger reasons to care that your central projects and relationships are successful. Our lives would be unrecognizable if we behaved as if each of us had reasons of the same strength to care about each person's child and about each person's friends, relationships, and projects.[24]

This appeal to the agent-relative perspective is the source of certain agent-relative moral *permissions*, and not merely the grounds for *excuses*.[25] We are excused when we act in a way that we should not have, but mitigating circumstances mean that we aren't fully culpable for our act. Sceptics of the agent-relative view might believe this is what happens if you kill a non-responsible threat in self-defence. You should not have used lethal force under those circumstances, but panic and/or self-interest made it very difficult to act in accordance with morality's requirements. I believe, however, that agent-relative reasons can do more than provide the grounds for excuse: they can affect the boundaries of what is permissible.

Consider the following case:

Boulder Redirection: A boulder is rolling at high speed towards Albert and it will kill him unless he redirects the boulder. He has the ability to redirect the

---

[24] My sketch of the agent-relative perspective follows Samuel Scheffler's influential formulation. See Scheffler, *The Rejection of Consequentialism: A Philosophical Investigation of the Considerations Underlying Rival Moral Conceptions* (Oxford: Clarendon Press, 1982), chap. 3.

[25] This account of agent-relative prerogatives thus differs from several other ways such prerogatives might be justified. Saba Bazargan-Forward helpfully identifies at least three different types of arguments for agent-relative prerogatives: (1) *derivative* arguments such as those offered by some consequentialists, (2) *deontic* arguments that appeal to the fact that a life or project is one's own, and (3) *axiological* arguments that appeal to the intrinsic personal value of a project. See Bazargan-Forward, 'Vesting Agent-Relative Permissions in a Proxy', *Law and Philosophy* 37, no. 6 (2018): 673.

boulder, but doing so means the boulder will crush Betty's spine, rendering her a paraplegic.

I believe Albert may permissibly redirect the boulder, but it would not be permissible for a morally motivated stranger to do so. The stranger would need a lesser evil justification for imposing this very serious harm on Betty, and saving one innocent person's life is not sufficient. If these judgements about this case are correct, then there must be agent-relative prerogatives to impose harm.

Sceptics of such prerogatives, however, are unlikely to share my intuitions about cases of this kind. An argument addressed to such sceptics must begin with less controversial premises. The following two sections provide an argument addressed to these sceptics.

Before moving on to that argument, however, three clarifications are in order. First, I will argue that we sometimes have an agent-relative prerogative to harm or kill non-liable persons, such as justified attackers and non-responsible threats. When we do so, we *infringe* the rights of the non-liable person. Justified attackers and non-responsible threats possess the same agent-relative prerogative. Since they have done nothing to waive or forfeit their rights, they have an agent-relative prerogative to use counter-defensive force. On my account, these cases involve parties who are symmetrically situated with regard to their moral rights and their permission to use defensive force. Each possesses an agent-relative justification for imposing harm on the other in self-defence. Second, the scope of the agent-relative prerogative is limited: it applies to the imposition of harm on people who retain rights against the imposition of the harm. It has no application in cases involving liability since in these cases there is a different justification and set of conditions for the permissible use of force.[26] Third, the agent-relative perspective is objectively, rather than subjectively, specified. That is, I do not hold that a person may permissibly attach any weight she likes to her own life. Rather, I claim there is an objective sense in which each person may permissibly attach much greater weight to their own life in comparison to the lives of others. Agent-relative prerogatives to impose harm thus cannot justify any amount of harm that might be needed to avert a threat to ourselves—there are limits.

3.4 The Violinist Argument: Part I

Here is a famous case:

Violinist: You wake up in the morning and find yourself back to back in bed with an unconscious violinist. A famous unconscious violinist. He has been found to

---

[26] As I make clear in Chapter 4, for example, the question of what constitutes proportionate defensive force will be answered very differently for liable attackers as opposed to non-liable threats.

have a fatal kidney ailment, and the Society of Music Lovers has canvassed all the available medical records and found that you alone have the right blood type to help. They have therefore kidnapped you, and last night the violinist's circulatory system was plugged into yours, so that your kidneys can be used to extract poisons from his blood as well as your own. The director of the hospital now tells you, 'Look, we're sorry the Society of Music Lovers did this to you—we would never have permitted it if we had known. But still, they did it, and the violinist is now plugged into you. To unplug you would be to kill him. But never mind, it's only for nine months. By then he will have recovered from his ailment, and can safely be unplugged from you.' Is it morally incumbent on you to accede to this situation?[27]

Almost everyone agrees that you are morally permitted to unplug yourself from the violinist. It seems obvious that you may do so, and I am going to take it as given that this is the correct answer. Now consider the following case:

Nonlethal Cushion: Carl is an innocent person who has been kidnapped and thrown by a villain from the top of a well towards the bottom of the well. At the bottom of the well stands Debbie. Carl will survive the fall unharmed *because landing on Debbie's body will cushion his fall*. If Debbie were not present, Carl would not survive the fall. If he lands on Debbie, it will painlessly damage her spine in such a way that she will be bedridden for nine months, after which she will make a complete recovery. Debbie can avoid Carl's falling body only by pulling a lever that will place a barrier between Carl and herself, causing Carl to land on the barrier rather than Debbie, resulting in his painless death.

In this example, Carl's survival depends on Debbie's body.[28] He needs her body to survive in much the same way the violinist needs your body to survive. Like the violinist, it is not credible to suppose that Carl is liable to be killed—he has done nothing that would constitute a forfeiture of his rights. If you are permitted to unplug yourself in Violinist, then I think Debbie must be permitted to act in Nonlethal Cushion: there are no relevant differences between the cases. The harms in the cases have been equalized, and what the agent can do to save her own life is structurally similar: she performs an action that is intended to stop the other person from making use of her body, in one case by disconnecting tubes, in the other case by pulling a lever that erects a barrier.

A critic might insist the cases differ, however, because in Violinist you merely let the violinist die, whereas in Nonlethal Cushion Debbie kills Carl. The best argument for this view appeals to the role that ownership or property rights play

---

[27] Judith Jarvis Thomson, 'A Defense of Abortion', *Philosophy & Public Affairs* 1, no. 1 (1971): 48–9.
[28] For a different analysis of cases that have this particular feature, see Burri, 'The Toss-Up'.

in distinguishing instances of killing from instances of letting die. When you merely deprive someone of something over which you have a rightful prior claim, the argument goes, you merely let that person die, you do not kill him. In Violinist, you merely deprive the violinist of something, your body, over which you have a rightful prior claim, and thus you merely let him die. But in Nonlethal Cushion, Debbie does not merely deprive Carl of the use of her body, she also kills him by ensuring that his body will hit the barrier.

But we can easily modify either Violinist or Nonlethal Cushion to eliminate this distinction in a way that should not affect our judgements regarding what is permissible. Suppose, for instance, that in order to unplug yourself from the violinist, you must first send an electrical current through the tube connecting you to the violinist, which causes the violinist to die before he is unplugged from your body, though he would die subsequently, as a result of being denied access to your body. It seems clear to me that this does not make a difference regarding what is permissible: you are still permitted to unplug yourself from the violinist.[29] Alternatively, we could change Nonlethal Cushion in the following way: suppose that Debbie's pulling of the lever opens a small trap door that lowers her beneath the floor of the well, so that now Carl lands on the floor of the well and is killed by the impact as he would have been had Debbie not been present. Again, changing the example in this way does not, I think, make a difference to permissibility. Whether Debbie acts permissibly cannot depend on whether she places the barrier above her head or places herself beneath a floor barrier.

To clarify, I'm not denying that there is a morally relevant difference between killing and letting die, nor am I denying that cases of letting die are distinguished by the fact that we deprive victims only of things over which we have rightful prior claims. I am only claiming that this distinction does not play an important role when comparing Violinist and Nonlethal Cushion. In both these cases the defensive agent can prevent another person from benefitting from her body. In this respect both cases share an important feature with paradigmatic letting die cases. The only difference is the mechanism by which the defensive agent prevents the other person from benefitting from her body. My claim is that these differences are not sufficient to change what is permissible in these cases. It cannot be true that you are permitted to unplug yourself from the violinist in the original version of the example but not in the version where you must first send a fatal electrical current through the tube.

I conclude that the appeal to the distinction between killing and letting die fails to identify a morally significant difference between the cases, and I can see no

---

[29] Others may disagree. John Finnis, for example, might see a decisive difference given his remarks about an 'assault on the body'. See his 'The Rights and Wrongs of Abortion: A Reply to Judith Thomson', *Philosophy & Public Affairs* 2, no. 2 (1973): 139–41.

other reason to resist the claim that Violinist and Nonlethal Cushion are morally on a par. The argument thus far is this:

P5   It is permissible to unplug yourself in Violinist.

P6   Violinist is relevantly analogous to Nonlethal Cushion.

Therefore,

C3   It is permissible for Debbie to pull the lever in Nonlethal Cushion.

Now consider another case:

> *Lethal Cushion*: Carl is an innocent person who has been kidnapped and thrown by a villain from the top of a well towards the bottom of the well. At the bottom of the well stands Debbie *who will be killed by Carl's falling body unless she shoots him with her trusty ray gun first.* If she doesn't shoot, Carl will survive the fall unharmed because landing on Debbie's body will cushion his fall. If Debbie were not present, Carl would not survive the fall.

How does this case differ from Nonlethal Cushion? One difference might be this: in Lethal Cushion Debbie must *intend* to shoot and vaporize Carl, whereas arguably the harm in Nonlethal Cushion and Violinist is merely *foreseen*.

Even if we grant, for the sake of argument, that there is a moral difference between intended versus merely foreseen harms, I doubt that this difference is enough to make a decisive difference regarding what is permissible in the two cases. The reason is this: in Lethal Cushion, Debbie's *life* (not merely nine bedridden months) is at stake. It is difficult to believe that the distinction between intended versus foreseen harms is so significant that it can explain why it is permissible to foreseeably bring about the death of an innocent person to save oneself from nine months of being bedridden, but impermissible to intentionally bring about the death of an innocent person to save oneself from death. The difference between being bedridden for nine months as opposed to being killed is very great, particularly if the person in question is reasonably young. In my view, this difference must be of greater moral significance than the difference between intended versus foreseen harm.

But even if you do not share this view, there is surely *some* variant of Lethal Cushion where the harms Debbie would suffer would be great enough to outweigh the moral salience of the fact that she would be intending to shoot Carl. Suppose that if Carl lands on Debbie he will not simply kill her, but she will suffer in agony for nine months before dying. Is the moral salience of the intending versus foreseeing distinction so great that it can explain why it is permissible for you to foreseeably bring about the violinist's death to save yourself from nine painless months in bed, but impermissible for Debbie to intentionally bring about Carl's death to save herself from nine months of agony followed by death? I find that very hard to believe.

The argument thus far is as follows:

P5   It is permissible to unplug yourself in Violinist.

P6   Violinist is relevantly analogous to Nonlethal Cushion.

Therefore,

P7   It is permissible for Debbie to pull the lever in Nonlethal Cushion.

P8   There is some amount of harm that Debbie could suffer such that the difference between this harm and being bedridden for nine months morally outweighs any difference between intending a person's death and foreseeing a person's death.

Therefore,

C4   There is some variant of Lethal Cushion where it is permissible for Debbie to shoot her ray gun and vaporize Carl.

If this argument is sound, then there are cases where it is permissible for one person to intentionally kill another person in self-defence when there is no liability-based justification for doing so, and no consequentialist justification for doing so. This conclusion conflicts with the views of McMahan, Otsuka, and other proponents of the moral responsibility argument. These philosophers claim that it is impermissible to intentionally kill a non-liable person in self-defence. If the argument above is sound, however, these philosophers are either mistaken about the range of cases in which it is permissible to intentionally kill an innocent person, or else they should, counterintuitively, declare that it is impermissible for you to unplug yourself in Violinist.

You might worry that I've moved too quickly in reaching this conclusion. Proponents of the moral responsibility argument do not deny that it is sometimes permissible to intentionally kill a non-liable person if there are sufficiently weighty consequentialist reasons for doing so. It might thus be open to these philosophers to make the following reply: it is impermissible for Debbie to shoot Carl simply to avert her own death. It is only permissible for Debbie to shoot Carl in the version of Lethal Cushion where she would suffer nine months of agony prior to death; in this version there is a sufficiently weighty consequentialist justification for what she does (nine months of agony + death is much worse than death). P8 above, suitably interpreted, thus only shows that you can intentionally kill a non-liable person when there is a sufficiently weighty consequentialist justification for doing so. One can therefore accept all the premises and the conclusion of the argument above, while maintaining that it remains impermissible to intentionally kill a person when there is no liability-based or consequentialist justification for doing so.

But those who endorse a strong presumption against intentionally killing non-liable people typically present this presumption as one that is not outweighed even when multiple lives could be saved. For example, those who endorse the presumption are very unlikely to believe that it is permissible to intentionally shoot one innocent person even if doing so would result in saving the lives of three other innocent people. But if saving three lives is an insufficiently good consequence to render it permissible to intentionally shoot an innocent person, then saving one person from nine months of agony and death is also an insufficiently good consequence.

3.5 The Violinist Argument: Part II

I will now argue that the permissibility of unplugging you from the violinist (and by implication, the permissibility of Debbie's shooting Carl) must be agent relative because it cannot be agent neutral.

There is no lesser evil justification for unplugging you from the violinist since the death of the violinist is a much worse outcome than your being involuntarily connected to him in the hospital for nine months. There is also no rights-based or justice-based justification. Non-responsible threats such as the violinist are incapable of violating rights since they exercise no agency, and—following McMahan, Otsuka, and others—the exercise of agency is a necessary condition for being a rights violator. Claim rights correlate with duties, and since the violinist exercises no agency, he violates no duties with regard to you, and thus cannot threaten your rights. Something bad happens to you in Violinist, to be sure, and the Society of Music Lovers is guilty of violating your rights, but the unconscious violinist is no more guilty of violating your rights than any innocent bystander. And thus, just as there is no agent-neutral, justice-based rationale for harming an innocent bystander when you face the threat of harm, there is no agent-neutral, justice-based rationale for unplugging you from the violinist; doing so is not a way of using defensive force against a would-be rights violator.[30] Those who agree that non-responsible persons cannot be rights violators thus must agree either that there is an agent-relative justification for unplugging you from the violinist or else it is impermissible to do so.

Sceptics of the agent-relative explanation may protest that the preceding argument wrongly conflates doing harm with allowing harm or withdrawing aid. Even if there is never a justice-based argument for imposing harm on a non-responsible threat, there is a justice-based rationale for allowing harm to

---

[30] This point applies in equal measure to those who insist that you have a right not to be used as a means, and that this right explains the permissibility of unplugging you from the violinist.

befall a non-responsible threat. The rationale is this: no person is required, at the bar of justice, to provide aid to another person when doing so would be unduly burdensome. Since being attached to a person in the hospital for nine months is unduly burdensome, you do not act unjustly by unplugging yourself and thereby refusing to provide this aid.

This argument, however, is not an agent-neutral rationale for unplugging you from the violinist. It is true that *you* are not, at the bar of justice, required to provide aid to others when doing so would be unduly burdensome, but this doesn't entail that *other* people may unplug you from the violinist, thereby causing his death. To see this clearly, let's consider a variation on the case:[31]

> *The Enemy*: The initial circumstances are the same as in Violinist, except that you are temporarily unconscious and unaware of what's been done to you. The violinist's enemy sneaks into the hospital and detaches you from the violinist with the aim of causing the death of the violinist.

It seems clear that the enemy in this case wrongfully kills the violinist; he cannot claim to be acting permissibly by appealing to the view that, at the bar of justice, you are not morally required to provide unduly burdensome aid to others.

Now suppose that you are temporarily unconscious, and by the time you wake up it will be impossible to detach yourself from the violinist: the only opportunity to detach you is now, while you are unconscious. Would it be permissible for a morally motivated stranger (rather than the violinist's enemy) to unplug you from the violinist, having received no instructions from you? I cannot see that it would be. The third party would be performing an act that results in the death of one innocent person in order to save another from nine months in a hospital bed. Given the relative harms involved, the action cannot be permissible in terms of averting a greater harm. What could make it permissible for the third party to act in a way that brings about a much more harmful consequence? This question is particularly difficult to answer given that, if the third party unplugs you from the violinist, he will be killing the violinist, and not merely letting him die. The violinist will survive unless the third party unplugs you, and if the third party unplugs you, this cannot be construed as the third party failing to aid the violinist: he is not depriving the violinist of his own body or efforts, but rather someone else's. It's true that the morally motivated third party—unlike the enemy—would not act on the basis of a bad intention, but that is hardly sufficient to render it permissible for the third party to kill an innocent person. Even if one acts with the best of intentions, it is wrong to kill one innocent person in order to save another from nine months in bed.

---

[31] I borrow this example, with slight modifications, from McMahan, *The Ethics of Killing*, 379.

Now suppose you are conscious and you *ask* the morally motivated stranger to unplug you from the violinist because you are unable to do so yourself: under these conditions is it permissible for the third party to act? Put differently, if A has an agent-relative prerogative to countenance harming B, may she transfer the prerogative to any third party C? In one sense, I think the answer is no. A cannot grant a morally motivated stranger C the discretion to decide whether to exercise the prerogative: the decision must rest with A and is nontransferable. If the prerogative could be wholly transferred to any person C—if C could gain the power to decide whether to impose harm on B—then it could no longer plausibly be regarded as an agent-relative prerogative. It's hard to understand how allowing A the power to transfer the decision about whether to harm B to C could be justified by appeal to the disproportionate weight A's life has from A's own perspective. Of course, many moral rights can be entirely transferred—e.g., the bundle of ownership rights typically associated with property—but the agent-relative prerogative to impose harm is different. It is, by virtue of its special, agent-relative character, tied to the agent who possesses it. Because the basis for the permission is the agent-relative weight A may attach to her own life when compared to the lives of others, I think A must typically be the person who chooses whether to exercise the prerogative.

That said, I believe a limited class of people—those who stand in certain relationships to A—can act as the authorized agent of A when A decides to exercise her agent-relative prerogative. If, for example, C is A's spouse or parent, it seems C could permissibly impose the harm on A's behalf (either at A's request or when A's consent can reasonably be inferred). A sceptic might protest that in these cases there is no need to assume that C exercises A's prerogative on A's behalf. Instead, says the sceptic, these cases are better explained by the fact that the parent or spouse has her own agent-relative reasons to impose harm in defence of her child or spouse.[32] But even if some cases can be explained this way, others cannot. Some people occupy the role of legal guardian for a child, for example, without developing the special ties that exist between most parents and children. But legal guardians who fall into this category are, I believe, permitted to exercise an agent-relative prerogative on behalf of the child for whom they are responsible.[33]

---

[32] These agent-relative prerogatives could be one of two types. First, they could be the same type we have been considering thus far, that is, a prerogative to accord disproportionate weight to your own life and central projects. Second, they could be prerogatives grounded in the value of particular relationships, such as those between a parent and child, or between spouses.

[33] To be clear, even if there are cases where C may act as A's authorized agent in exercising the agent-relative prerogative, C may also be free to decline to assist. And of course there may be a variety of further variables that bear on the permissibility of C's decision. For alternative discussions regarding the possibility of transferring or vesting agent-relative prerogatives, see Bazargan-Forward, 'Vesting Agent-Relative Permissions in a Proxy'; Helen Frowe, 'If You'll Be My Bodyguard: Agreements to Save and the Duty to Minimize Harm', *Ethics* 129, no. 2 (2019): 204–29; Davis, 'Abortion and Self-Defense', 195–6; Fabre, 'Permissible Rescue Killings'; Lazar, 'Associative Duties and the Ethics of Killing in War',

Why should the ability to act as the authorized agent of the person with the agent-relative prerogative be limited to those with whom the person stands in some sort of special relationship? The agent-relative view involves adopting an evaluative standpoint in which, for example, your relationship with your spouse or your child is more important than a stranger's similar relationships. It makes sense to suppose that those with whom you share such relationships can, to a certain extent, share in your agent-relative evaluative perspective. It's also not difficult to understand why people who occupy certain special institutional roles, such as legal guardian, may share in this perspective: this is constitutive of the role. This suggestion is distinct from the claim that there are moral duties or requirements that arise in virtue of our special relationships with others (though it is compatible with it). My suggestion is that those with whom one stands in the right sort of relationship can permissibly come to adopt, within limits, your agent-relative perspective as their own, and thus, if authorized by you (or when such authorization can reasonably be inferred), such persons can act on the basis of your agent-relative reasons in a way that others cannot. The justification for the prerogative remains the same—the disproportionate weight A may attach to her own life when compared to the lives of others. But if A is unable to perform the relevant act, she may authorize those with whom she stands in a special relationship to do so on her behalf.[34]

Setting aside this complexity about third parties, the important point is this: a morally motivated stranger cannot permissibly decide to unplug you from the violinist. Such a third party would simply be killing a non-liable person to save you from being connected to someone in a hospital bed for nine months. This cannot be justified from an agent-neutral perspective. And so the moral permission for you—or those with whom you have particular relationships—to be unplugged from the violinist is agent relative.

Contrast Violinist with the following case: Albert is about to murder Betty to inherit her fortune and the only way to save Betty's life is to kill Albert. In this case, it's obvious that a morally motivated stranger may intercede and shoot Albert to save Betty. Because Albert wrongfully threatens Betty's life, he renders himself

Journal of Practical Ethics 1, no. 1 (2013): 3–48; and Lazar, 'Authorization and the Morality of War', *Australasian Journal of Philosophy* 94, no. 2 (2016): 211–26.

[34] In this way, among others, my account of agent-relative prerogatives differs from the one recently proposed by Bazargan-Forward. He argues, following Thomas Nagel, that agent-relative permissions are grounded in our status as inviolable beings who 'cannot be permissibly sacrificed at the bar of just any greater good'. In light of this fact, he seems to suggest that agent-relative prerogatives can be vested in any willing third party and he argues that this more permissive view of vesting might be justified in a contractualist manner. See Bazargan-Forward, 'Vesting Agent-Relative Permissions in a Proxy', 688–90. My view is different: I think the prerogatives are a function of our agent-relative reasons, and these reasons only apply to people who can coherently occupy the evaluative perspective from which the reasons arise.

liable to defensive harm, and thus the stranger may shoot him if necessary to save Betty. In Violinist, by contrast, a morally motivated stranger cannot permissibly kill the violinist because there is no sufficient agent-neutral justification. In sum:

P5   It is permissible to unplug yourself in Violinist.

P6   Violinist is relevantly analogous to Nonlethal Cushion.

Therefore,

P7   It is permissible for Debbie to pull the lever in Nonlethal Cushion.

P8   There is some amount of harm that Debbie could suffer such that the difference between this harm and being bedridden for nine months morally outweighs any difference between intending a person's death and foreseeing a person's death.

Therefore,

P9   There is some variant of Lethal Cushion where it is permissible for Debbie to shoot her ray gun and vaporize Carl.

P10   The permission to unplug yourself in Violinist is an agent-relative moral permission.

Therefore,

C5   The permissibility of Debbie's vaporizing Carl in some version of Lethal Cushion igrounded in an agent-relative prerogative to impose harm.

The prior steps do not, strictly speaking, entail the conclusion. The prior steps only establish that some version of Lethal Cushion is sufficiently similar to Violinist such that the two cases do not differ in terms of moral permissibility, but this leaves open the possibility that they differ in some way that means the moral permission to act in one case is agent relative, whereas in the other it is not. But this is very unlikely: there is no obvious way in which the cases differ that supports this alternative view.

   The argument above, if successful, constitutes a decisive objection to those who deny that it is ever permissible, for agent-relative reasons, for one person to deliberately kill a non-liable person to save herself.

3.6 The Means Principle

An obvious concern about the agent-relative prerogative is that its scope might be implausibly broad. If the prerogative allows defenders to kill non-responsible threats, why isn't a defender also permitted to grab an innocent bystander and use her body as a protective shield against a lethal projectile? Without some limits on its scope, the agent-relative prerogative will yield a host of highly counter-intuitive results.

I believe that the means principle provides the solution to this worry:

Provisional Means Principle: It is morally wrong to harm an innocent person, Y, in the pursuit of an objective if doing so involves using Y's body to successfully achieve your objective, unless Y is duty bound to allow this harmful use or has consented to this harm.

This principle captures part of the Kantian idea that there is something particularly wrong about treating another person as a mere means to your own ends. Warren Quinn proposes something similar, distinguishing between those cases where the harmed person's presence presents an opportunity or advantage, as opposed to those cases where the harmed person's presence is an obstacle. Quinn suggests that when we harm or kill in the former cases our agency is 'opportunistic', whereas in the latter cases our agency is merely 'eliminative', and he argues that the former acts are more difficult to justify.[35]

Many believe it is wrong, other things being equal, to profit or gain from someone else's suffering, but I think this intuition is strongest when the person who has been harmed can complain, 'You were just using me!' This complaint makes sense and has moral force when the person who acts could not have successfully executed the act *but for* the presence of the person who is harmed. A non-responsible threat cannot plausibly complain, 'You were just using me' if he is harmed or killed by someone acting in self-defence. In these cases there is no sense in which the acting agent takes advantage of, or exploits the presence of, the threat for her own gain. But if a defensive agent uses a bystander's body as a shield to stop a lethal projectile, the defensive agent does exploit the bystander for her own gain.[36]

I thus disagree with Otsuka when he says that killing a non-responsible threat is 'analogous to those most deplorable cases in which you kill a Bystander in order to

---

[35] Warren Quinn, 'Actions, Intentions, and Consequences: The Doctrine of Double Effect', *Philosophy & Public Affairs* 18, no. 4 (1989): 344. Others who endorse principles in the same family include Larry Alexander, 'The Means Principle', in *Legal, Moral and Metaphysical Truths: The Philosophy of Michael Moore*, ed. Kimberly Kessler Ferzan and Stephen J. Morse (Oxford: Oxford University Press, 2016), 251–64; Gerhard Øverland, 'Moral Obstacles: An Alternative to the Doctrine of Double Effect', *Ethics* 124, no. 3 (2014): 481–506; Ketan H. Ramakrishnan, 'Treating People as Tools', *Philosophy & Public Affairs* 44, no. 2 (2016): 133–65; Tadros, *The Ends of Harm*, chap. 6; and Alec Walen, 'Transcending the Means Principle', *Law and Philosophy* 33, no. 4 (2014): 427–64, and 'The Restricting Claims Principle Revisited: Grounding the Means Principle on the Agent–Patient Divide', *Law and Philosophy* 35, no. 2 (2016): 211–47.

[36] Shelly Kagan considers this method of explaining the normative difference between aggressors and threats as opposed to bystanders and shields, and while he declares that it is 'a promising possibility', he ultimately rejects it for reasons I consider below. See Kagan, *The Limits of Morality* (Oxford: Clarendon Press, 1989), 140–4.

eat her body to prevent yourself from starving or in order to replace your failing vital organs with healthy ones.'[37] There is a morally salient disanalogy since in killing the non-responsible threat you do not exploit his presence as a means of doing something you could not do without him, but this *is* what you do when you eat a bystander or steal a bystander's vital organs.[38]

I believe there can be no justification for violating the means principle.[39] Even when we have a powerful reason to harm an innocent person, for example, that doing so is necessary to avert harm to some larger group of people, this reason is defeated by the prohibition against harmfully using another person as a means. The same is true of agent-relative reasons: they are defeated by the constraint imposed by the means principle. If this is correct, then the scope of the agent-relative prerogative is suitably limited. Defensive force can typically be used against justified attackers and non-responsible threats because doing so does not violate the means principle. But cases where imposing harm is intuitively impermissible—like Otsuka's deplorable cases—are prohibited by the means principle.

The provisional means principle, however, is inadequate, as the following example illustrates:

> *Alcove*: You are in a tunnel and see a runaway trolley headed straight for you and it will kill you if do not escape. You can only escape the trolley by squeezing into a small alcove in the tunnel. Unfortunately for you, there is already someone in the small alcove. You could pull him out of the alcove and onto the tracks, where he will die, so that you may fit in the alcove and save yourself.[40]

The person already in the alcove is a *non-responsible obstructor*: someone who is not morally responsible for what threatens your life, but blocks your path to safety, and is not duty bound to move since moving would come at some significant cost. I believe it is clear that it is impermissible to kill the obstructor in Alcove. The difficulty, however, is that if you kill the obstructor in Alcove, you would not be taking advantage of, or exploiting, his presence: you would be safe from the oncoming trolley if he were not there. Cases like this pose a serious problem for the provisional means principle.[41]

Those who deny that it is permissible to kill non-responsible threats might therefore try to appeal to cases like Alcove to support their view.[42] In Alcove, it is

---

[37] Otsuka, 'Killing the Innocent in Self-Defense', 87. Note that Otsuka has subsequently retracted this claim in 'The Moral-Responsibility Account', 54–5.

[38] Frowe independently developed this objection to Otsuka. See Frowe, 'Equating Innocent Threats and Bystanders', *Journal of Applied Philosophy* 25, no. 4 (2008): 277–90.

[39] I defend this view in Chapter 7.

[40] This example is borrowed from Thomson, 'Self-Defense', 291.

[41] See Kagan, *The Limits of Morality*, 140–4.

[42] McMahan offers this objection as a means of showing why Quinn's distinction between eliminative and opportunistic agency cannot ground a permission to kill Innocent Aggressors and Threats

impermissible to kill the obstructor even though doing so apparently does not violate the means principle. If it is impermissible to kill obstructors even though doing so does not violate the means principle, then surely, the argument goes, it is also impermissible to kill non-responsible threats.

The means principle can, however, be reformulated to avoid this objection. The objection assumes that it is always impermissible to kill non-responsible obstructors, but this is false. Consider the following example:

> *Meteor*: A small meteor is falling towards you and will kill you if it lands on you. The only safe place where you can avoid the meteor is your very tiny one-person car. But there is already someone in your car: a third party placed this person there involuntarily. You could, however, pull the person out of the car to save yourself, thereby ensuring that he will die.

I think it is clear that you may act in this case. It is, after all, *your* car. It is unfortunate that you and the other person cannot both survive the oncoming meteor, but you have a prior claim to your car, and so can permissibly remove the other person from the car to save your life. Here we have a case where it is permissible to kill an innocent obstructor to save your own life.[43]

Now we must identify the relevant difference between Meteor and Alcove. I suggest the relevant difference is this: in Meteor you have a prior claim to the space being occupied by the obstructor, whereas in Alcove you do not. This explains why acting in the former case is permissible, whereas acting in the latter case is not. Before elaborating on that thought, let me first defend the claim that the person in the alcove has a prior claim to that space.

It makes sense to suppose we each have at least a prima facie claim to the space we occupy, provided that we have not entered someone else's private property without consent. Suppose Albert and Betty are in a public park, and Albert wants to get a better view of the lake, but can only do so if Betty moves from her present location where she is enjoying a picnic. Albert cannot simply move Betty, even if this causes her no harm, and even if he is somehow able to do this without touching Betty (thus avoiding violating any claims she might have against non-consensual touching). Betty has a presumptive right to her location even though it

---

in self-defence. See McMahan, *Killing in War*, 170–1. Also see Otsuka, 'The Moral-Responsibility Account', 56–7.

[43] Some might protest that you do not kill the person in Meteor, but rather you let him die since he only dies because you deny him something that belongs to you (your car). But the example can be modified. Suppose the car is on the edge of a cliff and the only way to remove the person from the car is to throw him out the door and off the edge of the cliff. In this case you certainly kill the Innocent Obstructor, but I think you are still permitted to do so.

is a public park, and even though it is more or less arbitrary that Betty arrived at that particular spot first. Of course, Betty's rights may sometimes be permissibly overridden if the benefits to some other person or persons are much greater than any interest of Betty's in remaining where she is. But we cannot simply ignore Betty's rights whenever there might be some small overall good in doing so. The same consideration that supports the view that a person has presumptive rights over their body motivates the thought that a person has presumptive rights over the physical space their body occupies. Without such rights we would lack one of the most basic elements of human agency—we would be unable to control our physical location. It would be strange to assert rights over the body grounded in a view of persons as self-directing agents, yet insist that individuals lack any claim against others from having their bodies moved without their consent.

If these remarks are sound, we are now in a position to see how this informs the means principle. Suppose it is permissible to kill in Meteor, but impermissible to kill in Alcove. We have identified the consideration that distinguishes the two cases: in the former case, but not in the latter, the acting agent does not require space to which the obstructor has some legitimate claim.[44] I therefore suggest that killing in Alcove is relevantly analogous to using a bystander's body as a shield to save yourself from some oncoming lethal projectile. In both cases your act cannot succeed *but for* something to which the bystander or obstructor has a prior claim. To kill in such cases would be to take advantage of, or exploit, the body or the physical space of someone else. In both cases you take advantage of things over which the bystander or obstructor has a rightful claim, and in doing so you shift the burden of death from yourself onto them. This, I think, is why killing in such cases is impermissible. However, in cases involving non-responsible threats, as well cases such as Meteor, the acting agent does not take advantage of, or exploit, the body or the physical space of someone else. This calls for a modification of the means principle:

> *Means Principle*: It is morally wrong to harm Y in the pursuit of an objective if doing so involves using Y's body or other things over which Y has a rightful prior claim,[45] unless Y is duty bound to suffer this harm, or has consented to this harm.[46]

I will not, in this chapter, provide a detailed argument for this version of the means principle. I pursue that objective in Chapter 7. For now, I'll simply note

---

[44] Note that our focus here is on cases where people have *legitimate* prior claims. As I emphasized in Chapter 1, it's a further very difficult and underexplored question how we should understand principles like the means principle under conditions where rights over bodies and other property have not been rightly allocated, or where we do not know what constitutes a just allocation.

[45] Or at least a claim that is stronger than any claim of the agent who might harm Y.

[46] Your failure to save Y also counts as harming Y, in my view, when Y has a right to be saved by you. When Y lacks this right, your failure to save Y is not a case of you harming Y.

that this principle coheres with many of our considered convictions; in particular it enables us to distinguish between intuitively permissible and impermissible instances of defensive force. In considering whether it's permissible to use defensive force and in doing so harm an innocent person, Y, we can ask the following question: If Y and all the things currently belonging to Y were suddenly to disappear, would you be safe?[47] If you would be safe, either because the act of self-defence is no longer necessary or because you can still successfully perform the very same act of self-defence, then you do not exploit or take advantage of Y by performing the harmful act. You merely keep what you would have without Y. If the answer is no, however, this shows that you do exploit or take advantage of Y in order to save yourself. Your act of successful self-defence depends on the presence of Y or other things over which Y has a rightful claim. Since your successful defence depends on things over which Y has a rightful claim, to use them and thereby harm Y would be to exploit Y's entitlements for your own benefit, and as such it is impermissible.

Several things are worth noting about this idea. First, the means principle depends on a theory of justice to tell us who has prior claims over which parts of the world. In other words, whether an infringement will be permissible depends on other judgements about moral rights or justice but, as I emphasize throughout the book, the best account of the morality of defensive force must depend on wider claims about justice in this way. Second, although the means principle restricts the scope of the agent-relative prerogative to impose harm on innocent persons, it does not always prohibit the harming of bystanders. Suppose, for example, there is a lethal projectile headed towards you and the only way to save yourself is to divert or deflect the projectile, though doing so entails the projectile will kill a bystander instead. I believe you may permissibly redirect the projectile, since you have an agent-relative prerogative to give greater weight to your own life, and you do not violate the means principle by redirecting the projectile.

3.7 Objections

I have defended an agent-relative prerogative to impose harm on innocent people, provided doing so does not violate the means principle. This section confronts

---

[47] There are, of course, interesting and difficult questions regarding how to define the counterfactual where the space occupied by an innocent obstructor or bystander is removed. I don't consider this issue in detail here, though I say more in Chapter 7. Note that because the relevant counterfactual is whether you would be safe if the innocent person and all their property were absent, you *are* permitted to use the property of a non-responsible threat to defend yourself from them. If such a person and their property suddenly vanished, you would be safe, and thus if you do need something that belongs to them (e.g., their gun) to defend yourself from them, you may make use of it since you do not take advantage of the threat in doing so.

several objections to agent-relative prerogatives (objections to the means principle are considered in Chapter 7).

3.7.1 Impartiality

Each innocent person's life has the same objective value: no one is morally more important than anyone else. Aren't agent-relative prerogatives inconsistent with this fact? Such prerogatives apparently permit you to behave as if your life is more important than the lives of others, and moreover they permit you to harm or kill innocent others on this basis. This conflicts with the conviction that morality demands a certain kind of impartiality, and so we should reject agent-relative prerogative to do harm.

The conception of impartiality to which this objection appeals, however, is vulnerable to a dilemma. Consider a very strict conception of impartiality according to which it is never permissible to prioritize your own life and projects over those of others. Such a conception condemns too much. It condemns a parent who chooses to rescue her own child from drowning rather than two children she does not know. It condemns the person who refuses to throw himself on a grenade when doing so could save several others. It condemns the person who chooses to be a philosophy professor when she could have done much more to improve the lives of others as an investment banker. If some of these choices, and many others like them, are morally permissible, the strict conception of impartiality must be false. But once we concede that our conception of impartiality must allow people to sometimes prioritize their own life and projects over those of others, it's no longer obvious why an agent-relative prerogative to do harm is ruled out. It becomes an open question as to whether the space morality opens up for non-impartial behaviour includes harm-imposing behaviour.

3.7.2 Arbitrary Facts

Some may object that agent-relative prerogatives to impose harm enable arbitrary facts—who is stronger, or who happens to have the required skills or weapons—to play a decisive role in determining who will be harmed and who will be saved in cases where not all can avoid harm. The weak have good reasons to reject a principle that permits conflicts to be resolved in this way.[48]

This objection proves far too much. Many moral principles permit arbitrary facts, including facts about who is stronger or has greater skills, to decisively determine who can avoid harm. For example, suppose a villain is trying to kill

---

[48] Tadros, *The Ends of Harm*, 207–8.

both of us. You are strong enough to climb a large wall to safety, but I am not. You could instead help me climb the wall, but if you do then the villain will kill you rather than me. You are not morally required to flip a coin in cases like this to decide who should be killed: you can permissibly climb to safety. Similarly, if it is impermissible to violate the means principle, this will benefit those who are better able to defend themselves without needing to make use of other people's powers or resources. But no one, to my knowledge, presents this as a good objection to the means principle.

A proponent of the initial objection, Tadros, anticipates this problem, but his response is puzzling. Tadros argues that the appeal to an agent-relative perspective does not explain why duties of rescue are not very demanding or why there is a morally important difference between doing harm and allowing harm. As he puts it, 'it is not at all plausible that agent-relative values drive the distinction between acts and omissions. Things are the other way around. The fact that there is no duty to rescue grounds our entitlement to prefer our own survival, health, and projects in our decisions.'[49] But this is a non sequitur. The question is not whether agent-relative prerogatives can explain the alleged distinction between acts and omissions. The question is whether it is a good objection to agent-relative prerogatives that they sometimes allow the arbitrarily strong to prevail over the weak. If it is a good objection to agent-relative prerogatives, then it is also a good objection to the moral principle that declares it to be permissible to refuse to help those in need when doing so is costly. There is no burden on the proponent of agent-relative prerogatives to establish that agent relativity is what grounds the distinction between doing and allowing.

3.7.3 Conflicts

A different objection focuses on the way agent-relative prerogatives generate conflicts. In standard cases of self-defence against a wrongful attacker, you are permitted to use necessary and proportionate defensive force, and the attacker is prohibited from interfering with your efforts. In standard cases, there is thus never a conflict of permissions or liberties: if you are at liberty to ϕ, then the wrongful attacker is not at liberty to prevent your ϕ-ing. But on the account defended in this chapter, conflicts can arise. You may permissibly use defensive force against a non-responsible threat or a justified attacker, but that does not entail that the threat or attacker is precluded from fighting back. On my view, these cases result in a conflict of permissions, where each side is permitted to use defensive force to try and save herself from the other. There are two objections to allowing such conflicts to arise.

---

[49] Ibid., 209.

The first objection is conceptual. It might seem incoherent to declare that X has a right of self-defence against Y, and yet that Y also has a right of self-defence against X. This charge of conceptual incoherence is easily dismissed. There is nothing incoherent about two people each being morally at liberty to attack the other. Boxers are each at liberty to throw punches at each other and to try to use certain means to prevent the other from landing punches—there's no incoherence here.

This response may seem too quick. Boxers are each at liberty to throw punches at the other because each boxer also waives his normal claim rights against being punched by voluntarily participating in the boxing match. Conflicting liberties of this kind are not incoherent because the alleged liberty (being under no duty to refrain from throwing the punch) does not conflict with anyone else's claim right (a claim against being punched). Things are different when defensive force is used against a non-responsible threat or justified attacker. In these cases, the threat or attacker retains his claim not to be harmed, and yet I have argued that the defensive agent nevertheless may permissibly impose defensive harm. Isn't this conceptually incoherent? The defensive agent cannot both be at liberty to ϕ and yet also be under a duty to refrain from ϕ-ing.

This charge of conceptual incoherence would apply if an agent-relative prerogative established that the defensive agent possessed a moral liberty in the Hohfeldian sense—that is, if the defensive agent were under no duty to refrain from harming the threat or attacker. But the claim is rather that the disproportionate weight that Betty is permitted to accord her own life entails that she can, within certain limits, permissibly infringe the claim that Albert retains against her. In this respect, agent-relative prerogatives are similar to lesser evil justifications. When Betty has a lesser evil justification for harming Albert, this doesn't entail that Albert no longer has a claim against Betty not to be harmed or that Betty is no longer under the correlated duty. Rather, the importance of averting the greater evil *outweighs* the duty that Betty owes to Albert, thereby rendering it morally permissible for Betty to harm Albert despite Albert's claim not to be harmed. Similarly, when Betty has an agent-relative prerogative to harm Albert, this doesn't entail that Albert no longer has a claim against Betty not to be harmed or that Betty is no longer under the correlated duty, only that the claim is outweighed by her agent-relative concerns.

The charge of conceptual incoherence thus fails. Agent-relative prerogatives do not entail that the defensive agent is both under a duty and not under a duty to refrain from performing an act. Rather, like lesser evil justifications, agent-relative prerogatives presuppose that our moral duties to others can sometimes be outweighed by competing considerations.[50]

---

[50] Some argue that moral rights cannot be permissibly infringed without contradiction. See, for example, Hillel Steiner, *An Essay on Rights* (Oxford: Blackwell, 1994), 86–101. I address this argument in 'Rights', in *The Routledge Companion to Social and Political Philosophy*, ed. Gerald Gaus and Fred D'Agostino (New York: Routledge, 2014), 625–7. Also see Thomson, *The Realm of Rights*, chap. 3.

3.7.4 Permissibility

This leads to the second conflict-based objection, which is substantive and not conceptual. This objection denies that it can be permissible to defend oneself against someone else who acts permissibly (the objection thus applies only to the agent-relative view as applied to justified attackers). Here is the argument:[51]

P11   If A's ϕ-ing is permissible despite causing harm to innocent B, then there must be

weighty reasons (WR) that justify A's ϕ-ing.

P12   If WR are weighty enough to justify A's ϕ-ing, then WR are typically weighty enough to justify prohibiting B from preventing A from ϕ-ing.

Therefore

C6   It is typically impermissible for B to use defensive force against A when A acts permissibly in threatening harm against B.

The problem with this argument, however, is that the second premise stipulates what proponents of an agent-relative prerogative deny. Moreover, there are good reasons to suspect that the second premise is false since the reasons that apply to one agent don't always apply to another agent. For example, Albert may have weighty reasons to grab the nearest life jacket so that he can save his child from drowning, even though doing so will foreseeably cause a stranger's child to drown. But Albert's weighty reasons in this case don't serve to prohibit Betty from trying to stop Albert from grabbing the jacket: she is permitted to try to grab it for her child instead. The special reasons that permit Albert to perform an act that will cause harm to Betty's child aren't the sort of reasons that apply to Betty (they are relative to Albert's special relationship to his child), and thus they cannot (at least not without further assumptions) ground restrictions on Betty's behaviour. Examples like this one cast serious doubt on the plausibility of P2. They also illustrate the sense in which the argument only seems to succeed by assuming what needs to be shown, namely, that there are typically never agent-relative reasons for action that entail different agents can have conflicting moral permissions.

A different problem with the proposed argument can be illustrated with the following case:

Defensive Trolley: There is an empty runaway trolley headed towards five people who are trapped on the main track, and the trolley will kill these people unless it is stopped or diverted. Fortunately, there is a side track onto which the trolley can

---

[51] For this argument see Tadros, *The Ends of Harm*, 203–6.

be diverted, though Betty is trapped on this side track and will be killed if the trolley is diverted. Albert is a bystander who has seen and understood everything, and stands next to the switch that can divert the trolley. Albert diverts the trolley onto the side track with the intention of saving the five people from being killed. Betty sees what Albert has done, and realizes the only way to save herself from being killed is to throw the grenade she is holding at the oncoming trolley, which will redirect the trolley away from her and towards Albert.

According to the argument above, if Albert has a lesser evil justification for redirecting the trolley, then Betty cannot defend herself by throwing the grenade. This conclusion seems implausible. Imagine Albert's attempt to explain to Betty why she may not throw the grenade that redirects the trolley away from her and towards him: 'You cannot make me pay the cost of saving the five with my life even though I am permitted to make you pay this cost with your life. Once the five have been saved, the costs are fixed and cannot be permissibly shifted from you to me.'

Now imagine Betty's rejoinder: 'I agree you had the moral permission to redirect the trolley away from the five and towards me. I'm simply insisting that you and I are then symmetrically situated: there is no reason that saving the five should come at the expense of my life rather than yours, and so each of us has an agent-relative prerogative to redirect the trolley away from ourselves (and towards the other) if possible.' Betty's claim seems more plausible. Her claim seems to correctly reflect the fact that Albert and Betty are morally on a par. As she says, there is no particular reason the price of saving the five should be Betty's life rather than Albert's; there's no reason the cost of saving the five should be fixed at the moment Albert turns the trolley. But while I believe it would be permissible for Betty to kill Albert to save herself, it would clearly be impermissible for a morally motivated stranger to do so: the stranger has no sufficient reason to intervene on Betty's behalf. And so Betty's permission to kill Albert must be agent relative.

3.7.5 Bodies and Spaces

Consider the following objection. The fact that one person arrived at a public location first is often arbitrary from the moral point of view, and thus it cannot ground a claim over the space, particularly when occupation of the space is essential to avoid some harm. Thus, in cases like Alcove, the fact that one person is the initial occupant of the alcove is morally irrelevant. The fair thing to do is flip a coin to decide who can safely occupy the alcove. Contrary to what I claim, it would thus be permissible to move the one person out of the alcove after winning a fair coin toss.[52]

---

[52] This argument is presented in Otsuka, 'The Moral-Responsibility Account', 60–1.

I have two responses to this objection. First, even if everything claimed in the previous paragraph is true, this doesn't constitute an objection to agent-relative prerogatives or to the means principle. Accepting this objection would only entail that I have reached the wrong conclusion about what is permissible in cases like Alcove on the basis of a mistaken view about persons' claims over the spaces they occupy. The main conclusions of the chapter would thus be unaffected.

But I also don't accept what is claimed in the objection. I agree that whether someone arrives at a public location first can be, in one sense, arbitrary, but many of our most important rights are arbitrary in this way. It is just a matter of luck, for example, that some people have healthy vital organs and others do not, but this doesn't entail that we should flip a coin to decide who should keep the organs. It may also be just a matter of luck that one person is standing at the top of an overpass under which a runaway trolley must pass whereas another person is trapped on the main tracks below and will be killed by the trolley unless we push the first person off the overpass, but this doesn't entail that we should flip a coin to decide whether to push the person off the overpass. The objection thus seems to prove far too much.

The proponent of the objection is likely to protest that the preceding reply ignores a crucial distinction: rights over our bodies are different from rights over other things in the world. Arbitrariness regarding rights over bodies is fine, but it's not fine when it comes to rights over other parts of the world.

I don't find this rejoinder persuasive—I doubt there is a compelling explanation for the proposed asymmetry between rights over the body and rights over other parts of the world. Persons typically have very stringent rights over their bodies for a variety of reasons—for example, we are more likely to be harmed by violations of our bodily rights, and we are more likely to have our freedom compromised by violations of our bodily rights when compared to violations of property rights. But these are contingent facts that don't obtain in all circumstances. Rights over an umbrella are not typically stringent because usually not much is at stake regarding the possession of an umbrella. But if possession of the umbrella is somehow essential to your survival things are different: if someone else seizes the umbrella this will kill you, and thus your right over the umbrella under these conditions is as stringent as your right against being killed.[53] Consider the following case:

Shipwrecked: After a ship has been destroyed at sea in a violent storm, one of the passengers, Betty, finds herself stranded on a small deserted island. When she was in the water, Betty's body was cut open by some sharp rocks, and she now has a large open wound that is bleeding. If she isn't able to close the wound soon, she will die. Fortunately, she finds a large and unusually adhesive piece of

[53] In the next chapter I elaborate on the view that the stringency of our moral rights depends on a plurality of factors, including how much harm the right-holder will suffer if the right is contravened.

seaweed on the beach, and she is able to attach this to her wound, effectively closing the wound with the seaweed and saving herself. Ten minutes later another passenger, Albert, washes ashore. Albert has sustained exactly the same type of injury as Betty, and the only way he can avoid dying is with the large piece of seaweed that Betty is already using. The seaweed is not large enough to save both of them.

The proponent of the objection must hold that Albert can seize the seaweed from Betty and kill her if he wins a fair coin toss. I think, however, this is obviously unacceptable. Doing this is no different from seizing one of Betty's vital organs. The seaweed is as crucial to Betty as a vital organ, and the fact that she currently possesses the seaweed is no less arbitrary than the fact that some people have healthy organs and others do not. In my view, if a person non-culpably comes into possession of some previously unowned or public part of the world (an object or a location) and needs this resource to survive, her claim to this resource is roughly as stringent as a claim to a vital organ.[54] Our bodies are not the only things that we arbitrarily possess and over which we have stringent claims. I thus deny that it is permissible to seize the physical space of the one person in Alcove.

3.7.6 Prerogatives and Liability I

Let's consider an objection that focuses on an apparent tension between agent-relative prerogatives to impose harm and the moral status account of liability to defensive force defended in Chapter 2. The moral status account, recall, tells us that a person is liable to defensive harm when he acts in a way that results in a threat of harm to innocent people if and only if the act meets the minimum conditions of moral responsibility, and the evidence-relative permissibility of performing the act depends on the assumption that those who are harmed (or might foreseeably be harmed) by performing the act lack rights against the imposition of the harm. One of the virtues of this account, I argued, is that it can explain why mistaken aggressors are liable to defensive force. Recall:

Mistaken Attacker: The identical twin brother of a notorious mass murderer is driving during a stormy night in a remote area when his car breaks down. Unaware that his brother has recently escaped from prison and is known to be hiding in this same area, he knocks on the door of the nearest house, seeking to phone for help. Resident has been warned by the authorities that the mass

---

[54] Note that this conclusion is compatible with the view that if a vital resource has not been appropriated by anyone, two people who both need the resource to survive and arrive on the scene at the same time should use a fair lottery to decide who can use the resource.

murderer will certainly attack anyone he meets on sight. On opening the door, Resident justifiably believes the harmless twin is the murderer and lunges at him with a knife.

The moral status account, I argued, deems Resident liable to defensive force since the evidence-relative permissibility of lunging at the twin with his knife depends on the justifiable but false assumption that the twin is liable to defensive force.

But, says the sceptic, if we accept that there are agent-relative prerogatives to impose harm, it's no longer true that the evidence-relative permissibility of Resident's act depends on the assumption that the twin is liable. Suppose that Resident believed that the apparent murderer at his door was a non-responsible aggressor: Resident would still have an agent-relative justification for using defensive force. Thus, Resident's evidence-relative justification doesn't depend on the assumption that the person at his door is liable; even without the assumption of liability, there would still be an agent-relative prerogative to use force. But this entails, counterintuitively, that mistaken aggressors like Resident are never liable to defensive force. We thus face an apparent dilemma.[55] If we accept both the moral status account of liability and the existence of agent-relative prerogatives, then justifiably mistaken aggressors are never liable to defensive force. Alternatively, if we are confident that justifiably mistaken aggressors are sometimes liable to defensive harm, we must reject either the moral status account of liability or the existence of agent-relative prerogatives.

This dilemma, however, is illusory. It relies on a mistaken view of what it means for a person's evidence-relative justification to depend on a particular fact. As the example is described, Resident has sufficient evidence to believe that there is a liable attacker at the door. Given his evidence, Resident has a liability-based justification but no agent-relative justification, since Resident has no reason to believe that he faces a non-responsible threat. If we ask whether Resident would have an evidence-relative permission to use defensive force absent the premise that the person at the door is a liable murderer, it seems clear the answer is no. Without the reports that a dangerous murderer is on the loose in his neighbourhood, Resident would have no reason to believe that the person at his door poses any threat.

In considering whether a defensive agent's justification depends on the assumption that a target is liable, we must hold constant the other facts of the case, and only eliminate the evidence that supports the assumption of liability. In most cases of mistaken aggression, when we do this, the defensive agent will no longer have an evidence-relative justification for using defensive force, and so the dilemma pressed above dissolves. Moreover, to say that a person's justification for using

---

[55] Ketan H. Ramakrishnan presses this dilemma in 'Quong on Defensive Harm' (unpublished manuscript).

defensive force depends on a particular premise is to make a claim about the defensive agent's justification in the world as it is. There may be close possible worlds where the defensive agent would have a different justification for acting, but this doesn't change the fact that, in the current world, the particular premise plays an essential role in the justification for using defensive force.[56]

3.7.7 Prerogatives and Liability II

Consider the following case:[57]

> *Mistaken Attacker II*: An innocent person in Resident's town, Unlucky, has been involuntarily administered a drug that forces him to walk around shooting people on sight, without any agency whatsoever (the drug has commandeered his body, bypassing all of his deliberative and intentional faculties). From the news and the authorities, Resident knows that Unlucky (or his body) has killed several people and is still on the loose. Meanwhile, Unlucky's harmless twin brother—who doesn't know, and has no way of knowing, about Unlucky's plight—is driving through Resident's town when his car breaks down. The twin knocks on Resident's door to ask for help, whereupon Resident forms the fully justifiable belief that the twin is Unlucky, and is about to kill him (Resident has been warned by the authorities that Unlucky will almost certainly attack anyone he meets on sight). Resident thus lunges at the harmless twin with a knife, attempting to kill him in (perceived) self-defence.

In this case Resident is justified, in the evidence-relative sense, in believing that he has an agent-relative prerogative to use defensive force, but he is unfortunately mistaken. Since the evidence-relative permissibility of Resident's use of force does not depend on assuming anyone is liable to defensive harm, the moral status account of liability deems Resident non-liable in this case. Ketan H. Ramakrishnan argues that this is problematic since, intuitively, Resident is just as liable to defensive force in this case as in the original version of Mistaken Attacker. He concludes that we must either reject the moral status account of liability, or else abandon agent-relative prerogatives to harm non-liable threats.[58]

---

[56] The same is true when we consider reasons for belief as opposed to reasons for action. If I look at my broken watch and it says that it is 2 p.m., I reasonably but mistakenly believe that it is 2 p.m. If I didn't have a broken watch, I might have asked someone for the time, and that person might have mistakenly told me it was 2 p.m. This counterfactual doesn't change the fact that, in the current world, the justification for my belief that it is 2 p.m. depends on the evidence from my watch.

[57] This case, along with the objection it supports, is presented by Ramakrishnan in 'Quong on Defensive Harm

[58] Ibid.

Unsurprisingly, I disagree. I believe there is an important moral difference between the two variants of Mistaken Attacker. It is morally significant how one treats the people one harms—whether one treats them as having forfeited their claims or not. Of course it might seem the cases are too similar to be treated differently. But the cases are different, and the difference will affect what evidence Resident must have before being permitted to use defensive force. In particular, what constitutes necessary and proportionate force in the two cases will differ. Even if one accepts that there is an agent-relative prerogative to harm non-liable threats, defensive agents are still required to bear greater risks to avoid seriously harming a non-liable threat than to avoid harming a fully liable attacker. For example, since Resident justifiably believes the twin to be non-liable in Mistaken Attacker II, it's less plausible to suppose that he would be evidence-relative permitted to immediately lunge at him with lethal force without any visual evidence that the person he perceives as a threat has pulled a weapon or indeed possesses one. He might be evidence-relative required to take a greater risk—for example, wait to see what the twin does with his hands—before being evidence-relative permitted to use defensive force. In the original version of the case, by contrast, because Resident is evidence-relative justified in believing the person at the door is liable, he is evidence-relative permitted to take fewer risks before imposing serious defensive force. If we accept the plausible assumption that the necessity and proportionality conditions apply differently with regard to liable and non-liable threats, and thus affect what defensive agents can permissibly do, this provides support for the more general idea that the two cases are importantly different, and thus it shouldn't be surprising to discover that Resident may be liable in one variant of the case, but not in the other.

3.8 Conclusion

An agent-relative prerogative, constrained by the means principle, to impose harm on non-liable persons when protecting what is rightfully yours, resembles the permission to allow other people to be harmed under certain conditions. When it is permissible to allow someone to be harmed, an important part of what makes it permissible is the fact that the harmed person loses only what he would have had by virtue of your efforts, or other things that belong to you. In these cases you merely keep what belongs to you in order to avoid a risky or costly action. To permissibly kill or harm a non-liable person in self-defence, a related idea applies. It must be true that saving your life does not require the presence of the non-liable person, or the presence of anything to which he has a rightful claim. To act when this condition is not met would involve wrongfully harming that other person as a means. You would be exploiting things over which he has a claim in order to shift harms from yourself onto him. Your use of a person in this way renders the act impermissible. The moral distinction between doing and allowing harm and the means principle share a common rationale, one where each person is an independent agent whose rightful entitlements cannot be used as a means for another's ends. Chapter 7 defends this view in greater detail.

4

Proportionality

Albert is angry with Betty because she won't go out on a date with him. He's advancing towards her and is going to wrongfully harm her unless she uses defensive force against him. Under these conditions, we've seen, Albert is *liable* to defensive harm. Now suppose that the only thing Albert is going to do is break her finger. In order to prevent him from breaking her finger, she kills him. Albert, I hope you'll agree, is not liable to *this* level of defensive harm. There may be a variety of lesser harms Betty can impose on Albert to defend her finger, but killing him is clearly far too severe. Put another way, killing Albert in order to defend Betty's finger is not proportionate.

This example illustrates that a person is never liable to defensive harm generally; rather, a person can only be liable to some particular proportionate level of defensive harm. As David Rodin says, 'for a person to be liable to a harm, just is for that harm to be narrowly proportionate in the circumstances. Proportionality and liability, far from being independent factors, are two manifestations of the same underlying normative relations.'[1] Proportionality, in the sense that will be the focus of this chapter, thus refers to the degree or amount of defensive harm to which a person is liable. Proportionality judgements are an essential part of the individual morality of defensive force. Even if we know *who* is liable to attack in self-defence, or in defence of others, we also need to know *how much* harm it is proportionate to impose in order to assess the moral permissibility of different courses of action.

I have two main aims in this chapter. The first is to explain and criticize a very widely accepted view about proportionality. On this view, the amount of harm it is proportionate to impose on an attacker should depend on the extent to which the attacker is *morally responsible* for creating a situation where someone suffering harm is unavoidable. The greater the attacker's degree of moral responsibility, the greater the degree of defensive harm it can be proportionate to impose. This idea, in some form, is endorsed by many, probably most, philosophers currently working in this area, but I'm going to argue that we should reject it.

The second aim is to offer a positive account of proportionality: the *stringency principle*. On this view, the independent variable that explains what counts as

---

[1] Rodin, 'Justifying Harm', 79. For a similar statement see for example McMahan, *Killing in War*, 10.

The Morality of Defensive Force. Jonathan Quong, Oxford University Press (2020). © Jonathan Quong.
DOI: 10.1093/oso/9780198851103.001.0001

proportionate defensive harm is the stringency of the right that the attacker threatens to violate. The more stringent the right that is threatened, the greater the degree of defensive harm that is proportionate. I believe the stringency principle provides the best explanation of the essential features of proportionality, and explains our judgements in paradigm cases. It explains, for example, why it is disproportionate for Betty to kill Albert in order to prevent him from breaking her finger: the harm she imposes on him far exceeds the stringency of the right that he threatens to violate.

Before proceeding to the main arguments, let me clarify a few things. First, I rely on examples where all plausible conceptions of liability agree that the attacker is liable to *some* level of defensive harm so that we may concentrate on the issue of proportionality. Second, I focus only on the issue of proportionality as it applies to those who are liable to at least some defensive harm. The arguments in this chapter thus do not apply to determining when harming non-liable persons may be proportionate in the wide sense, that is, when harming innocent persons is justified all things considered. Harm to non-liable persons is justified either by lesser evil considerations or by agent-relative prerogatives. Third, proportionality in defensive harm differs in crucial respects from proportionality in punishment, and it's important to keep these domains distinct. For example, some people believe that proportionate punishment is *deserved*, but moral desert plays no role in liability to defensive force as I understand it. Fourth, some accounts of liability to defensive harm include a necessity condition, that is, they hold that an attacker can only be liable to some particular act of defensive harm if imposing that harm is necessary to avert the threat that the attacker poses. In Chapter 5 I argue that making liability to defensive harm depend on meeting the necessity condition in this way is a mistake, but I will not argue for or assume that view here, and nothing in the arguments in this chapter turns on this issue.

The chapter proceeds as follows. Section 4.1 sketches the way moral responsibility might provide an account of proportionality. In section 4.2 I provide reasons to be sceptical of the appeal to moral responsibility. Sections 4.3–4.5 develop and defend my preferred account of proportionality: the stringency principle. In section 4.6 I consider various objections to the stringency principle, and section 4.7 concludes.

4.1 The Responsibility Principle

Compare the following two cases:

Stroll: Albert is out for a stroll, lost in thought. He negligently fails to heed the sign warning him not to walk any further, since there is a danger of creating rockslides that might injure those below. Albert is about to step forward into this dangerous area, and this will dislodge some rocks that will fall on and break Betty's leg. Carl happens upon the scene. He sees what will occur if Albert steps forward, and he also realizes that the only way to stop him in time is to tackle him to the ground, though this will result in some injuries to Albert.

Revenge: Albert is angry that Betty has refused to go on a date with him. He decides to take his revenge by waiting until Betty is walking along the footpath beneath his house, and pushes some rocks down the hill towards her, threatening to break her leg. Carl happens upon the scene and realizes that the only way to stop Albert in time is to tackle him to the ground, though this will result in some injuries to Albert.

Although the harm that Betty might suffer in each case is the same—a broken leg—it is plausible that our proportionality judgements in these two cases should differ. The amount of harm it might be proportionate for Carl to impose on Albert in Stroll should be lower than the amount it would be proportionate for him to impose in Revenge. Several differences between the two cases, or the conjunction of these differences, might explain why. In Stroll, Albert is unaware that he poses any threat to Betty, whereas in Revenge Albert is very much *aware* of the threat he poses. In Stroll the harm Albert threatens to impose is not intended, whereas in Revenge Albert's threat is *intended*. Albert's action is also a much *graver wrong-doing* in Revenge than in Stroll. And as a result of these considerations, Albert is also much *more culpable* in Revenge than in Stroll. It's not clear whether all of these considerations, or only some of them, bear on proportionality, but what does seem clear is that the correct account ought to reflect the fact that these two cases are different. There is more to proportionality judgements than the degree of harm the victim faces.

Some argue that there are many different considerations that bear on proportionality judgements. Rodin, for example, identifies fourteen different variables that he believes are relevant to proportionality.[2] But it's also true that we want more from an account of proportionality than a list of the different moral variables that may be relevant. I believe a successful account of proportionality should, ideally, do all of the following:

1. Explain our intuitive judgements about proportionality in paradigm cases.
2. Be sensitive to the way multiple considerations bear on proportionality judgements, and not misrepresent or distort the way these different considerations matter for proportionality.

---

[2] Rodin, 'Justifying Harm', 80–1.

3. Offer a coherent framework that unifies these different considerations, explaining why *these* considerations, rather than others, belong together in an account of proportionality.
4. Explain the relationship between (a) the necessary and sufficient conditions for any degree of liability, and (b) the considerations that determine the degree of liability.

Here is where the appeal to moral responsibility enters the picture. The moral responsibility account of liability looks as if it might meet the four conditions listed above. This account, recall, typically holds that in order for a person to be liable to defensive harm, it must be the case that the person voluntarily acted in a way that foreseeably might result in a threat of impermissible harm, and the impermissible threat eventuates. As I said in Chapter 2, at the heart of the moral responsibility account is an appeal to a particular responsibility-sensitive conception of distributive justice: that individuals ought to bear the costs for their own choices, but should not be held liable for the costs of brute luck, or the responsible choices of others.

Its proponents offer this as an account of the necessary and sufficient conditions for a person to be liable to *any* degree of defensive harm. But given the connection between liability and proportionality, it's natural to see the moral responsibility account as offering us a way to understand proportionality as well as liability. To the extent that one person is wholly responsible for the creation of some unavoidable harm, that person should bear the entire amount of harm. But some of our choices are made under conditions of limited knowledge, or partial duress, or panic, or diminished mental capacity, and thus it would be inaccurate to say that we are wholly responsible for those choices in the way we would be if the choices were made under conditions of full information, no duress, etc. The extent to which our voluntary agency is connected to some outcome can vary, and so responsibility, in this sense, comes in degrees. As McMahan puts it, 'The Responsibility Account treats liability as a matter of degree. Responsibility for an unjust threat can vary in degree, and liability varies concomitantly.'[3]

The variable we use to identify *who* is liable to defensive harm can thus also be the key consideration in explaining *how much* harm the person is liable to bear. Defensive harms are proportionate to the extent that they track an individual's moral responsibility for the creation of a situation where harm must unavoidably be imposed on someone. Notice that this account can explain the intuitive difference between the two cases I mentioned earlier: Stroll and Revenge. In Revenge Albert is fully responsible for the threat to Betty's leg, whereas in Stroll,

---

[3] McMahan, 'The Basis of Moral Liability', 395.

he only bears partial responsibility since the threat to Betty is not something that is connected to Albert's agency in the same strong way as it is in Revenge. There may be many variables that bear on proportionality judgements, but on the view proposed here, they can be partially, perhaps completely, unified and explained by reference to the single concept of moral responsibility. Whether the agent intended the harm, whether the agent was distracted or coerced, whether the agent was mistaken about key facts, whether he is someone with diminished mental capacity—all of these issues are united by the way they bear on the *degree* of an agent's moral responsibility for his actions.

Notice, however, that the appeal to moral responsibility cannot, on its own, generate intuitive judgements about proportionality. Consider, for example, the simple case described at the outset, where Albert is responsible for threatening to wrongfully break Betty's finger, and in order to avert his threat, she kills him. Clearly this constitutes a disproportionate level of defensive harm. Can the appeal to moral responsibility, on its own, explain this conclusion? Someone might argue that in wrongfully threatening to break Betty's finger, Albert foreseeably creates a situation where a certain amount of harm must unavoidably be distributed, an amount of harm roughly equivalent to a broken finger. For simplicity, let's give this level of harm a score of 5. What Albert foreseeably does, in other words, is create a situation where 5 units of harm must be distributed, and thus it's fair to hold Albert liable to suffer roughly 5 units of harm. But killing Albert, let's suppose, constitutes 1,000 units of harm. Albert, however, did not foreseeably create a situation where 1,000 units of harm must be distributed, and this is why Betty killing Albert in self-defence is disproportionate.

This might sound plausible, but there's an obvious problem. Suppose that the only way Betty can stop Albert from wrongfully breaking her finger is by killing him, and suppose this fact is foreseeable to Albert when he launches his wrongful attack—he knew she would need to kill him to save her finger. Since Albert is wholly responsible for the situation, why is it unfair to require him to bear 1,000 units of harm when the alternative will involve his imposing 5 units of harm on Betty (who bears no responsibility for the situation)? The appeal to moral responsibility cannot, on its own, explain why it's disproportionate to kill Albert. Other factors, such as the amount of harm that the victim might suffer, seem necessary to generate intuitively plausible judgements, at least with regard to setting the maximum amount of harm to which a person can be liable.

But moral responsibility might still play a central role in determining judgements of proportionality. This role is described by the following principle:

> *Responsibility Principle*: Other things being equal, the degree of defensive harm that it is proportionate to impose on a liable attacker varies in accordance with the attacker's degree of moral responsibility for creating a situation where at least one non-liable person is threatened with harm.

The simplest view of proportionality incorporating this principle might posit only two relevant variables: (i) the severity of harm an attacker threatens to impose, and (ii) the attacker's degree of moral responsibility. Holding responsibility constant, the less harm the attacker threatens to impose, the lower the attacker's level of liability. Similarly, holding the level of harm constant, the less responsible the attacker is, the lower the degree of defensive harm it is proportionate to impose on that attacker. More complex accounts will include more variables.

Although there are different ways of interpreting the responsibility principle, in one form or another it has been endorsed or proposed by many currently working on defensive force and just war.[4] I believe, however, that the principle is false. I agree that a minimal degree of moral responsibility is necessary for an agent to be liable to any level of defensive force since a person cannot be a potential right-violator unless she meets some minimal standard of responsibility, but I deny that further differences in the degree of an agent's moral responsibility above this threshold have a direct bearing on how much harm a person is liable to bear.

4.2 Why Responsibility?

Let's begin with some intuitive worries about the responsibility principle. Compare Dave, who decides to violently mug another person, and has no respon-sibility-diminishing excuse for doing so, with Eric, who threatens to do exactly the same thing to a different person, but is partially excused as a result of some mild coercion by others. The fact that Eric is somewhat less responsible for the threat he poses does not change the fact that he and Dave threaten to commit the same type of crime. Or consider another pair of cases. Frank did not plan to get drunk tonight, but his friends, as a prank, gave him three alcoholic drinks that Frank believed were nonalcoholic, and as a result he is now mildly drunk. He becomes aggressive and threatens to wrongfully assault a man at the bar. Gary has not had anything to drink, but he is an aggressive person, and he threatens to wrongfully assault a man at the bar with the same degree of force as Frank. Frank and Gary differ in their relative levels of moral responsibility, but the rights that they threaten to violate are the same.

It does not seem plausible, at least to me, that the total amount of defensive force to which Eric is liable should be less than Dave, nor that Frank should be

---

[4] The following is a partial list of those who suggest that a person's degree of moral responsibility or culpability for creating a situation where harm is unavoidable bears on the issue of proportionality: Saba Bazargan, 'Killing Minimally Responsible Threats', *Ethics* 125, no. 1 (2014): 114–36; Kaila Draper, 'Defense', *Philosophical Studies* 145, no. 1 (2009): 81; McMahan, 'Self-Defense and Culpability', 766, 'The Basis of Moral Liability', 395, and 'Who Is Morally Liable to Be Killed in War', 548; Rodin, 'Justifying Harm', 80–4; Tadros, *The Ends of Harm*, 332; and Suzanne Uniacke, 'Proportionality and Self-Defense', *Law and Philosophy* 30, no. 3 (2011): 265.

liable to less defensive force than Gary, yet this is what the responsibility principle apparently recommends. Of course, intuitions about such cases may differ: I don't present these cases as a decisive reason to reject the principle. But what can the proponent of the responsibility principle say to those of us who find such implications counterintuitive? Why must the degree of defensive harm it is proportionate to impose be sensitive to an attacker's degree of moral responsibility? Below I consider several possible answers, but I argue that none are satisfactory.

One rationale is rejected by almost everyone who works on the morality of defensive force, namely, any appeal to *moral desert*. Liability to defensive harm is not about giving people what they deserve; there is typically no positive reason to impose defensive harm on someone when doing so is unnecessary, and thus liability to defensive harm is unlike the classic retributive picture of liability to punishment.[5] If the responsibility principle is true, it has nothing to do with the ways in which degrees of moral responsibility might reflect differential levels of moral desert.

The responsibility principle might seem to be more clearly justified by appeal to the *fair distribution of harm* between an attacker and his potential victim. As McMahan puts it: 'the determination of liability to defensive harm is a matter of justice in the *ex ante* distribution of unavoidable harm'.[6] When Albert wrongfully threatens Betty, the fact that he is morally responsible for creating a situation where harm is unavoidable—either he will harm Betty or Betty will harm him in self-defence—entails that it's only fair that he, rather than Betty, should suffer the relevant harm. And this, it might seem, is why an attacker's degree of moral responsibility matters in determining his level of liability. The greater the attacker's degree of responsibility for a wrongful threat, the more harm he can justly be liable to bear.

Whether the appeal to fairness in the distribution of unavoidable harm can ground the responsibility principle depends on further details about the conception of fairness or justice being invoked. McMahan has argued, for example, that Albert is liable to the entire amount of some unavoidable harm even if Albert is only minimally responsible, provided that Albert is *more responsible* for the threat of harm than Betty, and the harm is not divisible.[7] On this view, justice in the distribution of unavoidable harm involves selecting the option from the feasible

---

[5] See McMahan, *Killing in War*, 8–9. For similar remarks see, for example, Frowe, *Defensive Killing*, 106; and Tadros, *The Ends of Harm*, 176–7. For an exception to this consensus, see John Gardner and François Tanguay-Renaud, 'Desert and Avoidability in Self-Defense', *Ethics* 122, no. 1 (2011): 111–34.

[6] McMahan, 'Self-Defense against Justified Threateners', 117.

[7] This is, as we saw in Chapter 2, the way McMahan proposes dealing with the case of the conscientious driver who experiences a freak accident and whose car now threatens to kill a pedestrian. See McMahan, 'The Basis of Moral Liability', 394–8.

set that best approximates the relative levels of responsibility of attackers and victims. Let's call this the *feasibility account* of fairness in the distribution of harm.

Whatever its other advantages and drawbacks might be, the feasibility account does not provide clear support for the responsibility principle. According to the feasibility account, two attackers who are differentially responsible for equally serious threats of harm may be liable to exactly the same amount of defensive force because degrees of liability are heavily determined by the distributive options that happen to be feasible. A conscientious driver who foreseeably imposes a tiny risk of harm on an innocent pedestrian when driving to work can be liable to be killed even though she is far less morally responsible for the threat than a person who culpably threatens to murder someone for the sake of an inheritance. Thus, the feasibility account of fairness does not support the proposition that, other things being equal (e.g., degree of harm threatened), changes in an attacker's degree of moral responsibility ground changes in the attacker's degree of liability to defensive harm. Of course the appeal to moral responsibility plays a role in determining *who* is liable to defensive force, but in any situation where the harm is indivisible—where either a responsible attacker or a non-responsible victim must suffer harm—the attacker's *degree* of moral responsibility becomes irrelevant since any degree of responsibility on the attacker's part makes him liable to bear the entire harm: all that matters is that the attacker bears more responsibility for the unavoidable harm in comparison to the potential victim.

Suppose, then, that we endorse an *idealized account* of fairness in the distribution of unavoidable harm.[8] On this view, the fair or just distribution is one where each person cannot be liable to any greater harm than the percentage of unavoidable harm for which he or she is morally responsible.[9] If Albert is partially excused for his wrongful attack on account of duress, and so is only 40 per cent responsible for the unavoidable harm, then he can be liable to no more harm than he would be liable to bear if he were fully responsible for a harm 40 per cent as severe as the one he threatens to impose.[10] On this view, it is irrelevant that it may not be possible to allocate this less severe harm to Albert.[11] Principles of just distribution are not constrained by facts regarding what is currently feasible: instead they identify an

---

[8] Bazargan develops and defends an account of liability and proportionality that depends upon this view. See Bazargan, 'Killing Minimally Responsible Threats'. McMahan also proposes this view in 'Duty, Obedience, Desert, and Proportionality in War: A Response', *Ethics* 122, no. 1 (2011): 155.

[9] Though note that this account need not conceptualize moral responsibility for unavoidable harm as a zero-sum issue.

[10] Bazargan, 'Killing Minimally Responsible Threats', 122.

[11] But how then do we decide what it is permissible to do when a harm is indivisible, and no person is liable to the entire amount? Bazargan argues that, at least in many cases of this type, the defensive agent may permissibly impose the entire harm on the attacker by combining a liability justification with a lesser evil justification. See Bazargan, 'Killing Minimally Responsible Threats'. McMahan has also suggested this method of combining liability and lesser evil justifications. See McMahan, 'What Rights May Be Defended by Means of War?' in *The Morality of Defensive War*, ed. Cécile Fabre and Seth Lazar (Oxford: Oxford University Press, 2014), 138–40.

ideal distribution of harm that best reflects the relative degrees of moral responsibility of those involved.[12]

The difficulty, however, is that it remains mysterious why we should endorse
this view and apply it to proportionality in defensive harm. In other contexts
where costs are distributed we do not adhere to this conception of fairness.[13] If
I drive negligently and injure a pedestrian, the amount of compensation to which
the pedestrian is entitled, at least in American tort law, does not depend on the
extent to which I am excused for my negligent driving, provided I meet the
minimum conditions of voluntary agency. Of course the *punitive* damages that
I may face if, say, I acted with great recklessness, can differ depending on the
nature and extent of my excusing conditions, but punitive damages are a different
matter, and liability to defensive harm is not a form of punishment or blame.

Consider another context. A group of people cooperates to produce some
resources that can be shared among them. But their levels of moral responsibility
differ. Some members of the group are fully committed to the project and their
participation is wholehearted. Others participate only grudgingly, under some
considerable duress—they only participate because their other options are very
bad or because they are threatened with sanctions. But in the end, each person
performs an equal share of the work. The fact that some participate wholeheartedly while others do so only because they face some duress seems irrelevant to the
question of what justice requires in distributing the benefits of the project. We are
not tempted to say (at least I am not tempted to say) that the relative degrees of
moral responsibility for participation bear on the just distribution of the resources,
at least so long as everyone's participation meets some minimal standards of
voluntariness. In both this domain and the domain of tortious liability, what
seems to matter is whether a person's voluntary conduct meets, or violates, a
certain standard of conduct. The extent of a person's responsibility-diminishing
excuses seems irrelevant, at least above a certain threshold.[14]

[12] Note that the feasibility account and the idealized account might be combined to yield a
constrained version of the responsibility principle, one where changes in the degree of an attacker's
moral responsibility should result in changes in the degree of liability to defensive harm
whenever the harm can feasibly be divided in this way. On this view, there is an ideal distribution of
harm that ought to reflect an individual's degree of moral responsibility, and a person's degree of
liability to defensive harm ought to track this ideal distribution whenever feasible. The rationale for this
constrained responsibility principle would, however, inherit the main objection to the idealized
account. The constrained principle would also, I believe, be vulnerable to the charge that it depends
on an unstable conception of liability.
[13] To be clear, I don't think distributive principles directly apply to the morality of defensive force,
but since most proponents of the moral responsibility account do, it seems appropriate to consider
other distributive contexts when evaluating the responsibility principle.
[14] Some might object that there are other cases of distribution that more closely resemble cases of
self-defence, and where moral responsibility does bear on how the good should be distributed. For
example, one sailor tosses a ration of food overboard out of spite. Another sailor does so because he
misjudges a storm and skittishly thinks that cargo needs to be jettisoned. It seems fair that the first
sailor should go without a ration, if the crew is left a ration short. But it's less intuitively obvious that the
second sailor should be denied a full ration. Isn't this best explained by their differing degrees of moral

To be clear, I'm not suggesting that a proponent of the responsibility principle is committed to applying the principle in other contexts, such as the cooperative one being considered. The point is rather that the proposal—that the just distribution of burdens or benefits should be sensitive to each person's degree of moral responsibility—is not intuitively appealing in other contexts, and thus it remains mysterious why it should be true in the domain of liability to defensive harm.

The idealized account of fairness as applied to liability to defensive harm may gain some plausibility from a conflation of two different senses of 'morally responsible'. Sometimes when we say that Albert is morally responsible for certain costs, we simply mean that Albert can be justly held liable for those costs. But this is not the sense of moral responsibility that proponents of the responsibility principle are invoking—if it were, the principle would be tautological and not explanatory. Rather, proponents of the principle are using moral responsibility to mark the extent to which the consequences of a person's act can be appropriately connected to her voluntary agency. The question is why liability to defensive harm ought to reflect changes in degrees of this kind of responsibility. I've suggested that neither appeals to fairness nor punishment can persuasively answer this question.

But there is one further rationale worth considering. A proponent of the responsibility principle might argue that proportionality in defensive harm must be sensitive to changes in degrees of moral responsibility because proportionality is determined by the *wrongfulness* of the threatened harm, and other things being equal, the less responsible the attacker is, the less wrongful the threatened harm.

To evaluate this proposal, we need to distinguish between two senses of wrongfulness. Sometimes when we talk about an act being more or less wrongful, our focus is on the *agent* who performs the act. In this sense, when we say an act is more or less wrongful, we are in fact describing how culpable or blameworthy the agent is who performs the act. It may be true that, holding other things equal, being less morally responsible always makes the act less wrongful in this sense. But it's not at all clear why judgements about proportionality in defensive harm should be sensitive to changes in this kind of wrongfulness. Defensive harm is not a form of blame or punishment.

Alternatively, sometimes talk of degrees of wrongfulness refers to the seriousness of the wrong done to the *victim*. Murder is, in this sense, more wrongful than the theft of a laptop computer. I believe that this sense of wrongfulness, appropriately defined, *does* ground judgements of proportionality in defensive harm

responsibility? I believe the intuitive difference between these cases is best explained by appeal to the fact that the two sailors violate different duties of justice with different degrees of stringency. The first sailor simply destroys property that is not his to destroy, whereas the latter sailor makes a mistake borne of panic in executing his duties. But our intuitive sense that some types of panicked mistakes are less serious violations of justice when compared to equally harmful deliberate acts of wrongdoing is not grounded in prior, pre-justicial notions of moral responsibility; rather, our judgements about moral responsibility lie downstream from our wider judgements about rights and duties. See the further defence of this claim in section 4.3.

but, as I argue in the following sections, this does not support the responsibility principle because changes in an attacker's degree of moral responsibility do not necessarily ground changes in the wrongfulness of a potential threat.

4.3 The Stringency Principle

In this section I develop and defend the following idea: proportionality is explained by the stringency of the moral right that the attacker threatens to violate.

The stringency of a right, as I will use the term, refers to the strength or weight of the right-holder's claim. In most cases, the more stringent a right is, other things being equal, the more difficult it is to justify infringing the right in question.[15] For example, it might be permissible to infringe right R1 only if we could, at a minimum, save one innocent person from having his legs broken. But it might be permissible to infringe right R2 only if we could, at a minimum, save fifty innocent people from being killed.[16]

I assume that two main facts determine the stringency of a right. First, the stringency of a right depends on the *severity of the harm* that will befall the right-holder if the right is infringed or violated. Consider the right I have against you that you refrain from taking my umbrella, as opposed to the right I have against you that you refrain from cutting off my arm. The latter is typically more stringent than the former because the harm of losing an arm is typically much greater than the harm of losing an umbrella.[17] Second, the stringency of a right depends on the way in which the right protects or reflects the *moral status* of the right-holder. Consider the rights to vote and run for elected office in liberal democratic societies. Even if someone would not be materially harmed by having one of these rights violated or revoked, the rights are stringent partly because of the way they reflect our moral status as free and equal participants in the democratic process. Similarly, we have rights against others *using* our bodies or our property not merely because doing so may cause us harm, but also because doing so is inconsistent with our moral status as free or independent. Our moral status, and

---

[15] I discuss exceptions to this formulation later in the chapter.

[16] Note that we can either individuate rights in a relatively fine-grained manner by appeal to differences in stringency, or we can opt for a more coarse-grained individuation of rights (e.g., the right not to be murdered or the right not to be assaulted), but then allow that different violations of the same type of right will vary in gravity by appeal to differences in stringency. There are things to be said in favour of each approach, but I will not try to settle the issue here. The stringency principle should be compatible with either approach.

[17] I believe the account of harm used in calculating the severity of rights infringements must be objective and non-perfectionist, though I won't defend that further claim here.

the stringency of our rights, is thus sensitive to the mode of agency by which an aggressor threatens us.[18]

I believe the severity of harm and the moral status of the right-holder are the central considerations that determine the stringency of a right.[19] But even if you think I'm mistaken about this, this needn't be fatal for the stringency principle, so long as you accept the idea that rights can vary in their stringency and that a plurality of considerations bear on the stringency of rights.

With this brief sketch of stringency in hand, we can now introduce the first version of the stringency principle:

Stringency Principle (Harm Focused): If an attacker threatens to violate a right with a harm-focused stringency level X then, other things being equal, the level of defensive harm it is proportionate to impose on the attacker is equivalent to X.[20]

This is not a general statement of the stringency principle, since it focuses exclusively on the degree of harm that a defensive agent may proportionately impose and excludes consideration of moral status. Once I have explained this harm-focused version of the view, I will provide a statement of the more general principle.

Clearly you can harm someone without violating her rights (e.g., when the success of my business causes the failure of yours), and you can also violate someone's rights without harming her (e.g., when I enter your house without your permission and leave without your knowledge, having damaged nothing). Given that they mark distinct moral categories, how can we make sense of the idea that the amount of defensive harm that can be imposed on a wrongful attacker can be calibrated relative to the stringency of the right that is threatened?

The harm-focused stringency of a right is determined by asking the following question: Other things being equal, how much harm to an innocent stranger (or strangers) would need to be averted to render it permissible to infringe the right in question? Virtually all rights-based moral theories agree that a right cannot be permissibly infringed whenever the beneficial consequences of doing

---

[18] In previous work I assumed that mode of agency was a distinct consideration bearing on the stringency of a right, but I now believe that was a mistake: mode of agency matters because of the way it bears on the moral status of the right-holder. For example, rights violations that also violate the means principle are particularly serious forms of wrongdoing because these acts treat other people as if they lack a certain moral status. Chapter 7 provides a more detailed defence of this idea.

[19] I remain neutral here as to whether other distinct variables also bear on stringency, for example, whether standing in a special relationship to the right-holder is an independent consideration that bears on the stringency of the right.

[20] Thomson seems to endorse something roughly like the stringency principle in 'Self-Defense', 302–3, note 13. But Thomson mentions the view only in a note and does not explain how stringency ought to be determined, nor why the stringency principle is preferable to other ways of conceptualizing proportionality. Uniacke also emphasizes the severity of the injustice the attacker threatens to commit in her discussion of proportionality, but she does not agree that the stringency of the right should be the exclusive independent variable in determining the proportionality relationship. See Uniacke, 'Proportionality and Self-Defense', 271.

so marginally outweigh the bad consequences. The benefits produced by infringing a right must be significantly greater than the costs before doing so can be permissible, and I will assume this is correct.

Suppose Albert is threatening to wrongfully violate Betty's right against having her arm broken. Let's assume, for simplicity, that having her arm broken causes her 30 units of harm. Given our assumption about the amount of harm that needs to be averted to justify infringing a right, it would not be permissible for Albert to break Betty's arm merely if doing so was necessary to avert 31 units of harm to someone else: the beneficial consequences need to be significantly greater to justify infringing the right. Let's stipulate that Albert could only permissibly infringe Betty's right if doing so averted *more than* 120 units of harm to some innocent stranger.[21] The harm-focused stringency of Betty's right is thus 120 units of harm. Under these conditions, it would be proportionate for Betty to impose *up to* 120 units of harm on Albert to avert his wrongful threat. Albert is liable to this amount of defensive harm because he is not justified in breaking Betty's arm unless doing so would avert more than 120 units of harm, and thus he has no standing to complain when up to 120 units of harm are imposed on him to prevent him from breaking Betty's arm.

The stringency principle is an account of how to measure whether a particular use of defensive force is disproportionate, that is, how to measure whether the amount of defensive force used morally exceeds (in some sense) the value of what is being defended. The proposal is this: the value of the right that is being defended is measured by considering how much harm would need to be averted to render infringing the right permissible. If it is permissible to break Betty's arm to avert 121 units of harm befalling someone else, then Betty's right not to have her arm broken is not more important than someone suffering 121 units of harm. This provides a useful way of identifying disproportionate uses of defensive force. If Betty imposed 121 units of defensive harm on her attacker to prevent her arm from being broken, she would be treating her right against having her arm broken as having greater moral importance than it does when we assess whether breaking it would be permissible. But if it is impermissible to break Betty's arm to avert 120 units, then there is one sense in which Betty's imposition of 120 units on her attacker to defend her right does not look disproportionate. Protecting the right is 'worth' 120 units when we assess whether it would be permissible for someone to break the arm.[22]

---

[21] I focus on the harm to an innocent stranger to bracket agent-relative prerogatives or special ties. The purpose of the proposed test is to find a way of measuring the impartial value of the right, and this is achieved by setting aside special agent-relative reasons one might have for imposing harm.

[22] Here's a possible worry. When deciding how much harm would need to be averted to make it permissible to infringe some right, R, it may matter how the harm that could be averted is distributed. That is, it might be permissible to infringe R to avert 50 units of harm befalling a single person, but not permissible to infringe R if doing so averts 50 units of harm equally distributed across fifty different people. If the distribution of harm matters in this way, this might seem to create a fatal indeterminacy

By wrongfully threatening Betty's right, Albert loses the standing to complain against being forced to bear the entire value of Betty's right, where the value is measured by considering how much harm would need to be averted to make infringing the right permissible. Typically, you cannot be forced to bear great costs to come to the aid of others. But if Albert threatens Betty's right, this has a transformative effect. Albert now becomes responsible for the full value of the right he threatens: Albert cannot plausibly insist that being forced to bear this cost is unjustified since Albert is acting in a way that fails to show due regard for Betty's right. On what basis could Albert claim that making him bear such costs is a violation of his rights or is otherwise unduly demanding? He is merely being made to bear the costs equivalent to (or less than) the value of the right that he himself threatens. He cannot plausibly argue that these costs should fall on Betty, or even be shared between him and Betty.

To avoid misunderstanding, it's important to be clear regarding the role of the stringency principle. It does not purport to explain who is, and is not, liable to defensive force. The stringency principle's role is instead to explain *how much* defensive force those who wrongfully threaten the rights of others are liable to bear. In this way, for example, the stringency principle differs from Tadros's duty view of liability. Tadros claims that 'a person is liable to be harmed for some goal if she has an enforceable duty to bear that harm for that goal'.[23] This claim, I believe, is best understood as a proposal regarding what it usually is, or what it usually means, for a person to be liable to some amount of harm: being liable to bear some amount of harm H, for the sake of goal G, means being under an enforceable duty to bear H for the sake of G. But this proposal, on its own, says nothing regarding what determines the size of H. The stringency principle, however, aims to explain how the size of H is determined in cases of threatened wrongful attacks: the size of

for the application of the stringency principle. If it is sometimes, but not always, permissible to infringe R to avert 50 units of harm, how do we know what degree of defensive force is proportionate to avert violations of R? We can, however, answer this question. The stringency principle focuses on how much harm to a single person (with no special ties to anyone involved) would need to be averted to justify infringing a given right. It makes sense to use the single person as a comparison since we are focused on the amount of harm a single attacker can be liable to bear. This gives us a nonarbitrary reason to focus on the single-person comparison, whereas I cannot see a nonarbitrary basis for selecting any other larger number of people as the relevant comparison. It can still be helpful, as a heuristic, to use comparisons that involve multiple persons as a way of getting a sense of the stringency of a given right, particularly since some rights are so stringent that we have difficulty imagining any realistic amount of harm we could avert to a single person that would justify infringing the right. The right not to be killed in some very painful manner, for example, is so stringent that it's difficult to imagine what amount of harm a single person might suffer that we could avert that would justify infringing this right. It's easier to imagine permissibly infringing this right if doing so is necessary to save five others from suffering a similar fate. Doing this may give us a better grip on the stringency of the right, and may help to explain why many are inclined to think there's no realistic way for a defensive agent to impose disproportionate harm on a wrongful aggressor who is threatening to violate a right of this type.

[23] Tadros, 'Duty and Liability', 262.

H is determined by measuring the stringency of the right that the attacker threatens.

The stringency principle should also not be confused with more general proposals regarding when it is permissible to impose harm on others. The stringency principle does not, for example, entail that if A would be acting impermissibly in φ-ing in order to avert harm H, then it is permissible for others to impose H on A to prevent his φ-ing. The stringency principle does not have this implication since many acts are morally wrong or impermissible but do not involve the violation of individual rights. It may be, for example, morally wrong to refuse to attend my friend's play in order to avoid the inconvenience of spending thirty minutes in traffic. This does not entail that a third party could permissibly force me to attend the play at the cost of thirty minutes in traffic, since my failure to attend the play is not a rights violation. The stringency principle also does not imply that if it would be wrong for A to infringe B's right to avert suffering harm H, then B may permissibly impose H on innocent third parties to avoid having her right violated by A. The stringency principle provides a way of determining how much harm wrongful attackers are liable to bear, but this doesn't entail that the equivalent harm can be permissibly imposed on those who have done nothing to make themselves liable. The fact that it would be wrong for A to violate B's right to avert H clearly does not imply that some bystander, C, can be forced to bear the full value of protecting B's right. C is in a different normative situation. C hasn't threatened anyone else's rights, and so there's no rationale for imposing any more harm on C than the minimal duties of rescue that bystanders are required to bear to help those in urgent in need of assistance.

In sum, the amount of defensive harm to which a wrongful attacker is liable is determined by the amount of harm that would need to be averted to justify infringing the right that the attacker threatens. Since Albert would not be justified in breaking Betty's arm unless doing so was needed to avert more than 120 units of harm, he cannot justifiably have a claim against having 120 units (or less) imposed on him to prevent him from breaking Betty's arm.[24] Notice that this proposal explains why a person acting in self-defence against a wrongful attacker is, other things being equal, permitted to impose far more harm on the wrongful attacker than the wrongful attacker threatens to impose on her. It follows from the widely

---

[24] Suppose Albert wrongfully threatens Betty's right in order to avoid suffering 30 units of harm. If Betty successfully uses defensive force on Albert, he will suffer these 30 units *in addition to* whatever defensive harm Betty imposes. Should these additional 30 units be taken into account when determining how much harm Albert is liable to bear? I think the answer is no. By acting unjustifiably, Albert demonstrates a disregard for the stringency of Betty's right and so he should be liable to the full amount of defensive harm as measured by the harm-focused stringency of the right. Put differently, the fact that Albert will suffer 30 units of harm unless he breaks Betty's arm does not diminish the stringency of the right he threatens, and thus does not diminish the amount of defensive harm Betty may proportionately impose. Of course the additional 30 units he will suffer does bear on the issue of *wide* proportionality.

accepted idea that rights cannot be permissibly infringed unless significantly more harm will be averted by doing so when compared to the amount of harm caused. This proposal also makes clear why the stringency of the right that an attacker threatens to violate determines the degree of defensive harm it can be proportionate to impose on an attacker. The more stringent the right, the greater the amount of harm that would need to be averted to make infringing the right permissible, and thus the greater the amount of harm any would-be rights violator can be forced to suffer to prevent an unjustified transgression of a right.[25]

Thus far I have focused, for the sake of simplicity, only on the harm the defender might suffer and the harm that might be imposed on an attacker, but it's important to remember that both moral status and severity of harm are relevant in our measurement of what a defensive agent may proportionately do. The general statement of the stringency principle (i.e., one that does not focus exclusively on harm) is thus:

> *Stringency Principle (General)*: If a wrongful attacker threatens to violate a right with stringency level X, then the level of defensive *force* it is proportionate to impose on the attacker is equivalent to X.

I use 'force' as a metric that combines the variables of moral status and degree of harm. We measure the right that the attacker threatens to violate by considering both variables, and we also measure the amount of defensive force the defensive agent might impose on the attacker by considering both variables. In this initial comparison, we must gauge the degree of defensive force imposed on the attacker as if the attacker retains all his rights, though of course if we subsequently determine that the amount of defensive force is proportionate, then we will conclude that the attacker does not, in fact, retain rights against the imposition of this force.

Let's suppose that Albert threatens to break Betty's arm. Following the earlier discussion, assume that breaking Betty's arm would cause 30 units of harm. We must then combine the amount harm Betty would suffer with our judgements about the moral status that is protected or reflected by the right in question to

---

[25] A further issue: What are the implications for cases involving multiple victims, for example, where A threatens to violate the rights of B, C, D, and E? I believe the stringency principle allows each defender to impose what would be individually proportionate on A, and as a result A is liable to the combined or aggregate level of defensive harm that results from considering the threatened rights violation that each individual potential defender faces. Suppose A is threatening to unjustly impose 10 units of harm on each of B, C, D, and E, and A is thus liable to 40 units of defensive harm by each of B, C, D, and E because 40 units is a measure of the stringency of the right of each that he is threatening. A is thus potentially liable to 160 units of harm in defence of *all of* B, C, D, and E. If A's liability to defensive harm could not be aggregated in this way, then each of his potential victims would be proportionately permitted to do less in self-defence than she would if A were attacking her alone. In other words, A could decrease his liability to defensive harm with regard to any particular individual by wrongfully threatening to attack more people. This conclusion seems perverse.

reach an overall judgement about the amount of force Albert threatens to impose. Of course it may not be possible to assign precise numerical values to these different considerations.

For the sake of illustration, assume Albert threatens to impose 60 units of force on Betty. Betty has a right against Albert imposing 60 units of force in this way. We should assume (as we did earlier) that it would not be permissible for Albert to infringe this right for a mere marginal gain, for example, if doing so was necessary to avert someone else suffering 61 units of force. Instead we should assume it would only be permissible for Albert to infringe Betty's right if doing so is necessary to avert significantly more force being imposed on someone else. Let's stipulate that this amount is more than 240 units of force. The stringency of Betty's right taking all the relevant variables (not merely harm) into account is thus 240 units of force. We should conclude that it would be proportionate for Betty to impose up to 240 units of defensive force on Albert. Again, the rationale appeals to the fact that Albert would only be justified in breaking Betty's arm if doing so was needed to avert more than 240 units of force. Since he lacks a justification for his wrongful attack, he thus lacks the standing to complain when anything up to 240 units of force is imposed upon him to avert his unjustified threat.

Notice that when we ask whether the action taken by the defensive agent is proportionate, we must ask not only how severe the harm is that she might impose on her attacker, but also the way in which her act would threaten the moral status of the attacker if the attacker retained all of his rights. This is why the harm-focused stringency principle states that *other things being equal*, the level of defensive harm it is proportionate to impose on the attacker is equivalent to X. When we hold moral status constant, then the amount of harm a defensive agent may impose on her wrongful attacker increases as the stringency of the threatened right increases. But when other things are not equal, for example if the defensive agent must harm an attacker in a manner that constitutes a more serious threat to the attacker's moral status, then the relative degree of harm the defensive agent may proportionately impose will decrease.

The stringency principle has a number of virtues in addition to those already identified. First, it can explain paradigm cases, like the one where you disproportionately kill Albert to stop him from breaking your finger: the force you use on Albert clearly exceeds the stringency of the right of yours that he threatens to violate.

Second, it provides a unified explanation of why certain variables bear on our judgements about proportionality. Given that a number of different considerations may affect the way a right protects or reflects a right-holder's moral status, there will typically be a number of variables that bear on our proportionality judgement in any given case. But the list of considerations that bear on proportionality judgements is not ad hoc: we do not simply draw up a list of things that seem relevant. Rather, the variables are united by the way in which they explain the relationship between the seriousness of the injustice the attacker threatens to commit, and the degree to which the attacker forfeits his own rights. The more serious the injustice the attacker threatens, the greater the degree of his rights forfeiture. This also nicely explains the relationship between liability and proportionality. The condition for liability to defensive force is that a person must be threatening to violate the rights of someone else, and the amount of force that is proportionate varies in accordance with the stringency of the threatened violation.

4.4 Rights That Cannot Be Infringed

I have suggested that the stringency of a right, R, can be measured by asking how much harm or force would need to be averted in order to render it permissible to infringe the right. This way of measuring the stringency of a right gives us the upper limit of what constitutes proportionate defensive force against a wrongful aggressor threatening to violate R.

But what if some rights cannot be permissibly infringed, no matter how great the benefits of doing so would be? What does the stringency principle imply about the proportionate use of defensive force against an aggressor who threatens rights of this type? Perhaps there is no limit to how much force can be imposed on wrongful aggressors who threaten such rights. But this is a very extreme view, and so we should consider whether there are other solutions.

We could, of course, avoid this extreme view by insisting that all rights can be permissibly infringed if the beneficial consequences of doing so are great enough. But I reject this view. In Chapter 7 I argue that it is never permissible to violate the means principle. This principle, recall, states:

> It is morally wrong to harm Y in the pursuit of an objective if doing so involves using Y's body or other things over which Y has a rightful prior claim, unless Y is duty bound to suffer this harm, or has consented to this harm.

Thus, the rights against harmful use protected by the means principle cannot be permissibly infringed no matter how much good might be produced by doing so. This conclusion, however, is less dramatic than it might initially appear since we can be duty bound to use our bodies and resources to rescue others under certain conditions.[26] Whether Y is duty bound to allow X to use some resource, P, over which she has a rightful claim depends in part on how costly it would be for Y to allow this use, and also what the benefits of allowing such use will be. For example,

---

[26] I explore some of the further implications of the right to be rescued in Chapter 5.

if X can save the lives of two people by using Y's arm in a way that will break Y's wrist, it may be that Y is duty bound to suffer this break for the sake of rescuing the two people. Thus, although the rights described by the means principle cannot be permissibly infringed, these rights do not generate cost-insensitive duties. If the costs to Y are not too great, and the benefits of allowing P to be used by others are sufficiently great, Y can be duty bound to allow others to use P.

I propose that we measure the stringency of rights that have this structure by asking the following question: How much harm or force would need to be averted for Betty to be duty bound to allow others to use P at some cost, C, to herself? Suppose the answer is this: Betty would be duty bound to allow this use only if doing so was necessary to avert more than 200 units of force to others. The stringency of Betty's right against the use of P at cost C to herself is thus 200 units of force, and thus this sets the upper limit of how much force it would be proportionate to impose on an attacker who wrongfully threatens to violate Betty's right. The stringency of rights against harmful use is measured by asking when the right-holder would be duty bound to allow this use, whereas the stringency of other rights (i.e., those whose violation would not violate the means principle) are measured by asking when it would be permissible to infringe the right.[27]

Some might worry that there's something ad hoc about measuring the stringency of different rights in different ways. But I think this worry is misplaced. We need a way of measuring the value or weight of each moral right. One plausible way of doing so is by asking the following general question: When are the benefits to others sufficiently great that the right no longer constrains the duty bearer? For some rights—rights against mere harm—this threshold is reached when it is permissible for the duty bearer to infringe the right. For other rights—rights against harmful use—this threshold is reached when the right-holder is duty bound to allow the use of her body or property. Thus, although in one sense the stringency of the different types of rights are measured differently, in a more fundamental sense they are measured in the same way, by asking when the benefits to others are sufficiently great that the right no longer constrains the duty bearer.

Moreover, this way of measuring the stringency of the different rights has a further advantage: it reflects the fact that rights against harmful use are, other

---

[27] There is another way in which some rights cannot be permissibly infringed. We have rights, for example, against being harmed by others' negligence. But we can't, it seems, meaningfully ask how much good would need to be done to render it permissible to negligently harm someone: a negligent act is by definition one that isn't done deliberately. What does this imply for the stringency principle? I think we can solve this apparent problem by using a slightly modified version of the test that I've proposed. We can ask instead: How much harm or force would need to be averted to render it permissible to bring about a world where another person negligently violates a given right? It's true that this introduces a new layer of complexity, but I think it preserves the basic idea of the original formulation.

things being equal, much more stringent than rights against mere harm. For example, it may be permissible for Albert to redirect a lethal threat towards Betty in order to save three other people from death, but Betty is not duty bound to allow others to use her body at the cost of her life if doing so could save three others from death. Thus, the account proposed in this chapter has the plausible implication that, other things being equal, it is proportionate to use significantly more force in defence of rights against having one's body or property wrongfully used when compared to rights against mere harm.

4.5 Stringency and Responsibility

Suppose the stringency principle is roughly correct. Does this entail that the responsibility principle is false? It might seem that there are two ways of reconciling the responsibility principle with the stringency principle, but neither succeeds. The first option is to insist that an agent's degree of moral responsibility for an unjust threat is always a further consideration that directly affects the stringency of the right being threatened. Other things being equal, the less responsible an attacker is for a threatened rights violation, the less stringent the right in question actually is.

But this suggestion seems clearly false. Recall the examples introduced at the beginning of section 4.2:

> *Muggings*: Dave decides to violently mug another person and has no responsibility-diminishing excuse for doing so. Eric threatens to do exactly the same thing to a different person, but is partially excused as a result of some mild coercion by others.

As I suggested earlier, the fact that Eric is somewhat less responsible for the threat he poses does not change the fact that he and Dave threaten to violate the same type of right with the same degree of stringency. Also recall:

> *Assaults*: Frank did not plan to get drunk tonight, but his friends, as a prank, gave him three alcoholic drinks that Frank believed were nonalcoholic, and as a result he is now mildly drunk. He becomes aggressive and threatens to wrongfully assault a man at the bar. Gary has not had anything to drink, but he is an aggressive person, and he threatens to wrongfully assault a man at the bar with the same degree of force as Frank.

Frank and Gary differ in their relative levels of responsibility, but the stringency of the rights that they threaten does not differ. Frank may be less blameworthy than Gary, and he may not deserve to be punished as severely, but those are not our questions. Our question is whether Frank's victim has a weaker claim not to be assaulted than Gary's victim. I think it's clear that the answer is no.

But there is a second way the responsibility principle might be reconciled with the stringency principle. A proponent of the responsibility principle may argue that the stringency of a right is affected by the attacker's mode of agency, for example, whether the threatened rights violation is intended or merely foreseen. Proponents of the responsibility principle typically assume that an attacker is, other things being equal, less responsible for foreseen as opposed to intended harm. So, although an attacker's degree of responsibility may not always affect the stringency of a right, responsibility still plays a significant role once we acknowledge the relationship between modes of agency and degrees of responsibility.

This argument, however, depends on conflating two very different senses of moral responsibility. The type of moral responsibility to which proponents of the responsibility principle appeal is meant to capture the degree to which some outcome, O, can be connected to the voluntary agency of some agent, A. The greater the extent to which O can be connected to some voluntary decision made by A, the greater A's moral responsibility for O. Various facts—duress, diminished mental capacity, or failure to intend O—can diminish the agential connection between A and O without severing it. This conception of moral responsibility presupposes very little in terms of pre-existing moral judgements. For example, to know the extent to which A is responsible for O in this sense we do not need to know whether it was permissible for A to bring about O; whether A violates a duty in bringing about O; or whether A can bring about O using only things to which A has a rightful claim. The property identified by proponents of the responsibility principle is thus a relatively nonmoralized, descriptive fact about the degree of A's agential involvement in O.

But this kind of moral responsibility is not what matters when we assess the stringency of a right.[28] Consider, for example, the following pair of cases:

Alley Panic: Henrietta sees a man in a dark alley approach, and having been mugged recently, she is easily panicked in such situations. Although the man has done nothing threatening, Henrietta panics and is about to shoot and seriously injure the man. The man is innocent and poses no threat.

Negligent Driver: Ike is driving through a residential neighbourhood. He is not speeding, but he becomes distracted by thinking about a problem at work. As he turns a corner he fails to notice a pedestrian, and is now about to hit and seriously injure the innocent pedestrian.

---

[28] A further problem is that it's not clear that changes in modes of agency always entail changes in an attacker's degree of responsibility, at least as understood by proponents of the responsibility principle. For example, there's no obvious sense in which an attacker's degree of agential involvement is any greater when he harmfully uses a victim as opposed to when he harms the victim without using the victim.

Even if we hold constant the degree of harm that each victim faces, there may be a sense in which it's true that Henrietta bears a greater degree of moral responsibility for her threat than Ike does for his. But this difference in moral responsibility is not a difference in the simple descriptive sense—the degree of agential involvement in the outcome—to which proponents of the responsibility principle appeal. Indeed, it may be that Henrietta's panic diminishes her agential involvement to exactly the same extent as Ike's negligence. Rather, the difference in moral responsibility is explained by appeal to our broader moral judgements. The duty not to intentionally shoot a loaded gun at someone is a very stringent duty not merely because of the serious harm that results, but also because doing so shows a particular type of disregard for the moral status of others. This may partly be because the activity of shooting a loaded weapon at another person is not one that delivers general social benefits, thus making it reasonable to demand that others refrain from engaging in this practice except in extraordinary circumstances, circumstances that do not include 'when panicked'. Negligent driving, on the other hand, though wrongful, is not easily separated from a practice that is central to our current way of life, and thus does not appear to show the same disregard for the moral status of others.

It's not important, however, that you accept the particular account I've offered as to why rights against being harmed by negligent drivers are less stringent than rights against being shot, even by someone who is panicked. The more general point is that insofar as we are tempted to say that an attacker's mode of agency sometimes seems relevant to our assessment of the attacker's moral responsibility and also the stringency of the right being threatened, it's a very different sort of moral responsibility from the one deployed by proponents of the responsibility principle. If we judge Henrietta to be more morally responsible than Ike, this judgement lies downstream from a host of other moral judgements regarding what activities we can justly demand others refrain from engaging in, and which considerations seem morally relevant in assessing the type of injustice or wrong-doing an attacker threatens to commit. The resulting claims about relative degrees of moral responsibility do not *ground* our judgements about liability and proportionality, they are rather the *conclusions* we reach after taking into account all the considerations that seem relevant in devising a scheme of rights and duties with which each person can reasonably be expected to comply. Just as many are rightly sceptical that there is a pre-institutional conception of moral desert that partly grounds individual claims of justice, we should be similarly sceptical that there is a pre-justicial conception of moral responsibility that partly determines the stringency of rights not to be harmed or attacked.[29]

---

[29] Arthur Ripstein and Samuel Scheffler make similar claims about the place of responsibility in a theory of social or distributive justice. See Ripstein, *Equality, Responsibility, and the Law*, esp. 12–18; Scheffler, 'What Is Egalitarianism?' *Philosophy & Public Affairs* 31, no. 1 (2003): 26–8.

4.6 Objections

This section confronts four objections to the stringency principle.

4.6.1 Too Restrictive

The stringency principle measures the severity of a potential rights infringement by asking the following question: How much good would need to be produced to render it permissible to infringe the right? This sets the upper limit for how much defensive force can be imposed on a liable attacker. If breaking Betty's arm would only be permissible if doing so averted more than 120 units of harm, then Albert is liable to 120 units of harm when he wrongfully threatens to break Betty's arm.

A critic may protest that this method of identifying the upper limit is too restrictive since it fails to distinguish between harm imposed on innocent persons as opposed to liable attackers. It would only be permissible to break Betty's arm to avert more than 120 units of harm to some innocent person but Albert is not innocent, he's a wrongful attacker, and thus harm to Albert should be discounted relative to harm that might be suffered by innocent persons. In sum, if the value of Betty's right is equivalent to 120 units of harm suffered by a non-liable person, then the equivalent for Albert should be much higher, since he is liable.

This objection, however, rests on a mistake. Harm to others is only discounted when we make judgements about wide proportionality, and the only harm that is discounted is harm to which a person is liable or against which he has no claim. But this chapter's focus is narrow proportionality or the degree of an attacker's liability. We cannot begin by assuming that any harm imposed on a wrongful aggressor should be discounted since that assumes what needs to be shown, namely, that the harm imposed is harm to which he is liable. We first need an independent account of how much harm a person is liable to bear, since only that amount is discounted relative to harm imposed on an innocent person. The stringency principle would be seriously flawed if it began—as this objection supposes it should do—by discounting all harms imposed on a wrongful attacker in the course of determining how much harm the attacker is liable to bear.

4.6.2 Too Permissive

Some critics, conversely, might worry that the stringency principle is too permissive. In support of this view, these critics might make the following argument. In many cases the amount of good needed to render it permissible to infringe a right far exceeds our intuitive sense of how wrongful it would be for someone to violate that right. Thus, in many cases, the stringency principle mistakenly entails that wrongful attackers are liable to degrees of defensive force far in excess of our intuitive sense of the wrongfulness of the attacker's threat. Suppose, for example, you believe that it would only be permissible for Albert to paralyse Betty if doing so saved more than twenty innocent lives. This doesn't mean that if Albert wrongfully threatens to paralyse Betty, the wrongfulness of his threat is equivalent to twenty innocent persons' lives. If this were true Albert would be liable to a counterintuitively enormous degree of defensive force.

For this objection to succeed, however, it requires some plausible alternative way of measuring the wrongfulness of the attacker's threat, one that would be an appropriate way to determine how much defensive force is proportionate. One proposal, considered at the end of section 4.2, is this: the more culpable or blameworthy an attacker is for posing a threat, the more wrongful the threat. But we rejected this view for a good reason. Liability to defensive force is not a means of identifying what people deserve in virtue of their culpability or blame. And I don't see any other compelling alternative in the offing.

Of course the sceptic might insist that, even if we lack a clearly defined alternative means of measuring the wrongfulness of a threat, the stringency principle yields sufficiently counterintuitive results that we have good reasons to reject it. But this version of the objection is difficult to evaluate, in part because people's intuitions regarding how much good would need to be averted to render it permissible to infringe a given right are likely to diverge. I also doubt that many people have clear intuitions about the relative seriousness of potential rights violations that do not track how much good would need to be produced in order to render infringing the right permissible.

4.6.3 The Costs Defenders Should Bear

Some critics will argue that we should reject the stringency principle because it does not distinguish between fully culpable attackers and those who are significantly, though not entirely, excused for posing a wrongful threat. The stringency principle, for example, does not distinguish between Resident in Mistaken Attacker (who has a significant epistemic excuse) and a fully culpable murderer. Other things being equal, both are liable to the same degree of defensive force according to the stringency principle. This, insists the critic, is too counterintuitive to accept. To support this conclusion, the critic asks us to consider what costs the defensive agent can be required to bear to avoid harming Resident, as opposed to a fully culpable murderer. Intuitively, the defensive agent should go to greater lengths and bear greater costs to avoid harming Resident as opposed to a fully culpable murderer. Perhaps, for example, the defensive agent should suffer two broken legs to avoid killing Resident, but it doesn't seem true that this is a cost that a defensive agent has to bear to avoid killing a culpable murderer. This, says the critic, provides support for the conclusion that significantly excused attackers are not liable to the same degree of defensive force as attackers who lack any excuses.

I think we can reject this objection for several reasons. First, the intuitions to which the critic is appealing are intuitions about necessity and not proportionality. Whether it's necessary to impose defensive force on an attacker depends on what alternatives are available to the defensive agent, and whether those alternatives are ones whose costs are sufficiently modest that the defensive agent (or other affected persons) are duty bound to bear in order to rescue the attacker from harm. I defend this account of necessity in the next chapter. One of the further claims I make in that chapter is this: our duties to rescue others from harm do not vary according to the culpability or blame of the person we can rescue. The right to be rescued from harm is not something that varies in stringency according to the content of our character; it is rather something that each person possesses and cannot forfeit. Even the worst wrongdoers retain their right to be rescued from serious harm. I thus do not share the intuition that a defensive agent is duty bound to incur greater costs to avoid harming an excused attacker as opposed to a culpable attacker.

Second, setting the first response aside, the critic's view of proportionality also yields very counterintuitive results. Suppose, for the sake of argument, that significantly excused attackers are liable to much less defensive force than fully culpable attackers, all else being equal. Recall the following case from Chapter 2:

Duped Soldiers: A group of young soldiers is successfully fooled by a totalitarian regime into believing that the regime is good and just and is under repeated attacks from their evil neighbours, the Gloops. The regime's misinformation campaign is subtle and convincing—the soldiers are justified in believing what they are told by the regime. Once the misinformation campaign is complete, these soldiers are given orders to attack and destroy a Gloop village on the border, which, they are told, is really a Gloop terrorist camp plotting a major attack. In fact, everything the regime has said is a lie, and the Gloop village contains only innocent civilians. The soldiers prepare to shell the village and are about to (unknowingly) kill all the innocent civilians in it. A peacekeeping force from a neutral third country patrols the border and could avert the attack, but only by killing the soldiers.

Each soldier is significantly excused, and thus apparently liable to much less defensive force than someone who wrongfully kills without an excuse. Suppose each soldier is liable to something roughly half as serious as death.[30] Now assume that there are one hundred soldiers and only thirty Gloop civilians. Under these

---

[30] Of course it might be the case that each soldier, though significantly excused, is still liable to be killed because fully culpable killers are liable to harms far in excess of death such that the excuse only

conditions the neutral peacekeeping force cannot intervene to save the civilians. Such intervention is impermissible because it imposes on each solider non-liable harm roughly equivalent to something half as serious as death. Since there are one hundred soldiers this is equivalent to killing fifty non-liable persons. And it is clearly impermissible to kill fifty non-liable persons in order to save thirty. Accepting the critic's position thus has very counterintuitive implications in cases where a number of partially excused attackers pose a wrongful threat.[31]

4.6.4 The Aggregation of Small Harms

Consider the following case:

> *Deadly Drops*: Albert, along with two dozen others, decides to play a vicious prank on Betty. He puts a tiny drop of a hallucinogen in her morning coffee. Consuming one drop has a limited effect: it would cause Betty to suffer a momentary panic-inducing hallucination, but no further harm. But the cumulative effect of having more than two dozen drops in her morning coffee is very serious: it will kill Betty. Carl knows what is about to happen but cannot warn Betty—the only way for him to save Betty's life is to kill Albert and each of the others who are going to put a drop in Betty's coffee.

Intuitively, Carl is permitted to kill Albert and the two dozen others to avert their deadly threat to Betty. But each individual apparently only threatens a relatively minor rights violation: it's wrong to subject someone to a momentary panic-inducing hallucination, but it's hardly the sort of rights violation that renders a person liable to lethal defensive force. The stringency principle, a critic may argue, thus cannot deliver the correct result in cases of this type.

This claim is mistaken. If Albert and the two dozen others conspired to act together, and have sufficient evidence to understand the gravity of the threat that they pose, then each person is guilty of attempting to murder Betty, and thus each is potentially liable to lethal defensive force. On the other hand, suppose that each person acts alone, and has no evidence that anyone else is planning to put any

brings the degree of liability down to the point of death. Even if true, this doesn't affect the main point being made—there will be a version of the example where a large group of excused aggressors cannot be harmed to save a smaller number of innocent persons, even though it would be permissible to harm the aggressors if they were fully culpable.

[31] Bazargan argues that these cases can be handled in an intuitively satisfying way by proponents of the responsibility principle if they endorse a 'lesser evil discounting view'. See Bazargan, 'Killing Minimally Responsible Threats', 125–32. On this view, we discount even the non-liable harms that the excused attackers might suffer for reasons of comparative fairness. This view, however, seems to me to involve an objectionable form of double counting.

drops in Betty's coffee. Under these conditions, each person is not guilty of attempting to murder Betty; rather each person threatens to violate a less stringent right. Under these conditions, none of the individuals are liable to be killed by Carl. This seems like the correct result. Although the harm that Betty will suffer is the same in each version of the story, the evidence available to the attackers plays a role in determining the type of right that they threaten to violate.[32] Chapter 6 offers a defence of this view of the relationship between evidence and moral rights.

In sum, not only can the stringency principle accommodate intuitions about a range of cases involving the aggregation of small harms, it is better equipped to do so than the responsibility principle. The main reason is simple. Albert's degree of moral responsibility for posing a wrongful threat is—according to McMahan and others—partly a matter of the degree of Albert's causal contribution to the threat. If a number of people contribute to a threat, their causal contributions must be divided, and cannot equal more than 100 per cent. Proponents of the responsibility principle will thus always struggle to explain how it can be permissible to impose defensive force on a large number of attackers, each of whom makes only a small causal contribution to a serious threat.[33] By contrast, a person's degree of causal contribution is often irrelevant to the question of what type of right the person threatens to violate. An indefinitely large number of people can all work together to violate a person's right not to be killed, and in doing so each person threatens to violate the victim's right not to be killed. Cases involving the aggregation of small harms thus provide no objection to the stringency principle; they are in fact a further reason to endorse the principle.

4.7 Conclusion

At the outset I suggested that a successful account of proportionality should, ideally, meet all of the following conditions:

1. Explain our intuitive judgements about proportionality in paradigm cases.
2. Be sensitive to the way multiple considerations bear on proportionality judgements, and not misrepresent or distort the way these different considerations matter for proportionality.

---

[32] The cases here are, of course, greatly simplified. In many cases where a group of persons pose a threat of harm via the combination of their individual acts, there are further facts to be taken into account (e.g., whether the individual acts form part of an activity that is generally beneficial, or whether the agents face a collective action problem). I'm not claiming to address all of these complexities that are sometimes present in cases of collective harm—I'm only insisting that one of the relevant dimensions is the evidence that agents possess regarding the consequences of their acts.

[33] For an ingenious an attempt to resolve this problem on behalf of the moral responsibility account, see Kerah Gordon-Solmon, 'Self-Defence Against Multiple Threats', *Journal of Moral Philosophy* 14, no. 2 (2017): 125–33.

3. Offer a coherent framework that unifies these different considerations, explaining why *these* considerations, rather than others, belong together in an account of proportionality.

4. Explain the relationship between (a) the necessary and sufficient conditions for any degree of liability, and (b) the considerations that determine the degree of liability.

The stringency principle succeeds in meeting these conditions. The key to understanding liability and proportionality is the idea that one person has contravened a duty of justice he owes to others. Liability and proportionality judgements should be grounded in an account of this relationship between the wrongdoer and his victim. The more serious the breach of the duty is, the greater the degree of the rights forfeiture. The stringency principle provides the right explanation of this relationship. Other views, like the responsibility principle, do not. An attacker's degree of responsibility for his wrongful action is irrelevant to the question of how weighty or important the claim of justice is that the wrongdoer threatens. In a slogan, it doesn't matter how wholeheartedly an attacker threatens to violate someone's rights, what matters is the type of right he threatens to violate.

5

Necessity

Albert is attempting to wrongfully assault you. His assault will leave you partially
paralysed for life. You have two ways of averting his attack, both of which are
certain to succeed: you can shoot Albert in the chest, which you know will leave
him partially paralysed for life, or you can jump on your bike and ride to the safety
of the police station just around the corner.

It is wrong for you to shoot Albert. Why? Shooting him does not seem
disproportionate; after all, shooting him will impose the same degree of harm he
threatens to wrongfully impose on you. Instead, it is wrong to shoot Albert under
these circumstances because it is not *necessary*. You have an alternative means of
successfully averting his threat that will impose no harm. Shooting Albert thus
violates one of the most widely accepted conditions on the permissible use of
defensive force: the necessity condition.

Philosophers who work on the ethics of defensive force are nearly unanimous
in claiming that the imposition of defensive harm is permissible only if it meets
the necessity condition. This consensus mirrors views held by the general public.
For example, one of the most persistent recent criticisms of law enforcement in
many American cities appeals to the necessity condition. In a series of high-
profile cases, police officers have used lethal force against black citizens when
video evidence and eyewitness testimony strongly indicate that lethal force was
not necessary. Although the wrongness of the deaths in these cases may well be
overdetermined, the fact that the harm was unnecessary seems sufficient to
establish that the killings were wrong.

Despite the consensus, the necessity condition is still not very well understood.
Recent formulations present the necessity condition as a type of consequentialist
constraint on the permissible use of defensive force, a principle that weighs all the
harms that would be imposed by a defensive act against the benefits of averting the
attacker's threat, and then compares this moral weighting with other options
available to the defensive agent to determine whether a given use of defensive
force is indeed necessary. I think there are problems with this view. The most
important problem is that it cannot be reconciled with the idea that unnecessary
defensive force is something against which the target of the defensive force—
typically the attacker—has a distinctive complaint. Unnecessary defensive force,
I think, is presumptively wrongful because it wrongs the attacker in a particular
way, and so we need an account of the necessity condition that can make sense of
this fact.

The Morality of Defensive Force. Jonathan Quong, Oxford University Press (2020). © Jonathan Quong.
DOI: 10.1093/oso/9780198851103.001.0001

I propose that the necessity condition is an instance of a more general moral right that each of us possesses: the right to be rescued.[1] Even wrongful attackers have the right to be rescued from serious harm when others can do so at reasonable cost, and this right explains why there is a necessity condition on the permissible use of defensive force.

This conclusion has important practical implications. One implication concerns cases where the defensive agent correctly believes that if she exercises her liberties in a particular way—for example, a young African-American walking through a predominantly white neighbourhood, or a wife returning home to an angry and abuse-prone spouse—another agent will threaten unjust harm, and the defensive agent correctly believes that she will then need to impose defensive harm to avert the wrongful attack. The main existing formulations of the necessity condition can't reach intuitively plausible verdicts in cases of this kind, but an account grounded in the right to be rescued gets the correct results in these cases.

The chapter is organized as follows. In sections 5.1–5.3 I consider three formulations of the necessity condition, and explain why they are inadequate. Section 5.4 introduces the rescue-based conception of the necessity condition. In section 5.5, I show how the earlier formulations of the necessity condition struggle to explain cases where an attacker will only threaten wrongful harm if a defensive agent performs a permissible act. Section 5.6 shows that the rescue-based version of the necessity condition offers a better explanation of these cases. Section 5.7 responds to objections. In section 5.8 I consider the relationship between liability and the necessity condition. Section 5.9 identifies two further advantages of the rescue-based view, and section 5.10 concludes.

5.1 The Simple Account

Let's start with a simple account of the necessity condition. On this view, some amount of defensive harm is unnecessary whenever there is an equally successful alternative means of averting the attacker's threat that will impose less harm on the attacker. Put more precisely,

SIMPLE: The imposition of defensive harm H on attacker A is necessary to avert unjust threat T iff imposing H stands some positive chance of averting T, and there is no lesser degree of harm that could be imposed on A with the same (or higher) probability of successfully averting T.

---

[1] I first proposed a variant of this idea in co-authored work with Joanna Mary Firth. See Firth and Quong, 'Necessity, Moral Liability, and Defensive Harm', Law and Philosophy 31, no. 6 (2012): 693–6. In that paper Firth and I referred to the right as a humanitarian right to reasonable aid and protection. The argument in that paper departs from the argument in this chapter in several ways, and Firth bears no responsibility for the ways I have developed this idea here.

If the imposition of unnecessary defensive harm is presumptively wrongful, then SIMPLE is vulnerable to an obvious objection: it is insensitive to the costs that the defender or third parties bear under the different options. Suppose, for example, that Albert is threatening to wrongfully assault you, and you have two ways of successfully averting his attack: you can shoot him, or you can jump out the window and fall to the ground, which will result in your suffering serious injuries. Since the latter has the same chance of averting his unjust threat and imposes no harm on Albert, SIMPLE declares shooting Albert to be 'unnecessary'. But this cannot be right. You don't violate any plausible moral constraint in shooting Albert, provided shooting him is narrowly proportionate. Albert cannot complain that your shooting him is unnecessary because you ought to have jumped out the window and suffered serious injuries to avoid his unjust threat.

SIMPLE similarly fails to be sensitive to the costs to third parties. Suppose you have two ways to avert Albert's attack: shoot him, or jump out the window and fall to the ground below where your fall will be cushioned by an innocent third party who will suffer serious injuries. Again, the correct account of necessity should not deem that shooting Albert is unnecessary because you can instead seriously injure a bystander. The correct account of necessity must assess the different options not merely in terms of their probabilities of success and the harm imposed on the wrongful attacker—it must also weigh the costs suffered by the defensive agent and by third parties. This objection seems sufficient to reject SIMPLE.

5.2 The Weighted Account

How can SIMPLE be improved to avoid the objection? Here is one proposal:

WEIGHTED: The imposition of defensive harm H on attacker A is necessary to avert unjust threat T iff imposing H stands some positive chance of averting T, and there is no other defensive option with the same (or higher) probability of successfully averting T that imposes less morally weighted harm overall.

Instead of focusing solely on how much harm the different defensive options will impose on the attacker, WEIGHTED requires that we consider how much harm will be imposed on all those affected. Moreover, a moral weighting is used to reflect the fact that the wrongful attacker is to some extent liable to defensive harm, and thus harms imposed on him count for less than harms imposed on non-liable persons. To illustrate, suppose you have two ways to avert Albert's attack: shoot him, which will partially paralyse him for life, or jump out the window and land on a bystander below, which will partially paralyse the bystander for one year. Depending on the extent to which Albert's claims are discounted, it might be the case that shooting Albert imposes less morally weighted harm overall, and thus shooting Albert will satisfy the necessity condition, even though it causes more total harm.

Although WEIGHTED is in this way superior to SIMPLE, it's also vulnerable to a serious objection, first developed by Seth Lazar.[2] Consider:

Risky Shooting: You have two ways to try to avert Albert's wrongful attack: (i) you can shoot and kill Albert, which has a 100 percent chance of successfully averting his attack, or (ii) you can jump out the window (where you won't suffer any harm), which has a 99.8 percent chance of successfully averting his attack.

WEIGHTED declares that since the latter option has a lower chance of success, its existence doesn't render shooting Albert unnecessary. But this looks false. The chance of success in jumping out the window is very high and only slightly lower than shooting Albert, yet the difference in morally weighted harm between the two options is very great. The permissibility of using defensive force should require trade-offs between the chance of success and the amount of morally weighted harm imposed. If you have an alternative means of averting Albert's threat that is virtually certain to succeed and causes no harm to anyone, we should conclude that shooting Albert is not permissible because it's not necessary. Call this the *trade-off objection* to WEIGHTED.

5.3 The Trade-Off Account

In light of the trade-off objection, Seth Lazar and Jeff McMahan have each proposed something a bit like:[3]

TRADE-OFF: The imposition of defensive harm H on attacker A is necessary to avert unjust threat T iff H offers the lowest expected morally weighted harm when compared with all the feasible alternatives.

This view abandons the idea that we should focus only on the option, or options, with the highest probability of success. Instead, TRADE-OFF declares that all options should be compared in terms of expected morally weighted harm, that is, where the harm is not only morally weighted, but also weighted by its probability of eventuating. This means that it may sometimes be necessary for a defensive agent to choose an option with a lower chance of successfully averting

---

[2] Seth Lazar, 'Necessity in Self-Defense and War', *Philosophy & Public Affairs* 40, no. 1 (2012): 7–9. The objection is also developed in Jeff McMahan, 'The Limits of Self-Defense', in *The Ethics of Self-Defense*, ed. Christian Coons and Michael Weber (New York: Oxford University Press, 2016), 187–8.
[3] Lazar, 'Necessity in Self-Defense and War', 11; McMahan, 'The Limits of Self-Defense', 187–8.

the threat. As a consequence of this revision, TRADE-OFF also abandons the requirement that necessary options should have some positive probability of successfully averting the wrongful threat. To insist that necessary options must have some positive chance of success, no matter how small, and no matter how great the increase in morally weighted harm, seems arbitrary if we accept the main rationale for TRADE-OFF. As a result, TRADE-OFF will sometimes direct a defensive agent to *submit* to a wrongful attack—this will sometimes be the option with the lowest expected morally weighted harm.[4]

TRADE-OFF obviously avoids the central problem with WEIGHTED. For example, it yields the intuitively correct judgement in cases like Risky Shooting that proved awkward for WEIGHTED. But TRADE-OFF has a major drawback.[5] Consider the following case:

> *Too Many Bystanders*: Albert is threatening to wrongfully assault you. You have two options: (i) submit, and allow him to wrongfully assault you, or (ii) roll a large boulder towards Albert that will cause him injuries (similar to those he would cause you) and prevent him from harming you, but the boulder will also kill seven innocent bystanders nearby.

On any plausible account of moral weighting, rolling the boulder fails to minimize the morally weighted harm when compared to the alternative of submission. TRADE-OFF thus entails that rolling the boulder towards Albert imposes unnecessary defensive harm.

But this doesn't accurately describe the reason you have to refrain from rolling the boulder. The reason you should not roll the boulder is not that doing so is *unnecessary*. Rather, it is that doing so will impose *disproportionate harm on bystanders*: saving yourself from the assault is not so important that it can justify killing seven innocent people. But TRADE-OFF implausibly declares that rolling the bolder is unnecessary and not merely disproportionate.

This problem is particularly acute for those who endorse the view that necessity is internal to liability, that is, the view that an attacker cannot be liable at all to some defensive harm, H, if H is unnecessary. When this position is combined with TRADE-OFF, it yields the conclusion that Albert is not liable to the defensive harm

---

[4] The overall effect of these revisions, as Lazar notes, is that impositions of defensive harm cannot be necessary unless they are widely proportionate. If an act of self-defence is widely disproportionate, this means the morally weighted benefits of acting are not sufficient in light of the costs, and so you should refrain from acting. These disproportionate acts will also be condemned by TRADE-OFF, since disproportionate acts do not impose the lowest expected morally weighted harm: one can always choose to refrain from performing the harmful act instead. Lazar points out there may be unusual cases where the defender lacks the option of doing nothing—where no matter what choice the defender makes she will cause widely disproportionate harm. In these cases, Lazar argues that a particular choice may be necessary and justified as a lesser evil (rather than justified as self-defence), though it will be widely disproportionate. See Lazar 'Necessity in Self-Defense and War', 19–20.

[5] Nicola Kemp has independently developed this objection in unpublished material.

you would impose by rolling the boulder in Too Many Bystanders. But this seems implausible. If the only harm caused were the harm to Albert, rolling the boulder wouldn't violate the necessity condition. It cannot be the case that a wrongful aggressor like Albert gains a right against the imposition of defensive force that he would otherwise lack by virtue of the harms that third parties will suffer. Any claims Albert has must be grounded in something to do with Albert—some way in which the act of defensive force harms him or mistreats him.

One of the necessity condition's main functions—I believe—is to identify cases where the wrongful attacker has the standing to complain that the defensive agent used more force than was necessary. But in Too Many Bystanders it's only the bystanders, not Albert, who can complain if you roll the boulder. Any adequate formulation of the necessity condition should ground the presumptive wrongness of imposing unnecessary harms in something done to the attacker. TRADE-OFF abandons this idea: it abandons the idea that necessity represents a distinct constraint—distinct from wide proportionality—on the permissible use of defensive force.

But my concern is not simply that TRADE-OFF shares a rationale with the wide proportionality constraint. Instead, my concern is that we lose something important if we accept TRADE-OFF. What we lose is the notion that there are at least two distinct ways in which an attacker might be wronged by the imposition of defensive force. One way is that the force used on the attacker is disproportionate relative to the injustice that the attacker threatens to commit. But a different way the force might wrong the attacker is that the defensive agent could have avoided imposing it at reasonable cost. It's valuable to distinguish these as different ways that defensive force might wrong an attacker. In one case, the basis of the claim centres on the gravity of the wrong that the aggressor threatens to commit. In the other case, the basis of the aggressor's claim is grounded in how costly it would be to the defensive agent (and to third parties) to avoid imposing the harm. Because the claims have different bases, they also have different conditions under which the relevant duties are triggered, and different conditions under which the claims are forfeited or lost.

In sum, I think we have good reasons to look for a different account of the necessity condition, one that captures the distinct complaint an aggressor has when defensive force is imposed on him under conditions when this could have been easily avoided.

5.4 The Rescue Account

The formulations of the necessity condition considered so far focus exclusively on the consequences, or expected consequences, the act will produce when compared to the consequences, or expected consequences, of other possible courses of action. I think this approach is mistaken, or is at least seriously incomplete. The necessity condition is instead better conceptualized as a kind of interpersonal moral demand or claim right that attackers possess against defenders. Once we understand the condition in this way, it becomes clear that considerations apart from the consequences of the act bear on the question of whether the act satisfies the necessity condition.

Let's focus on a particular moral right that I believe we each possess: the right to be rescued from serious harm when others can do so at reasonable cost. Instances of this right and the correlated duty are familiar. If you can rescue Albert from drowning at the cost of ruining your nice new shoes, Albert has a right to be rescued by you, and you are duty bound to rescue him. You are not, however, duty bound to rescue him if the cost to you is too great—for example, if you would lose your arms in the course of the rescue.

I don't think we forfeit this right even when we are guilty of serious wrong-doing. I've argued for this conclusion in other work, and I won't rehearse the whole argument here.[6] In brief, two related facts explain why the right to be rescued cannot be forfeited.[7] First, the right is cost sensitive: it imposes only limited costs on duty bearers. Second, the net benefits of the right are large: the right-holder is rescued from serious harm, whereas the duty bearer suffers modest costs at most. Because the right is limited in these ways, it's a right that you cannot forfeit as a result of wrongdoing. If you could forfeit the capacity to make even such very limited moral demands on others, then you could almost entirely lose your moral standing, at least the moral standing to make claims of others. Suppose, for example, a fire breaks out in a prison and will kill some of the prisoners, each of whom has been correctly convicted of first-degree murder. If rescuing the prisoners does not pose unreasonable risks, we are duty bound to rescue them. We cannot leave them to die in the fire because they have committed violent crimes. Even the worst wrongdoers retain some moral standing and thus retain some claims against the rest of us. The right to be rescued is, I think, one of those claims.[8]

---

[6] The material in this paragraph summarizes an argument made at greater length in Jonathan Quong, 'Miller's Crossing', in *Political Philosophy, Here and Now: Essays in Honour of David Miller*, ed. Daniel Butt, Sarah Fine, and Zofia Stemplowska (Oxford: Oxford University Press, forthcoming).

[7] This is compatible with the possibility of waiving the right. Rights are waived when the right-holder deliberately chooses to release the duty bearer from the duty. Forfeiture is not deliberate in this way—the right is lost as a result of some act of the right-holder, but the right-holder doesn't perform the act with the aim of losing the right. The inability to forfeit the right to be rescued also does not entail that others are duty bound to rescue you even when doing so would involve serious harm befalling third parties—in these cases there is no individual claim to be rescued since the rescue comes at too great a cost to at least one other person. I say more about this issue in 'Miller's Crossing'.

[8] This is, of course, compatible with the thought that victims may often be excused for failing to fulfil the duties they owe to wrongful attackers.

With this assumption in hand, I suggest that the necessity constraint on the permissible use of defensive force is an instance of a more general duty: the duty to rescue those in need when doing so can be done at reasonable cost:[9]

> RESCUE: The imposition of defensive harm H on attacker A is necessary to avert unjust threat T iff the imposition of H is consistent with the duty of rescue that each person, including the defensive agent, owes to A.[10]

If Albert wrongfully threatens Betty with lethal force, and she can either avert his threat by killing him or by suffering some relatively modest cost (e.g., a sprained wrist), she owes Albert a duty of rescue to bear the modest cost. This is why killing Albert is, in the relevantly moralized sense, unnecessary and wrong. But when the costs of refraining from killing Albert exceed what Albert can demand in terms of his right to be rescued (e.g., Betty would be rendered a paraplegic), then killing Albert does not violate the necessity constraint on the permissible use of defensive force.

I think RESCUE has a number of advantages over existing formulations of the necessity condition. RESCUE can reach the intuitively plausible verdict in all the cases considered thus far. In particular, RESCUE can explain why rolling the boulder towards Albert in Too Many Bystanders is not a violation of the necessity condition. If you refrain from rolling the boulder, Albert will seriously harm you, and we do not have duties to bear serious harms in order to prevent someone else from suffering equally serious harms. Albert thus has no standing to complain if you roll the boulder (of course it remains wrong to roll the boulder because it is widely disproportionate).

RESCUE's most important advantage is that it identifies a range of cases where the attacker has the standing to complain about the imposition of defensive force, but the nature of the attacker's complaint is distinct from a complaint regarding the force being either narrowly or widely disproportionate. On this view, the imposition of unnecessary force is wrong because it violates a duty of rescue that the defensive agent (or others) owes to the attacker.

Before moving on, it's worth distinguishing between two different conceptions of the right to be rescued. On the first conception, we each possess a right to be rescued from any degree of harm, no matter how trivial, provided that others can

---

[9] Alternatively, some might prefer to say that the right to be rescued and the necessity constraint on defensive force are each manifestations of a more fundamental human right: the right to be spared from harm. Those who prefer this view can still, with only minor modifications, endorse all the main substantive claims I make about the necessity condition.

[10] On my view, defensive agents and bystanders are, other things being equal, symmetrically situated in terms of the duty to bear costs for the sake of the attacker. Thus, if the defensive agent would be duty bound to bear some cost, C, to avoiding harming the attacker, a bystander will also be under a duty to bear C for the sake of the attacker. It will thus sometimes be necessary for defensive agents to impose modest harms on bystanders to avoid imposing much graver harms on attackers.

do so at reasonable cost. If the harm is low, then the costs to the alleged duty bearer would have to be extremely low to trigger the duty, but in principle we may have rights to be rescued from mild bruises, or pinches, whenever others can do so at trivial cost or no cost. What matters is the ratio of the harm that can be averted relative to cost to the alleged duty bearer. We can call this view *No Threshold*. On the second conception, we do not have rights to be rescued from trivial or modest harms; we only have rights to be rescued from significant or serious harms when others can do so at reasonable cost. We can call this view *Threshold*.

These conceptions clearly have different implications. Most obviously, they differ as to whether we can ever have a right to be rescued from trivial harms. They also have different implications regarding which defensive options meet the necessity condition. Consider the following case:

Small Harm: Albert is wrongfully threatening Betty. She can avert his attack in one of two ways: (i) impose 100 units of harm on Albert and suffer no harm herself, or (ii) impose 99 units of harm on Albert and suffer a trivial degree of harm herself.

Let's assume that 1 unit of harm is below the bar set by Threshold. Thus, Threshold entails that Betty has no duty to rescue Albert from 1 unit of harm and thus she does not impose unnecessary harm if she chooses (i). If we accept No Threshold, however, then it may be true that Betty has a duty to rescue Albert from 1 unit of harm when she can do so at some trivial cost. This entails that Betty imposes unnecessary defensive harm if she chooses (i).

I believe Threshold is the better conception of the right to be rescued, but I won't try and defend that view here, and the arguments in the rest of the chapter don't depend on endorsing one of the more specific conceptions of the right to be rescued.

5.5 A Further Problem for Other Views

I now want to draw attention to another advantage of RESCUE in comparison to the alternatives. Consider the following case:

Dangerous Party: There is a party tonight, and Betty is deciding whether to go. A completely reliable person has warned her that Albert will be at the party, and he will assault Betty if she turns up.[11] Betty justifiably believes that if she goes to

---

[11] Note: Albert has not threatened Betty, nor performed any acts that would constitute an attempt to violate Betty's rights. We can suppose the reliable person has come by the information by reading Albert's diary or overhearing Albert talking to himself. We can further stipulate that Albert does not

the party, Albert will threaten to assault her, and she will then need to use (and be able to use) serious defensive force to avert his wrongful assault (such force is narrowly proportionate given the seriousness of Albert's threatened assault). Going to the party is not very important to Betty—she could also stay home and finish the novel she's reading.[12]

I believe that Betty doesn't violate the necessity condition if she goes to the party and then use defensive force against Albert when he attempts to assault her. This seems *clearly* true to me. But the earlier formulations of the necessity condition, such as WEIGHTED and TRADE-OFF, can't reach this conclusion. I'll first explain why these views can't reach this conclusion before turning to explain why RESCUE can.

Here is the argument for the conclusion that Betty's use of lethal defensive force in Dangerous Party is unnecessary, at least according to WEIGHTED and TRADE-OFF.[13] First, consider a different case:

> *Two Options*: Albert has initiated a wrongful attack on Betty. Betty has only two options, both of which will avert a wrongful assault by Albert: (i) leave a party and go home, or (ii) use serious defensive force against Albert.

All versions of the necessity condition will deem the use of defensive force unnecessary in Two Options. The next step in the argument is to deny that there are any relevant differences between Two Options and Dangerous Party. The argument thus has only two premises:

believe that Betty will be attending the party, to avoid any implication that Albert attends the party in order to assault Betty.

[12] Although they are similar in important respects, it's crucial to distinguish cases such as Dangerous Party from cases where an attacker makes a conditional threat, e.g., 'your money or your life'. In these cases, the issuing of the conditional threat is itself a moral wrong: the attempt to coerce the defensive agent by threatening wrongful force renders the attacker liable to a certain degree of defensive force even though the attacker has not yet attempted to assault or harm the defender. In Dangerous Party, Albert makes no such conditional threat; Betty is simply aware of what Albert is likely to do if she attempts to go to the party. Because Albert makes no conditional threat and has, I stipulate, not yet done anything that constitutes a threatened rights violation, he's not yet liable to any defensive harm at the point where Betty is deciding whether she should go to the party. I will return to the distinction between Dangerous Party and conditional threat cases in the concluding section.

[13] Jeff McMahan and Victor Tadros both seem to endorse arguments not too dissimilar to the one I sketch. See McMahan, 'What Rights May Be Defended by Means of War?' 148; Tadros, 'Resource Wars', *Law and Philosophy* 33, no. 3 (2014): 380–3. McMahan actually suggests that it would be wrong for Betty to act in escalation cases of this type because it would be disproportionate, rather than unnecessary. But given that McMahan endorses TRADE-OFF, he is committed to the conclusion about necessity as well. Cécile Fabre, on the other hand, shares my view that it is permissible for Betty to act in cases of this type, though she does not consider the necessity-based objection that is our focus here. See Fabre, *Cosmopolitan War*, 123.

P1   The use of defensive force is unnecessary in Two Options.

P2   There are no relevant differences between Two Options and Dangerous Party.

Therefore

C1   It is unnecessary for Betty to impose defensive force in Dangerous Party.

P1 is beyond dispute, and so if there is a problem with the argument, it must lie with P2. It might seem that there are several relevant differences between Two Options and Dangerous Party. One relevant difference might be uncertainty: in Dangerous Party, Betty has been reliably informed that Albert will assault her if she goes to the party, but she cannot be certain this will occur. So long as she is uncertain, then there is a third option available in Dangerous Party that isn't available in Two Options: (iii) go to the party, and have fun without being assaulted by Albert. Of course this outcome might not eventuate, but given her evidence, Betty can have some low credence that it will.

But does the possibility of this option really make a difference? Suppose Betty's evidence gives her reason to believe there is roughly a 10 per cent chance that Albert will not assault her if she goes to the party. Is the net benefit Betty gains by going to the party and having fun (rather than staying home and finishing the novel) sufficient to morally outweigh the serious harm imposed on Albert, particularly given that there is only a 10 per cent chance that Betty will be able to go to the party and have fun without harming Albert? The answer is clearly no. The benefits of going to a party are insufficient to risk a 90 per cent chance of seriously harming someone, even when we discount the weight of Albert's interests.[14] Betty's degree of certainty regarding the probability of Albert's assault is not going to help distinguish the two cases.

Perhaps instead the relevant difference is that in Dangerous Party, unlike Two Options, Betty faces two decisions at two different points in time. At t1, Betty must decide whether to go to the party or stay home. At t2, she must decide whether to harm Albert or allow Albert to seriously assault her. Suppose the decisions are treated as independent, with the necessity condition being applied separately to each one. Betty's decision at t1 to go to the party does not violate the necessity condition, provided the potential harm to Albert is bracketed and only considered at t2. And once Betty is at the party, her decision at t2 to impose force on Albert also meets the necessity condition, since at t2 her only alternative to the imposition of force is suffering serious harm herself, harm which, by hypothesis, is sufficient to render harming Albert proportionate.

---

[14] If you are inclined to think that Albert's interests can be so heavily discounted that the small chance of enjoying the party does morally outweigh the serious harm to Albert, you will embrace an extraordinarily permissive conception of the necessity condition, one that will entail that defensive agents need not make even very trivial sacrifices in order to avoid seriously harming wrongful attackers.

But there's a serious problem with this line of reasoning. Suppose that at t1 it is *certain* that Albert will assault Betty if she goes to the party. Given this assumption, it is disingenuous to treat Betty's decisions independently. At t1 Betty is making a decision about whether to stay home and read a novel, or bring about a situation where either she seriously harms Albert or Albert seriously assaults her. By bearing a trivial cost at t1, Betty can ensure that neither she nor Albert needs suffer any harm. When you face two choices, one of which involves no harm to anyone, and the other one of which involves serious harms befalling one or more persons, versions of the necessity condition such as WEIGHTED and TRADE-OFF require that you choose the option involving no harm, *unless* you can choose the harmful option and ensure that you alone bear the subsequent harms. WEIGHTED and TRADE-OFF don't allow Betty to ignore the harmful consequences of making any choice, even when the consequences are some way into the future. Considering an analogous case may be helpful:

Knockout Gas: Albert is wrongfully attacking you and you have two options: (a) escape at only trivial cost to yourself, or (b) use your knockout gas that will render you and Albert each unconscious for an hour, after which time you will each wake up and then you face two choices: allow yourself to be seriously harmed by Albert, or seriously harm Albert in self-defence.

WEIGHTED and TRADE-OFF do not allow you to use the knockout gas and subsequently harm Albert in self-defence. This is unnecessary since you can escape at only trivial cost to yourself. The same thing is true of Betty in Dangerous Party.

Consider one final attempt to resist the conclusion of the argument above. Suppose Betty decides to go to the party and Albert attacks. She now faces the choice of whether to use defensive force or allow Albert to assault her. Unlike in Two Options, Betty also bears some responsibility for creating this state of affairs. But who bears greater responsibility? Surely Albert. Even if we think Betty acted wrongly in choosing to attend the party, her mistake is not as serious as Albert's mistake of choosing to assault her. As we know, McMahan defends a view of liability on which the person who bears greater moral responsibility for creating a forced choice situation can be liable to bear the entirety of the harm when the harm cannot be divided in proportion to each person's degree of responsibility.[15] If we accept this conception of liability, and we also assume that Albert bears a greater degree of moral responsibility than Betty for the forced choice situation she confronts at the party, then Albert is liable to defensive force. And if Albert is liable to the defensive force, then it cannot be unnecessary for Betty to impose this force.

---

[15] See McMahan, 'The Basis of Moral Liability', 394–8.

There are at least two problems with this explanation of Dangerous Party. The first is internal to McMahan's view.[16] McMahan endorses the view that attackers can never be liable to unnecessary harm.[17] Thus, whether Albert is liable to defensive force in Dangerous Party depends on whether this harm is necessary. Whether the harm is necessary depends on whether it was necessary for Betty to attend the party and impose defensive force on Albert. But as the earlier argument makes clear, it seems unnecessary for Betty to do this—she could have stayed home with her book instead. Since going to the party and harming Albert is unnecessary (at least according to WEIGHTED and TRADE-OFF), this is harm to which Albert cannot be liable, but this contradicts the responsibility-based explanation of liability in the preceding paragraph. McMahan thus faces a stark choice: either he must abandon the view that attackers can never be liable to unnecessary defensive harm, or else he must accept that Albert is not liable to defensive harm in Dangerous Party.[18]

But setting McMahan's particular view aside, there is a more general problem with the proffered explanation. The question that is our focus is whether Betty violates the necessity condition by going to the party and using defensive force on Albert. Pointing out that Albert bears a greater degree of moral responsibility for the forced choice Betty faces once she is at the party seems irrelevant to answering this question. After all, in almost all cases where a defensive agent has been wrongfully attacked and has a choice regarding how to respond, the wrongful attacker bears greater responsibility for the forced choice that the defender faces. But the attacker's greater degree of responsibility doesn't entail that the necessity condition no longer applies. The necessity condition is surely supposed to constrain a defender's behaviour in cases where the wrongful attacker bears greater responsibility for the choice faced by the defender. If an attacker's greater moral responsibility for the situation could render apparently unnecessary forms of defensive harm necessary, this would amount to an abandonment of the necessity condition.

5.6 Rescue to the Rescue

RESCUE, however, offers a superior approach to cases like Dangerous Party. Does Betty owe a duty of rescue to Albert to refrain from attending the party, knowing his conditional intention to assault her? I believe not. Albert cannot—without denying his own agency—make the following moral demand of Betty at t1: 'I will

---

[16] Frowe also makes this objection. See Frowe, *Defensive Killing*, 116.

[17] See for example, McMahan, 'The Limits of Self-Defense', 195–206.

[18] McMahan considers a version of this objection as applied to a somewhat different case. The solution he offers, however, does not resolve the kind of case currently being considered. See McMahan, 'The Limits of Self-Defense', 201–2.

wrongfully attack you at the party—that's something that's going to happen—and so you now owe me a duty of rescue to avoid creating a situation where you will have to use defensive force against me.' Since he can't plausibly make this kind of moral demand, Betty can permissibly go to the party without transgressing any duty of rescue she owes to Albert.

Albert denies his own agency, in the sense I have in mind, when he treats his own future decisions as events over which he has no control or no responsibility. Borrowing an idea that G. A. Cohen uses in a different context, we can make this proposal a bit more precise.[19] If a moral demand depends on an empirical premise, and the person issuing the demand (or on whose behalf it could be issued) is also the person whose future decision will make the empirical premise true, then if that person cannot provide a satisfactory justification of why she will choose to behave in a manner that makes the empirical premise true, this undermines the moral demand that the premise supports. Following Cohen, we can call this the *interpersonal test*. I suggest that interpersonal moral demands, like claim rights, are not sound unless they can pass this test.[20]

We can illustrate this idea using one of Cohen's examples. Suppose a kidnapper tells the parents of the child he has kidnapped, 'If you don't pay me the ransom, I will kill your child. Therefore, it would be wrong for you to refuse my ransom demand.' If the kidnapper is telling the truth, then of course it can be true that the parents ought to pay the ransom. But the kidnapper cannot use this argument to demand the ransom—he cannot claim he is rightfully owed the ransom money. The empirical premise that makes it true that the parents should pay the ransom—that the kidnapper will kill their child if they refuse—is something the kidnapper makes true, but his decision to make this premise true is obviously something he cannot justify. This undermines any claim the kidnapper can make that he is owed the money, or that he would be wronged if he isn't paid. His demand fails the interpersonal test.[21]

The earlier formulations of the necessity condition fail to focus on a question that is central to a rights-based view such as RESCUE, namely, whether the

---

[19] See G. A. Cohen, *Rescuing Justice and Equality* (Cambridge: Harvard University Press, 2008), 39–44.

[20] Although the interpersonal test can be presented as part of a more general contractualist moral theory, it needn't be understood in this way. Even non-contractualists (like Cohen) can endorse the interpersonal test. Endorsement of the test reflects a weaker and far more widely accepted idea: that rights or moral claims are moral demands that are, in some sense, addressed to others. Thinking about what we can coherently demand of others is thus, at a minimum, a useful heuristic for determining what claims we possess.

[21] There's an elegant discussion of some cases that have this structure in Johann Frick, 'What We Owe to Hypocrites: Contractualism and the Speaker-Relativity of Justification', *Philosophy & Public Affairs* 44, no. 4 (2016): 223–65. Frick concludes that some of these cases—for example, where someone threatens to kill himself unless you hand over $20—show that contractualism can only represent one part of more complete normative theory. This is true, he argues, since the person who threatens to kill himself cannot be wronged in the contractualist sense by your refusal to hand over the money, and yet it remains true, Frick believes, that you are morally required to hand over the money.

wrongful attacker *has the standing to complain* about some act, φ, performed by the defensive agent. Whether the attacker has the standing to complain depends not only on how much morally weighted harm φ-ing will cause when compared to the other feasible alternatives, but also on whether the attacker can reasonably demand that the defensive agent refrain from φ-ing. And whether the attacker can make this demand depends on the extent to which the consequences of the defensive agent's φ-ing are still matters for which the attacker can be held responsible. Conceptualizing necessity this way gives us a clearer picture of how it works, and yields the intuitively plausible result in cases like Dangerous Party. Here is an argument summarizing how RESCUE delivers the correct result in Dangerous Party:

P3   The necessity condition is a manifestation of the right to be rescued.

P4   A only possesses a claim right against B when he can reasonably demand that B fulfil the duty that correlates with the right in question.

P5   A cannot reasonably make a moral demand of B when the demand fails the interpersonal test.

P6   A's demand that B refrain from exercising one of her liberties on the grounds that if she does exercise this liberty A will choose to violate her rights, fails the interpersonal test.

Therefore

C2   In Dangerous Party, the necessity condition does not prohibit Betty from choosing to go to the party, and subsequently using proportionate defensive force on Albert.

5.7 Objections

Let's consider some objections to this argument, and to the more general proposal that RESCUE is the best account of the necessity condition.[22]

5.7.1 Going to the Party Is Wrong

Some might be tempted to endorse the following objection:

---

[22] I don't consider two objections here that are discussed in other work. The first challenges the proposal that wrongdoers do not forfeit their right to be rescued. The second challenges the conceptual coherence of wrongdoers being at once liable to defensive harm while also having a right to be rescued from some of that defensive harm. The former is addressed in Quong, 'Miller's Crossing' and the latter in Firth and Quong, 'Necessity, Moral Liability, and Defensive Harm'.

P7   It is wrong for Betty to go to the party and use defensive force on Albert in Dangerous Party.

P8   RESCUE entails that it is not wrong for Betty to go to the party and use defensive force on Albert in Dangerous Party.

Therefore

C3   RESCUE is false.

This argument fails because the second premise is false. RESCUE does not entail that it is permissible for Betty to use defensive force in Dangerous Party. RESCUE only yields the more modest conclusion that if Betty uses defensive force in this case, she does not violate the necessity condition, and Albert has no standing to complain about her use of defensive force. It could still be wrong for Betty to go to the party and use defensive force for other reasons. For example, one might plausibly believe that there are reasons of wide proportionality (i.e., distinct from any claims or rights Albert might have) to refrain from harming Albert, and the benefits of Betty's attending the party are insufficient to outweigh these reasons. For example, seriously harming someone is a traumatic incident that likely ruins the party for everyone else and causes significant psychological distress to many of those at the party. It might be wrong for Betty to go to the party for these reasons. Some may also hold that Albert's life and well-being have an impersonal value over and above any interpersonal claims he can make, and this impersonal value is sufficient to make it wrong for Betty to attend the party.[23] I take no position here on this latter suggestion.[24] My point is simply that RESCUE, like other formulations of the necessity condition, is not a claim about what one may do all things considered. RESCUE more modestly states that Albert has no standing to demand that Betty refrain from going to the party and using defensive force. Thus, someone who endorses P7 need not reject RESCUE.

5.7.2 An Arbitrary Restriction

A sceptic might complain that the formulation of the interpersonal test is arbitrary, and once the arbitrariness is removed, RESCUE is vulnerable to a *reductio*. As formulated above, the interpersonal test requires that agents making moral demands on others must be able to justify any *future* decisions they make that play a role in the argument for the moral demand. But why is the interpersonal

---

[23] This, I think, is what Frick might argue. See Frick, 'What We Owe to Hypocrites'.
[24] I will say that even if Albert's life and well-being have impersonal value in this sense, this would also have to be weighed against all the reasons that might support Betty's attending the party (e.g., the benefits of deterrence of future wrongful aggression, the benefits of preventing a wrongful aggressor from limiting the freedom of a victim).

test temporally limited in this way? Shouldn't agents also have to justify any past decisions they have made, when those past decisions serve as premises in support of a moral demand? But if the interpersonal test applies to past decisions as well, then the necessity condition is eviscerated. Wrongful attackers must always appeal to the fact that they have made a decision to launch a wrongful attack as part of any alleged moral demand to be rescued from defensive force, but they cannot justify their past decision to launch a wrongful attack. Defensive agents will thus never have a duty to avoid imposing unnecessary defensive harms on wrongful attackers since wrongful attackers can never satisfy the condition in P5. But this conclusion is clearly unacceptable.

This objection, however, should be rejected. There is a good reason why the interpersonal test applies to a claimant's future decisions but not his past decisions. It's perfectly coherent to treat past decisions as fixed events that can't be changed, and sometimes to make claims on others in light of those decisions. You might say, for example, 'I've had too much to drink—can you please make sure I get home safely?' You needn't be denying your agency with regard to your past decision to drink too much; you might accept responsibility for this, recognize that you've made a mistake, etc. This is all compatible with taking it as given that you have had too much to drink, and making a claim on someone else's help in light of this fact. Your responsibility for the decision is perfectly compatible with my being duty bound to make sure you get home safely. We owe some duties of care and rescue to others even when others are responsible for needing our help.

Things are different, however, with regard to decisions we haven't yet made. We can't plausibly treat these decisions as settled facts without denying our own agency, and this is why Albert cannot demand that Betty refrain from performing a perfectly permissible act because of what Albert will do if she performs the act.

5.7.3 Another Temporal Worry

Consider a related objection. It might seem that the proposed view of the necessity condition lacks the resources needed to handle cases where a wrongful attack is ongoing, or where the attack occurs in a series of steps. Suppose, for example, that Albert is wrongfully attacking Betty by throwing a series of punches. At t1 he has already thrown one punch, and he intends to throw several more punches over the next sixty seconds. The question is what Betty may permissibly do at t1 to avert his attack. P5 states that Albert cannot reasonably make a moral demand of Betty when the demand fails the interpersonal test. Albert thus cannot make moral demands of Betty that take as given (i.e., outside of Albert's responsibility or control) the fact that he will throw future punches. But doesn't this implausibly entail that Betty owes no duty of rescue to Albert at all? Surely it can't be the case that Betty can use defensive force on Albert unconstrained by any requirement that the force be necessary merely because the rest of Albert's punches have yet to occur?

RESCUE does not have this implausible implication. At t1 Albert's past act of throwing a punch has, we can assume, already provided Betty with sufficient evidence that she is being physically assaulted by Albert, and thus is permitted to use proportionate defensive force. What Betty is permitted to do in self-defence depends in part on the evidence she already possesses regarding the severity of Albert's assault; that evidence has already been provided by Albert, e.g., by throwing the first punch, or by making sufficiently threatening statements. In the same way, what it is *proportionate* for Betty to do depends in part on the evidence Albert has provided through his actions, and what it is *necessary* for Betty to do depends in part on what Albert has already done. It's therefore straightforward to understand how Albert can make a moral demand of Betty without making reference to future decisions he has yet to make: 'By throwing the first punch and engaging in other threatening behaviour, I've given you sufficient evidence that I'm wrongfully assaulting you, and you are thus presumptively permitted to use proportionate defensive force against me. But you have a choice between imposing defensive harm H and H*. Since H* imposes much less harm on me and will not be costly for you relative to H, you owe me a duty of rescue to choose H* rather than H.'

As I argued in Chapter 2, whether Albert has rendered himself liable to defensive harm at the hands of Betty depends on some act that Albert has already performed. That past act is both the one that grounds Betty's presumptive permission to use defensive force, and also is the only act to which Albert needs to appeal in claiming a right to be rescued. Things are different, however, in cases like Dangerous Party. In this case, when Betty is deciding whether to go to the party, Albert has not yet done anything that would render him potentially liable to defensive force, and so there is not yet any defensive force from which he might have a claim to be rescued. This is why Betty owes no duty to Albert to refrain from attending the party, but she may owe Albert a duty to use a less harmful means of defensive force once Albert has already started throwing punches.[25]

5.7.4 Harming versus Aiding

Here is a different objection. A critic might protest that the necessity condition cannot be derived from a more general duty of rescue since duties of rescue

---

[25] A related issue concerns cases of automation or self-binding, where the wrongful attacker does something at t1 that guarantees he will perform the wrongful attack at some later time, t2. In cases with this structure, I think the defensive agent does have a duty of rescue to avoid the confrontation at t2 since the attacker's wrongful exercise of agency that initiates the attack is now in the past and not the future.

require duty bearers to *provide aid* or resources to the right-holder, whereas the necessity condition requires the defensive agent to *refrain from imposing harm* on the attacker. A duty to aid cannot ground a duty to refrain from harming—these are fundamentally different duties.

There are two ways of understanding this objection. One the one hand, the critic's point is purely conceptual: it's a conceptual error to suppose that a duty to provide aid can ground a constraint against harming. But this version of the objection is easy to dismiss since there are clear counterexamples. Suppose I have agreed to serve as your bodyguard, and as part of the contract I have a duty to rescue you from modest harms even at great cost to myself. Now suppose a runaway trolley is headed towards me, but I could redirect it towards you. The trolley will cause me great harm, but if redirected towards you, it will cause only modest harm. If I were not contracted as your bodyguard (e.g., if we were strangers) morality would permit me to redirect the trolley, but because I have a special duty to provide aid to you at great cost to myself, I am duty bound to refrain from redirecting the trolley. My duty to aid grounds my duty to refrain from harming in this case.

On the other hand, the critic's point might be more substantive. Drawing on the doctrine of doing and allowing, the critic might insist that, other things being equal, duties to aid are less weighty than duties to refrain from harming. If the duty of rescue were the basis for the necessity condition, then the duties imposed by the necessity condition would, other things being equal, be as weak as the duties a rescuer owes someone in need. But this is false, says the critic, because the necessity condition is a constraint *against harming*, and so it's more demanding than a duty of rescue.

But we can reject this version of the objection as well. The problem with this objection is straightforward: we should reject the assumption that the duties generated by the necessity condition must be stronger than the duties of a would-be rescuer in cases not involving defensive force. Compare the following cases:

Drowning: Albert wrongfully attempts to attack Betty, but he incompetently stumbles and falls into a lake. He is now drowning and will die without aid. Betty can rescue Albert at some cost, C, to herself.

Attack: Albert wrongfully attacks Betty. Betty has two ways of averting Albert's attack: using lethal defensive force (which is narrowly proportionate), which will cause no harm to Betty, or jumping to safety, at some cost, C, to herself.

In both cases Albert has wrongfully attacked Betty, and in both cases he will die unless Betty chooses to bear a certain cost, C. The only apparent difference is that, in Drowning, Betty must provide aid, whereas in Attack Betty must refrain from harming Albert. Intuitively, however, it does not seem to me that the cost Betty is duty bound to bear should be higher in Attack than in Drowning. If this intuition is sound, this undermines the second variant of the objection.

Here is the deeper explanation of the intuition. It is true that the duty to refrain from harming an innocent person is, other things being equal, more stringent than the duty to provide aid to an innocent person. But wrongful aggressors are liable to defensive force—they have forfeited certain rights against being harmed by the defensive agent that they would otherwise possess. Whatever remaining constraint there is against harming a liable attacker is thus not equivalent in stringency to the typical constraint against harming an innocent person. The demandingness of the duty the defensive agent continues to be under with regard to the wrongful attacker is instead equivalent to the demandingness of the duty to rescue. The demandingness of the duties does not track a nonmoral distinction between refraining from harming as opposed to providing aid; it rather tracks the moral rights that the wrongful aggressor retains against the defensive agent.

5.7.5 An Incoherent Duty?

Let's consider one final related objection. Some may be sceptical of the proposition that Betty can owe a duty of rescue to Albert, where what Albert needs to be rescued from is harm that Betty might otherwise impose. There's something incoherent, it might seem, about the proposal that you can have a duty to rescue people from yourself.

But there's nothing incoherent about the idea that we sometimes have a duty to rescue people from ourselves. Consider the case of Indira Gandhi, who was assassinated by two of her own bodyguards.[26] In addition to committing murder, these guards also violated a duty to rescue (in this case a contractual duty) Gandhi from attackers. We can clearly see this by imagining two variants of the case. Suppose in one variant, one of the bodyguards learns of the plot by the other, and could easily save Gandhi but chooses not to. This guard has clearly failed in a duty of rescue. Now suppose the guard is himself part of the group that's going to kill Gandhi. He could easily stop himself and the other guard, but chooses not. If the guard fails a duty of rescue in the first variant of the case then surely he does in the second. It's just that in the second case he also violates the more stringent duty not to kill.

In most cases of defensive harm, what the defensive agent does would be a violation of the attacker's rights against being harmed, but for the fact that the attacker has made himself liable to the defensive harm in question. The incoherence objection thus may rest on the following mistaken reasoning: 'the defensive

---

[26] Thanks to Cécile Fabre for drawing my attention to this case in connection with this issue.

agent has a choice about whether or not to impose defensive harm H, but since imposing H would be a violation of the attacker's right not to be harmed (e.g., the right not to be shot in the chest), if the defensive agent has a duty to refrain from imposing H, the duty must be correlated with the right against harm possessed by the attacker, and so cannot be correlated with a distinct right to be rescued'. The mistake here is clear: by virtue of his wrongful attack, the attacker does not possess the right against the imposition of H that he would standardly possess (e.g., the right not to be shot in the chest). Thus, if the defensive agent does have a duty to refrain from imposing H, it needs to be explained in some other way, and so nothing precludes the right to be rescued from providing the needed explanation.

5.8 Necessity and Liability

Some philosophers, most prominently McMahan, argue that a person cannot be liable, to any degree, to the imposition of unnecessary defensive harm.[27] On this view, necessity is an internal constraint on liability, and so I'll call this view *internalism*. At the other extreme, some might argue that there is no relationship between liability and necessity; the necessity condition is an independent constraint on the permissible use of defensive force, but a person can be fully liable to defensive force even when that force is unnecessary. Call this view *externalism*.[28] In between these options lies a middle position. On this view, a person cannot be *fully* liable to some defensive harm if imposing the harm violates the necessity condition.[29] But a person can be *partially* liable to such harm. You are partially liable to the imposition of some harm, H, when you have forfeited at least one of the claims you previously possessed against the imposition of H, but you retain some further claims against the imposition of H.[30] Let's call this view *partialism*.

RESCUE is clearly incompatible with externalism. According to RESCUE, the imposition of unnecessary defensive harm wrongs the attacker because it violates a duty of rescue that the defensive agent owes to the attacker. Since the attacker retains at least one claim right against the imposition of unnecessary defensive harm, he cannot be fully liable to such harm. This leaves us with a choice between

---

[27] See for example, McMahan, 'The Limits of Self-Defense', 195–206.

[28] For a defence of one version of externalism, see Frowe, *Defensive Killing*, 88–120.

[29] As a reminder, you are fully liable when you have no rights or claims against the harm being imposed.

[30] Although it might seem odd to suppose a person can forfeit some claims while retaining others with regard to the same act of harm imposition, this needn't be puzzling. We can have distinct claims—claims with different grounds—to the same good or resource. For example, I promise that you may use my car at a specific time tomorrow. When the time arrives, it turns out that you in fact need the car to rush your child to the hospital. You could lose the promissory claim to use the car (e.g., you waived the right or did something to forfeit it) without thereby losing the need-based claim to use the car. For further defence of this idea, see Firth and Quong, 'Necessity, Moral Liability, and Defensive Harm', 693–5.

internalism and partialism. RESCUE itself does not dictate which view we must choose. In previous work, Joanna Firth and I argued in favour of a version of partialism.[31] I won't repeat all those arguments here, or try to respond to all the objections that have been pressed against our view.[32] Instead I briefly focus on two of the strongest arguments to prefer partialism over internalism.

First, consider a case where Albert is wrongfully attacking Betty and she has three options: (i) she can seriously harm Albert and avert his attack, (ii) she can seriously harm a bystander and avert Albert's attack, or (iii) she can escape Albert's attack by incurring some minor cost. Assume that the availability of (iii) renders (i) unnecessary. The following seems clearly true: Betty would wrong Albert if she chooses (i), but not to the same extent that she would wrong the bystander if she chooses (ii). Partialism can easily explain this judgement. In virtue of his wrongful attack, Albert is partially liable to the harm Betty imposes, whereas the bystander is not liable at all. Internalism, on the other hand, says that Albert is not liable at all, and thus it yields the counterintuitive result that Albert and the bystander are equally non-liable to the harm that Betty might impose, and thus each would be wronged to the same extent.[33]

Second, consider whether a wrongful aggressor, A, should be permitted to use counter-defensive force when a defensive agent, D, threatens to impose unnecessary defensive harm, and if so, how much. The worry for internalism is that it looks as if A should be permitted to use the normal degree of proportionate defensive force against D (i.e., the same as any innocent person) since A not liable to the unnecessary force. This is counterintuitive.[34] Partialism, however, is better situated to handle such cases. Partialism tells us that A is partially liable to the unnecessary harm that D threatens to impose, and thus A may use limited defence against D, but cannot use the same degree of defensive force as someone who is not liable at all to D's threatened harm. For example, if D is threatening to kill A where this is unnecessary, partialism can explain why A may not be permitted to kill D in self-defence, even though it would be permissible for an innocent person to use lethal force to prevent herself from being wrongly killed by D.[35]

---

[31] Ibid.   [32] For some important objections, see Frowe, *Defensive Killing*, 94–105.
[33] Firth and I introduce this argument in 'Necessity, Moral Liability, and Defensive Harm', 687. McMahan responds to this objection by arguing that 'different people can be wronged to different degrees by being caused to suffer equivalent harms to which they are not liable ... because of [different] facts about the victims' (McMahan, 'The Limits of Self-Defense', 198). I don't find McMahan's response compelling for at least two reasons. First, some of the reasons he cites (e.g., opportunity to avoid the harm) do not reliably track the extent to which one is wronged by some harmful act. Second, and more importantly, if McMahan concedes that Albert is wronged to a lesser extent than the bystander, this amounts to conceding that some version of partialism is true. If Albert is wronged to a lesser extent, this means he has fewer claims, or less weighty claims, against the imposition of the harm than the bystander. By posing a wrongful threat, he has diminished the strength of his claims relative to the bystander: that's exactly what partialism tells us.
[34] Firth and Quong, 'Necessity, Moral Liability, and Defensive Harm', 689–90.
[35] RESCUE seems particularly well suited to handle these cases, if we assume that the right to be rescued is, other things being equal, less stringent or weighty than a negative right against harm or

McMahan suggests that the moral responsibility account of liability can handle these cases.[36] He suggests that, in cases where the harm is indivisible, the wrongful attacker's relatively greater degree of responsibility for the forced choice situation explains why a third party should allow D to impose the unnecessary harm on A, as opposed to using defensive force on A's behalf. From the third party's perspective, harm is unavoidable and indivisible: someone is going to suffer serious harm. But since A bears greater responsibility for this fact, A is liable to suffer the entire indivisible harm rather than D, even though the harm D imposes is unnecessary.

But this doesn't solve the problem. Rather, it exposes a tension between internalism and the moral responsibility account of liability, one that we previously identified in section 5.5.[37] If wrongful aggressor A bears a greater degree of responsibility for the forced choice situation, then the responsibility account yields the view that A is liable to the entire amount of indivisible harm. But this conflicts with internalism, the thesis that a person cannot be liable to unnecessary harm. Alternatively, we could insist that A is not liable to the harm because it's unnecessary, but this conflicts with the responsibility account, which tells us that when there is an indivisible and unavoidable harm, the person who bears greater responsibility is the one liable to bear the entire harm.

McMahan anticipates this objection. His response is to argue that liability is sometimes relative to persons. A is liable vis-à-vis the third party to suffer the harm because, for the third party, the harm is unavoidable and indivisible. But A is not liable to suffer the harm vis-à-vis D, since for D the harm is avoidable: by hypothesis D could easily avoid imposing the harm on A. Thus, we can apparently preserve the judgement that someone cannot be liable to unnecessary harm, while also concluding that, from the perspective of some agents, the wrongful aggressor is liable to suffer the entire harm in cases of this kind.

I don't believe this response succeeds. Liability cannot be relativized in the way McMahan proposes. If A is not liable vis-à-vis D to suffer the harm that D threatens to impose, then D threatens to wrongfully violate A's rights. By wrongfully threatening to violate A's rights, D makes herself liable to defensive force. The third party thus has a choice: (i) allow D to violate A's rights, or (ii) use proportionate force on D—force to which D is liable—to avert the rights violation. If choosing (ii) is not costly for the third party, he must choose (ii). To say that, from the third party's point of view, the harm is unavoidable and indivisible is a non sequitur. If one person is violating another person's rights, this is an agent-

interference. When this assumption is combined with the account of proportionality developed in Chapter 4, it yields the intuitive conclusion that when defenders threaten unnecessary harm against wrongful attackers, wrongful attackers can defend themselves against this unnecessary harm, but cannot use the same degree of force as a completely innocent person defending himself or herself from an equivalent level of wrongful harm.

[36] McMahan, 'The Limits of Self-Defense', 200–2.   [37] Also see Frowe, *Defensive Killing*, 116.

neutral moral fact, not something that shifts depending on whose perspective we adopt. The original dilemma thus remains. Either internalism is true, in which case D is violating A's rights, and thus a third party can justly impose proportionate harm on D to avert the violation, or else McMahan's preferred version of the moral responsibility account is true, in which case A can be liable to suffer unnecessary harm at the hands of D.

It's important to remember, however, that RESCUE is neutral between internalism and partialism. Thus, even if you don't find the arguments above for partialism compelling, this doesn't undermine the case for RESCUE.

5.9 Further Advantages

Let's return to RESCUE, and discuss a few further advantages it offers. First, compared to some conceptions of the necessity condition, RESCUE gives clearer guidance regarding how demanding the necessity condition is. That's because we already have rough judgements regarding how costly or demanding the duty of rescue is. Most agree, for example, that you are not duty bound to rescue a drowning person if the cost to you is paraplegia, but that you are duty bound to rescue the person if the cost is only ruining your shoes or bruising an arm. There will be a lot of disagreement about the cases in between, but at least the rough contours of the duty are widely accepted. We can use these rough contours to help us think about what costs defensive agents can be required to bear in order to avoid imposing certain harms on wrongful attackers. This approach has the additional advantage that the judgements to which we appeal are not judgements about the permissible limits of defensive force; rather we can appeal to judgements about rescue cases that have nothing to do with the use of defensive force. RESCUE is thus not merely a reflection of our existing intuitions about the permissible limits of defensive force—it draws justificatory support from a broader range of judgements about justice.

Another way in which RESCUE is different, and I think superior, concerns the aggregation of harms. The right to be rescued is a right *in rem*—held against everyone—and thus potentially imposing duties on everyone. A has a claim against B, and C, and D...etc. to be rescued when each of B, C, and D can fulfil the alleged duty at reasonable cost. If the cost to each person is reasonable, then each person cannot reasonably refuse to rescue A; the question of aggregate costs simply doesn't enter the picture. This has important implications. Consider the following example:

> *Bruising Bystanders*: Albert wrongfully threatens to harm Betty. She has two ways of averting his wrongful threat, both of which are narrowly proportionate: (i) paralyse Albert, causing no harm to anyone else, or (ii) sprain Albert's wrist in

a way that will also cause a mild bruise on the arm of each of some number, N, of innocent Bystanders.

TRADE-OFF may yield the conclusion that if N is large enough, the morally weighted harm in the latter option will be greater than in the former option, thus rendering the paralysis of Albert necessary.[38] But I think this is an unacceptable result. RESCUE avoids this result since it doesn't permit the aggregation of small harms in comparing different defensive options. What matters is whether the cost imposed on each person is sufficiently low that she is duty bound to bear the cost in order to rescue Albert from serious harm. Since we are each duty bound to suffer a mild bruise in order to rescue someone from a harm nearly as severe as paralysis, it is option (i), and not (ii), that is unnecessary according to RESCUE. This strikes me as the much more intuitive result. Just as it would be a mistake to aggregate all the pleasure that millions of viewers would gain from watching the World Cup final—in T. M. Scanlon's famous Transmitter Room example—as the justification for leaving a man to be electrocuted, it would also be a mistake to aggregate the mild bruises in Bruising Bystanders.[39] Each bystander owes a duty of rescue to Albert to suffer a mild bruise in order to save him from paralysis. The duty of each bystander does not disappear merely because there are many other bystanders who each happen to owe the same duty to Albert.[40]

5.10 Conclusion

I want to conclude by emphasizing some important practical implications with regard to two categories.

The first is domestic or spousal abuse, in particular violence against women. Women who are abused by their partners sometimes fight back, sometimes with lethal force. In some of these cases, the women are accused of using unnecessary defensive force. The accusations often take one of the following forms:

---

[38] I only say TRADE-OFF 'may' have this implication since this account could be combined with a theory of moral weighting where small harms to a large number of persons can never outweigh a large harm to a single person. But this idea—that small harms cannot be aggregated to outweigh a single more serious harm—is most commonly associated with rights-based or contractualist theories, and so it seems more difficult for a proponent of TRADE-OFF to arrive at this conclusion, whereas RESCUE can more naturally explain this result.

[39] Scanlon, *What We Owe to Each Other*, 235.

[40] Alex Voorhoeve appeals to a similar idea to defend a principle of limited aggregation regarding cases where only some people can be rescued from harm. See Voorhoeve, 'How Should We Aggregate Competing Claims?' *Ethics* 125, no. 1 (2014): 64–87. Whether principles of limited aggregation are coherent and defensible is the subject of an ongoing debate. See for example: Patrick Tomlin, 'On Limited Aggregation', *Philosophy & Public Affairs* 45, no. 3 (2017): 232–60; Victor Tadros, 'Localised Restricted Aggregation', *Oxford Studies in Political Philosophy* 5 (2019): 171-204 ; Seth Lazar, 'Limited Aggregation and Risk', *Philosophy & Public Affairs* 46, no. 2 (2018): 117–59; and Joe Horton, 'Always Aggregate', *Philosophy & Public Affairs* 46, no. 2 (2018): 160–74.

It's true that your husband was physically abusing you, and you did sincerely fear that he might kill you. But using lethal force on your husband on the night in question was unnecessary.... You did not have to come home from work that day: you could have gone to a friend's house or to a shelter.... You should not have confronted your husband with evidence of his infidelity because you knew he would react violently.... You should not have confronted him about his failure to pay child support when you know how violent he can get.

These accusations are outrageous. Abusive men cannot demand that their partners refrain from doing permissible things—such as returning home from work, or confronting them about unpaid child support—by pointing out that if their partners do these permissible things, they will become violent.[41] We won't understand the morality of defensive force unless we understand why these cases do not represent instances of unnecessary defensive force.[42]

The second category concerns wrongful violence by law enforcement officers. African-Americans are often justified in believing that they need to take additional steps (steps most other citizens don't have to take) in order to decrease the chances of a violent confrontation with police officers (to be clear, sometimes nothing helps avoid the violent confrontation). These steps include, among others, not wearing certain kinds of clothes, not driving certain kinds of cars, and avoiding certain neighbourhoods. In many instances, these additional steps are not objectively or subjectively costly for a given person. But the fact that these additional precautions aren't very costly is irrelevant, I think, to the question of whether a person who is wrongly attacked by law enforcement officers may permissibly use proportionate defensive force. It would be repugnant to tell someone who uses proportionate defensive force in such a case that the use of force was unnecessary since they could have easily avoided being in that neighbourhood or wearing those clothes. There may be other reasons why using defensive force against police officers in such cases is wrong or at least inadvisable; these cases raise complex issues about institutional roles. But whatever reasons there are to condemn using defensive force in cases like this, the fact that the defensive agents could have easily taken steps—*steps they should not have to take*—to reduce the risk of confrontation is not one of them. Understanding the necessity condition as an interpersonal moral demand that attackers are sometimes, but only sometimes, able to make of defensive agents enables us to see why this is true.

---

[41] See Ripstein, 'Self-Defense and Equal Protection', *University of Pittsburgh Law Review* 57 (1996): 700–1.

[42] There is a further issue that often has an important bearing on the necessary use of defensive force in cases of domestic abuse. In many such cases the abuser regularly makes conditional threats to the victim. In this way these cases differ from Dangerous Party. As I mentioned earlier, wrongdoers who make conditional threats are guilty of wrongful coercion, and thus are already liable to some defensive force. Since these wrongdoers are already liable to some defensive harm, their claims against the imposition of defensive harm are, other things being equal, weaker than someone who makes no conditional threat.

6
Rights and Evidence

You are about to drive to work. You always drive carefully and conscientiously and keep your car well maintained, but unbeknownst to you, a villain has tampered with your brakes, and as a result you will be unable to stop your car from hitting and killing an innocent pedestrian. Do you violate or infringe the moral rights of the innocent pedestrian?

Some philosophers—Judith Jarvis Thomson, for example—believe that the answer is yes. These philosophers endorse the *fact-relative* view of moral rights against harm:

> If B's φ-ing would contravene A's right not to be harmed if B had access to all the facts, then B contravenes A's right by φ-ing regardless of her epistemic position.

Although there has been a lively debate about whether moral permissibility or obligation is fact-relative or objective, there has been relatively little discussion of whether moral rights are fact-relative.[1] This is unfortunate. Whether or not A has a moral right that B refrain from φ-ing is one question, and what B is morally required or permitted to do all things considered is a different question. Some of the arguments—both for and against—the fact-relative answer to the latter question do not help us answer the former question, but the former question is still important, and indeed has major implications for the latter.

In this chapter I argue that the fact-relative view of moral rights is mistaken.[2] Our moral rights against being harmed are not determined against a backdrop of full or perfect information. Instead, I argue that many acts that do in fact cause harm to innocent others do not contravene anyone's claims not to be harmed, even if they would do if the acting agent knew all the facts. This is true because

---

[1] Proponents of the fact-relative view of moral obligation include Peter Graham, 'In Defense of Objectivism about Moral Obligation', *Ethics* 121, no. 11 (2010): 88–115; and Judith Jarvis Thomson, *Rights, Restitution, and Risk*, ed. William Parent (Cambridge, MA: Harvard University Press, 1986), 173–91. Proponents of evidence-relative conceptions of moral obligation include Frank Jackson, 'Decision-Theoretic Consequentialism and the Nearest and Dearest Objection', *Ethics* 101, no. 3 (1991): 461–82; T. M. Scanlon, *Moral Dimensions: Permissibility, Meaning, Blame* (Cambridge MA: Belknap Press of Harvard University Press, 2008), 47–52; Michael Zimmerman, 'Is Moral Obligation Objective or Subjective?' *Utilitas* 18, no. 4 (2006): 329–61, and *Living with Uncertainty: The Moral Significance of Ignorance* (Cambridge: Cambridge University Press, 2008).
[2] I concentrate on rights against acts that typically cause harm, but the arguments apply to moral rights generally.

whether A has a claim right that B refrain from performing some harmful act depends on whether A can *reasonably demand* that B refrain from performing the act. We cannot reasonably demand that people refrain from performing acts if they cannot reasonably be expected to know that the act has harmful consequences or is sufficiently likely to have harmful consequences. This doesn't mean that our moral rights are indexed to what others may *believe*. But it does mean that our moral rights are, in part, sensitive to the *evidence* we can reasonably expect others to possess regarding the consequences of their actions.

This conclusion has important implications for the morality of defensive force. To be liable to defensive force you must threaten to violate the rights of others. But if liability to defensive force depends on threatening another person's moral rights, and if moral rights are not determined by appeal to a fact-relative standard, then the range of persons who make themselves liable to defensive force is significantly narrower than some have suggested.

The chapter is structured as follows. Section 6.1 considers three reasons Thomson has advanced in favour of the fact-relative view of moral rights, but I show that none of these reasons are persuasive. In section 6.2 I offer a more general reason to reject the fact-relative view of moral rights, namely, that it is inconsistent with a view of moral rights as reasonable demands. Section 6.3 considers and responds to three objections to my view of moral rights as reasonable demands. In section 6.4 I confront a series of further objections pressed by Helen Frowe. Section 6.5 addresses a more general worry: that this chapter's focus on moral rights, rather than moral obligation, is an error. Section 6.6 concludes by drawing out some further implications for the morality of defensive force.

Before proceeding, let me make two clarifications. First, I assume that there is always a fact of the matter (rather than probabilistic information) regarding what will occur if an agent performs some act, and thus the fact-relative perspective includes this information, though of course particular agents often lack this information.

Second, although I reject the fact-relative view of moral rights, I do not defend an *evidence-relative view* of moral rights. On this view, A has a claim that B refraining from φ-ing if and only if B has sufficient evidence that φ-ing constitutes an infringement (or is sufficiently likely to risk infringing) of some claim of A's. This view is also false. The view I defend instead emphasizes the demands we can reasonably make of one another concerning types of acts. What we can reasonably demand of others depends in part on what evidence we can reasonably expect others to possess, but it also depends on other factors, including the control we can reasonably demand to have over our existing claims. As we shall see, this entails that the choice between the fact-relative and evidence-relative views is something of a red herring. The real question is *when* an agent's evidence has a bearing on whether she is under a duty, not whether evidence is ever relevant.

6.1 Thomson's Case

Day's End: B always comes home at 9:00 p.m., and the first thing he does is to flip the light switch in his hallway. He did so this evening. B's flipping the switch caused a circuit to close. By virtue of an extraordinary series of coincidences, unpredictable in advance by anybody, the circuit's closing caused a release of electricity (a small lightning flash) in A's house next door. Unluckily, A was in its path and was therefore badly burned.[3]

Thomson says that when B flips the switch, he violates a claim not to be harmed that A holds against him. This is true even though B had no way of knowing that his flipping the switch would have this consequence. Thomson thus endorses the fact-relative conception of A's right not be harmed by B.

Why does Thomson hold this view? First, she says that it would look 'weird if we were to say, "Look B, we know something that you don't know. If we tell you, then you will violate a right of A's if you flip the switch, but not if we don't."'[4] But, as others have pointed out, part of what makes this statement to B sound weird is that the statement falsifies the description of Day's End.[5] The initial description of the example stipulates that the harm that B's flipping of the switch will cause is unpredictable in advance by anybody. But if the statement is true, then the situation is no longer unpredictable in advance by anybody. More importantly, making the statement to B changes his epistemic situation by giving him a reason to believe that his act will harm A. This first argument can thus be set aside.

Second, Thomson suspects that some people reject the fact-relative view because it conflicts with

The Requirement-of-Fault Thesis for Claim Infringement: Y infringes a claim of X's in doing alpha only if Y is at fault for doing alpha.[6]

Thomson plausibly argues that this thesis cannot be true because there are cases where a person may faultlessly infringe the rights of others. For example, you might find yourself at the switch that can redirect a runaway trolley away from five innocent people who will otherwise be killed and onto a side track where the trolley will only kill one person. If you redirect the trolley, you act without fault, but you surely also infringe the claims of the one person on the side track. But even if the requirement-of-fault thesis is false—and I agree that it is—this provides no support for the fact-relative view of moral rights. One need not adopt the fact-relative view to endorse the uncontroversial thesis that there are sometimes lesser

---

[3] Thomson, *The Realm of Rights*, 229.   [4] Ibid., 233.   [5] Scanlon, *Moral Dimensions*, 51.
[6] Thomson, *The Realm of Rights*, 229. Thomson uses the term infringe to cover all cases where someone acts contrary to a right, whereas I reserve this term for cases where acting contrary to a person's right is permissible.

evil justifications—as in the trolley example—to infringe individual rights. If someone is guided by a lesser evil justification, she can act without fault and yet infringe a person's moral rights. But since many opponents of the fact-relative view can easily agree with this, rejecting the requirement-of-fault thesis is irrelevant to the question of whether we should endorse the fact-relative view.

Finally, Thomson points out that we can all agree that in Day's End if B *knew* that his flipping the switch would harm A, then he would be contravening A's claim not to be harmed by flipping the switch.[7] But how do we explain this? In particular, how can A have a claim that B refrain from flipping the switch *knowing* it will cause A harm unless A has a more fundamental claim that B refrain from flipping the switch? If the latter grounds the former, the fact-relative conception of rights will be difficult to resist.

But we can easily reject this conclusion. Those who believe that B must reasonably believe, or have sufficient evidence, that his act might harm A in order for his act to qualify as an infringement of A's claim can arrive at this view without assuming that A has a fact-relative claim not to be harmed by B. All they need to assume is that there are several necessary conditions that must be met before we can say that B contravenes a claim of A's. One of the necessary conditions might be reasonable belief or sufficient evidence, and the other might be that A does in fact suffer harm that is caused by B.

Consider a different example: most people believe that if A is dying and in need of urgent aid, A has a claim that B provide this aid *so long as doing so is not unduly burdensome for B*. When confronted with such an alleged claim, it would be implausible to say, 'How can A have a claim to be aided by B so long as doing so is not unduly burdensome for B unless A has a more fundamental claim to be aided by B?' To ask this question would be to misunderstand the nature of the claim right being described. The fact that providing the aid must not be unduly burdensome for B is an essential part of the moral story as to why A has a claim. A has no claim unless this condition is met. And those who reject the fact-relative view can rightly make the same complaint about Thomson's third argument. It might be the case that reasonable belief or sufficient evidence on the part of B is an essential part of the moral story as to whether B contravenes A's claim in Day's End. Of course we still need to know why some other variable is an essential part of the moral story, but Thomson's final claim provides no basis for doubting that this might be the case.

6.2 Moral Rights and Reasonable Demands

I've considered three arguments that Thomson offers, but none of them provide any positive reason to believe the fact-relative view. In this section I offer a more

---

[7] Ibid., 233.

general explanation as to why we should reject the fact-relative view. Let's begin with the following fact-relative thesis, endorsed by Thomson:

Harm Thesis: We each have claims against others that they not cause us harm.[8]

How should we understand this thesis and other similar fact-relative propositions about moral rights? Perhaps every time B performs any act that does in fact cause harm to A, B contravenes a claim of A's. But this leads to absurd results. If B opens a coffee shop on the same block as A's coffee shop, this may cause A great harm; his store may go out of business and A may lose his life savings. But we are not inclined to say that B therefore contravened a claim of A's.

A defender of the Harm Thesis may deny that cases like these involve harm; perhaps the thesis applies only to instances of physical harm. But narrowing the scope in this way doesn't eliminate the problem.[9] Suppose that A is in need of a kidney transplant or he will die. A does not receive the needed transplant and dies because B—who needs the same transplant—shows up at the hospital sooner and thus places himself ahead of A in the queue. Had B not acted in that way—had he shown up at the hospital slightly later—A would have survived. Let's call this *Transplant*. Does B contravene A's claim not to be harmed in Transplant? Assuming fair procedures were followed, surely not. Or suppose A has an unusual inner ear, the result of which is that whenever anyone speaks at a volume louder than a whisper within fifty feet, he suffers serious pain. Does this mean that if A stands at the intersection of Lexington and 42nd street in Manhattan for ten minutes, hundreds of people contravene his claim not to be harmed? Again, surely not. Let's call this example *Too Noisy*.

One way to modify the Harm Thesis so as to avoid the absurd implication that A's claims are infringed in the preceding examples is to stipulate that A's claim not to be harmed by B does not apply to acts that B has a moral right to perform. Since B has a moral liberty right to apply for a kidney transplant, or to speak at a normal volume on a busy city street, he cannot contravene any claim of A's when he performs these acts, even if doing so causes A harm. But this is obviously no solution. If A only has a claim not to be harmed by B when B performs acts he is *not* morally at liberty to perform, then we cannot appeal to A's claim not to be harmed to explain *why* B is not morally at liberty to act: to do so would be viciously circular. But the only alternative is to define the conditions under which B is morally at liberty to act without reference to A's claim not to be harmed, in which case the Harm Thesis cannot deliver many of the results that the proponent of the fact-relative view wants. In Day's End, for example, if we cannot appeal to

---

[8] Ibid., 248.
[9] There is another way that the scope of the Harm Thesis clearly must be limited—it must allow that we can waive, transfer, or forfeit our claims not to be harmed by others.

any potential claim that A has not to be harmed by B in deciding whether B is morally at liberty to flip the switch, then he might be at liberty to do so, in which case he contravenes no claim of A's when he flips the switch.

A different way to handle cases like Transplant and Too Noisy is to concede that individuals do not have an absolute claim not to be harmed by others, but only a claim not to be harmed by others when those others could easily avoid imposing harm. In Transplant, B cannot easily avoid harming A since he too will die without the kidney transplant, and in Too Noisy, perhaps it is too difficult for others to refrain from making any noise on busy city streets. But there are obvious problems with this move too. In many circumstances our claims not to be harmed are very stringent and apply even when it is extraordinarily costly for others to refrain from harming us. For example, if B will die unless he steals A's kidney, then it is not easy for B to refrain from harming A, at least if by easy we mean not too costly.

Maybe this problem can be circumvented by specifying that the relevant test is not how *costly* it is for B to refrain from harming A, but rather whether it would be *reasonable* for A to demand that B refrain from performing the harmful act, where reasonable is a moralized notion that takes into account the interests and status of all affected parties.[10] Even this modification might be insufficient, however, since there are cases where it might not seem reasonable for A to demand that B refrain from acting, and yet B will infringe a claim of A's if he acts. For example, some might argue that it is not reasonable (in the moralized sense) for A to demand that B refrain from turning a runaway trolley away from five innocent people and onto a side track on which A is trapped, but if he does so, he infringes a claim of A's not to be harmed. Reformulating the relevant test as follows might accommodate such cases:

Revised Harm Thesis: A has a claim right against B that B refrain from causing A harm only when A's demand that B refrain from performing the harmful act is reasonable, or else when A's demand that B refrain would be reasonable but for the existence of a lesser evil justification or an agent-centred or relational prerogative to impose harm.[11]

---

[10] Scanlon's well-known test of whether an act would be prohibited by a principle that no one could reasonably reject is one moralized conception, though I don't mean to invoke this specific conception here. See Scanlon, *What We Owe to Each Other*, chap. 5. For a different account of what we can reasonably demand of each other, with particular application to criminal law and tort law, see Ripstein, *Equality, Responsibility, and the Law*.

[11] I believe that interpersonal moral demands can be reasonable *despite* the existence of countervailing lesser evil justifications or agent-relative or relational prerogatives. But the Revised Harm Thesis is formulated to be neutral on this question. What's important is that the Revised Harm Thesis allows that lesser evil justifications and agent-relative or relational prerogatives can *outweigh* claims not to be harmed. Those who deny the existence of one or more of these justifications for harm imposition can adjust the thesis accordingly. Also, I set aside here the conditions under which one might waive, transfer, or forfeit one's claims not to be harmed, though I will return to this in the next section.

I think the Revised Harm Thesis, or something roughly like it, is correct. I don't believe any version of the Harm Thesis can plausibly deal with cases like Transplant and Too Noisy unless it includes some sort of moralized test, such as the one included in the Revised Harm Thesis. This poses a fatal problem for the fact-relative view of moral rights against harm. Whether it is reasonable for A to demand that B refrain from φ-ing can depend on a wide array of considerations, including, though not limited to (i) the importance of the activity B engages in by φ-ing, (ii) how costly it would be for B to refrain from φ-ing, (iii) whether B had sufficient opportunity to avoid finding himself in a situation where he faces the choice whether or not to φ, and (iv) whether A had sufficient opportunity to avoid finding himself in a situation where he might be harmed by B's φ-ing. It does not make sense to adopt the fact-relative perspective when asking and answering these questions about relative cost and the opportunity to avoid certain situations.

Consider Day's End: Is it reasonable to demand that B refrain from flipping any light switches unless he has assured himself that it's impossible that doing so will cause harm to others? Since B can never assure himself of this fact, such a demand imposes a substantial burden on B, and we can easily imagine that, from a suitably impartial perspective, all might agree that the miniscule risks posed by the act of flipping a light switch cannot justify imposing such a substantial burden on everyone who might do so. A similar story can be told for many everyday acts that impose very small risks of harm on others, but from which all, or many of us, derive substantial benefits (e.g., careful and conscientious driving, air travel).

Can a proponent of the fact-relative view accommodate this objection? Perhaps the proponent can say this: if B knew all the facts—if he knew that flipping the switch at that moment would harm A—it would be almost costless for him to refrain: he could wait a few seconds, or use a different light, or adopt any number of alternative strategies. And this explains why B contravenes A's claim not to be harmed. If B knew all the facts, it would be easy for B to avoid flipping the light switch, but the harm to A is serious, and this is why it is reasonable for A to demand that B refrain from flipping the switch.

But this response fails. Our imagined proponent of the fact-relative view tells us that *if* B knew all the facts it would be easy for B to refrain from flipping the switch, *therefore* it is reasonable for A to demand that B refrain from flipping the switch. But this doesn't help us resolve the problem of Day's End, since in Day's End B doesn't know all the facts. The fact that it would be easy for someone to perform (or refrain from performing) some act under one set of conditions has no immediate bearing or whether it's reasonable to require that he perform (or refrain from performing) that same act under different conditions.

Consider the following:

If B had Superman's special powers it would be easy for him to refrain from φ-ing, therefore it is reasonable for A to demand that B refrain from φ-ing.

The plausibility of the conclusion depends entirely on whether B has Superman's special powers. If he doesn't, then the truth of the premise does not support the conclusion. The same is true when the premise refers to what B knows or reasonably ought to know.

Someone might protest that physical abilities differ from epistemic limits. If B cannot fly, for example, then demanding that B ϕ, where ϕ-ing requires the ability to fly, is inconsistent with ought-implies-can and so the demand cannot be reasonable. But whether B can physically ϕ never depends on his knowledge of any particular fact, and thus assuming an agent has all the facts is not inconsistent with ought-implies-can in the way that assuming an agent has Superman's powers might be.

This reply, however, is of no help. Suppose an assassin is trying to kill A. The assassin is hiding behind one of a thousand doors. There is no time to open each door to see where the assassin is hiding. B has one chance to fire his weapon through the correct door to kill the assassin and save A. There is obviously a sense in which the demand that B shoot and kill the assassin does not violate the ought-implies-can principle: it is physically possible for B to do this. But it's clearly absurd to suppose that A could reasonably demand that B aim at the correct door. Showing that some alleged moral demand does not violate the ought-implies-can constraint is far from sufficient to establish that the demand is reasonable, at least in any plausible moralized sense of the term.

My argument can be summarized as follows:

P1   We only have claim rights against others that they refrain from causing us harm when our demand that others refrain from performing the harmful act is reasonable, or else when our demand that others refrain would be reasonable but for a lesser evil justification or an agent-centred or relational prerogative to impose harm (Revised Harm Thesis).

P2   Whether it is reasonable to demand that others refrain from the relevant act depends on a variety of considerations, including questions about the costs of refraining and the opportunities to avoid refraining.

P3   The questions referred to in P2 must be answered partly by reference to abilities and information that can reasonably be expected to be available to an agent in a given situation.

Therefore,

C1   The fact-relative perspective cannot determine the conditions under which we have claim rights not to be harmed by others.

I imagine proponents of the fact-relative view are most likely to respond by rejecting P1, and insisting that claims not to be harmed exist independently of whether it is reasonable to require others to refrain from harming us. But this rejection of P1 is problematic for at least two reasons. First, as we've already seen, P1 is necessary to explain cases like Transplant or Too Noisy.

Second, if we detach the existence of a claim right from any notion of whether it's reasonable to expect a duty bearer to comply, it's unclear what normative role claim rights play. In particular, if claim rights exist independently of whether it is reasonable to require duty bearers to comply, then they lack the distinctively second-personal character that seems to be an essential feature of claim rights. If A has a claim that B refrain from φ-ing even when it is not reasonable to demand this of B, then A lacks the standing to demand that B comply, and cannot complain that B has treated him disrespectfully, or failed to accord his claims or interests due weight. A proponent of the fact-relative view may reply that such second-personal features are inessential to claim rights. Thomson, for example, says that claim rights are, centrally, behavioural constraints: if A has a claim that B refrain from φ-ing, then, other things being equal, B ought not to φ.[12] But this sparse account of a claim right fails to identify its distinctive properties. If refraining from φ-ing would make someone happy, or make someone laugh, or increase the amount of beauty in the world then it is also true that, other things being equal, B ought not to φ. This is just to say that there is a reason for B to refrain from φ-ing. But although claim rights can provide duty bearers with reasons for action, this is not what distinguishes them as a normative kind, and so Thomson's definition cannot be the whole story about claim rights.

Because claims not to be harmed depend partly on what we can reasonably require of others, whether A has a claim not to be harmed by B depends on questions about relative costs and opportunities to have acted otherwise and, as I've argued, the answers to such questions depend partly on an agent's epistemic position. In Day's End, it's not reasonable to demand that B refrain from flipping the light switch in his hallway given the evidence available to him. Similarly, it's not reasonable to demand that individuals refrain from carefully and conscientiously driving their cars since the very small chance such acts may cause harm is outweighed by the benefits all of us derive from permitting this activity. Of course what exactly counts as 'reasonable' depends on one's broader moral views, but we don't need to settle that here.

Although we may sometimes speak loosely about general moral rights, such as the right not to be harmed by others, there is no general right entailing that others are always duty bound to refrain from harming us. Whether A has a claim that B refrain from performing some act depends on the type of act that B performs, and not merely on whether this act causes A harm. When the type of act that B performs is one that A cannot reasonably demand he refrain from performing— say, because it does not pose any undue risk of harm and refraining would be

---

[12] Thomson, *The Realm of Rights*, 232.

costly or damaging to B—then A has no claim that B refrain. This is true even if A would have such a claim if B's epistemic situation were different.

In sum, if some version of the Revised Harm Thesis is true, then the fact-relative view is false: many acts that do in fact cause harm to innocent others do not contravene anyone's claims not to be harmed, even if they would constitute a contravention of rights if the agent knew all the facts. Notice that the argument in this section undermines more than the fact-relative view of moral rights. It also undermines another somewhat weaker view: the *foreseeable risk of harm* view of moral rights. On this view, A has a claim against B's φ-ing whenever B can foresee that φ-ing poses any risk of harm to A (or to someone), and that risk does in fact eventuate. Like the fact-relative view, this view fails to be sensitive to the question of whether it would be reasonable for A to demand that B refrain from φ-ing.

6.3 Objections

Let's consider some objections to the preceding argument.

6.3.1 Third-Party Intervention

First, suppose B is about to innocently flip his light switch in Day's End, and doing so will cause severe burns to A. Now suppose that C, an employee at Omnicorp Electric who is working in the area, has just discovered the electrical fault that will cause the accident, and he can see through B's front window that B is about to flip the switch that will severely burn A. There isn't time for C to warn either B or A, but there is one thing he can do that will avert the accident: he can push a button that will prevent A from being harmed, but it will cause B to suffer an extremely painful electric shock when he flips the switch, though this will cause no lasting injuries. Many people may believe that C ought to press the button to save A from the very severe burns. But if, as I've argued, B does not threaten to contravene A's rights in Day's End, then how can C be justified in causing B to suffer a severe electric shock? Morality does not normally permit us to cause serious harm to one innocent person even if this is necessary to avert a serious harm befalling another innocent person. Some might insist we need the fact-relative view of moral rights to explain why it is permissible for C to push the button in this example.

This example does not, however, cast serious doubt on our conclusion. If the difference between the degrees of harm that A and B would suffer is sufficiently large, then there is a lesser evil justification for C to press the button. If, by contrast, the difference between the harms that A and B would suffer is not sufficiently great to ground a lesser evil justification, then I think it is impermissible for C to push the button. Suppose, for example, that if C does nothing, A will suffer a serious burn causing 100 units of harm, whereas if C pushes the button, B will suffer a slightly less serious burn causing 95 units of harm. I suspect that most people believe that it is not permissible for C to push the button to prevent B from causing 100 units of harm to A. But our standard views about proportionality when a person's rights are stake are very different. Most people believe that a person whose rights are being threatened (or a third party acting on her behalf) can impose at least as much, if not much more, harm on the potential rights violator than the potential rights violator is threatening to impose on the right-holder. If this were a case in which B is threatening A's right not to be harmed, it should thus be obvious that C may press his button to defend A, but I assume most people will not have this reaction. In sum, the intuitive force of the initial example reveals our commitment to a lesser evil justification, and not a commitment to the fact-relative view of moral rights against harm.

6.3.2 Evidence of Claims and Evidence of Forfeiture

Second, a critic might protest that, whatever its flaws, the alternatives to the fact-relative view are even less appealing. Recall the following example, introduced in Chapter 2:

> *Duped Soldiers*: A group of young soldiers is successfully fooled by a totalitarian regime into believing that the regime is good and just, and is under repeated attacks from their evil neighbours, the Gloops. The regime's misinformation campaign is subtle and absolutely convincing: the soldiers are justified in believing what they are told by the regime. Once the misinformation campaign is complete, these soldiers are given orders to attack and destroy a Gloop village on the border, which, they are told, is really a Gloop terrorist camp plotting a major attack. In fact, everything the regime has said is a lie, and the Gloop village contains only innocent civilians. The soldiers prepare to shell the village and are about to (unknowingly) kill all the innocent civilians in it. A peacekeeping force from a neutral third country patrols the border and could avert the attack, but only by killing the soldiers.

If the moral rights of the villagers not to be harmed depend purely on whether it is *permissible* for the soldiers to attack *given the evidence available to them*, then the soldiers do not contravene any claim rights of the villagers if they kill them, since they have sufficient evidence to believe their attack is permissible. And if the soldiers do not threaten to contravene any claims, the neutral peacekeeping force may not intervene to save the villagers if the number of villagers is roughly the same as the number of soldiers. But this is an unacceptable result.[13]

I agree that this is unacceptable. But rejecting the fact-relative view of moral rights does not entail that we must accept an account whereby A lacks a claim not to be harmed by B's φ-ing whenever B is evidence-relative permitted to φ. Instead the objection can be defused by separating two questions:

(i) Under what conditions does a person have a claim not to be harmed by a particular type of act performed by another person?

(ii) Has some particular person, A, waived, transferred, or forfeited this claim not to be harmed by another person, B?

The answer to the latter question depends on what A has actually done, and not on B's evidence about what A has done. Here are two reasons to accept this view. First, it coheres with many widely held convictions about the structure of rights. Suppose we want to know whether Alice still owns her blue Honda Civic, or whether she has transferred this right to Bert via a sale. To answer this question we do not ask what Bert (or anyone else) believes, or what evidence Bert, or anyone else, has. Rather, we ask whether Alice has in fact agreed to the sale of her car. Bert may reasonably but mistakenly believe Alice has done so—maybe a malicious third party has successfully fooled Bert into thinking so—but Bert's reasonable belief is irrelevant to the question of whether Alice retains ownership rights over the car. Second, there are good reasons why transfer, waiver, and forfeiture should depend on what the right-holder actually does: it grants the right-holder a more effective degree of control over the right, something that is typically of central importance in the justification of the right. The point, for example, in Alice having claim rights against certain forms of nonconsensual contact is to grant Alice an important element of control over her body. But if Alice can lose this right depending on what others reasonably believe she has done, rather than anything she has actually done, the right is less effective in securing one of its central aims. In sum, whether A has waived, transferred, or forfeited one of her rights depends on A's actual behaviour, and not on the beliefs of others.

But whether a person has any *type* of claim right in the first place depends on what it is reasonable for one person to demand of another under such and such conditions, and this does partly depend on what information individuals have about the expected consequences of their various options. So, in Duped Soldiers, we begin by asking whether people can reasonably demand that others refrain from firing mortar shells at their residences, taking various factors into account,

[13] The 'prospective' view of moral rights defended by Michael J. Zimmerman is vulnerable to counter-intuitive results like this one, though he accepts this implication of his view. See Zimmerman, *Ignorance and Moral Obligation* (Oxford: Oxford University Press, 2014), chap. 5.

including the very high chance that doing so will cause serious harm or death. The answer to this question is yes. Thus, the Gloops who live in the village have claim rights that the soldiers refrain from firing mortar shells at their village *unless* those Gloops have forfeited or waived those rights. And the soldiers ought to understand this, that is, they should understand that (given the absence of a lesser evil justification) the permissibility of their proposed course of action hinges on their assumption that the Gloops have forfeited their rights. The second question is then whether the Gloops have in fact forfeited their rights, and the answer to this question—despite what the soldiers might reasonably believe—is no. And so the Gloop villagers retain their rights not to be harmed in this example. Thus, if the soldiers shell the Gloop village, they wrongfully threaten the rights of the Gloops, and thus I believe they render themselves liable to proportionate defensive force. We reach this conclusion without presupposing the fact-relative view of moral rights; we only need to assume that rights forfeiture is a matter of what the Gloops have in fact done.

In sum, whether A forfeits her right against B's φ-ing does not depend on B's evidence. But whether A has a claim in the first place that B refraining from φ-ing does depend on what we can reasonably demand of each other, and what we can reasonably demand of each other is, in part, sensitive to the evidence we can reasonably expect others to possess. In determining what claims we possess against one another, we should ask, 'Could A possess a claim that others refrain from φ-ing under circumstances C?' where C does not include cases where A appears to have waived, transferred, or forfeited the claim under consideration. To include those cases within C would be to put the cart before the horse. Before we can determine the conditions under which A has waived, transferred, or forfeited an alleged claim, we need to know whether A can possess the claim in the first place. Once that determination has been made, I've argued that there are compelling reasons why waiver, transfer, and forfeiture should depend on what the right-holder actually does, and not on others' beliefs (however reasonable) about what she does.

6.3.3 Reasonable Demands and the Moral Status Account

Recall the following case:

Mistaken Attacker: The identical twin brother of a notorious mass murderer is driving during a stormy night in a remote area when his car breaks down. Unaware that his brother has recently escaped from prison and is known to be hiding in this same area, he knocks on the door of the nearest house, seeking to phone for help. On opening the door, Resident justifiably believes the harmless twin is the murderer. Resident has been warned by the authorities that the mass murderer will certainly attack anyone he meets on sight, and so Resident lunges at him with a knife.

In Chapter 2 I argued that Resident is liable to defensive force because the evidence-relative permissibility of his act depends on the assumption that the person at the door lacks moral rights that he in fact possesses.

But consider the following objection.[14] It is not reasonable to demand that Resident refrain from attacking the person at the door given his epistemic situation: he justifiably believes that he's about to be murdered. But if it's not reasonable to demand that Resident refrain from acting, then—given the view of moral rights defended in this chapter—the person at the door cannot have a right against what Resident does. And if the person at the door lacks a right against being attacked by Resident, then—contra what I argued in Chapter 2—the evidence-relative permissibility of Resident's act does not depend on treating the person at the door as lacking moral rights that he in fact possesses. Thus, if the view of moral rights that I've defended in this chapter is sound, then Resident is not liable to any defensive force, at least if the moral status account of liability defended in Chapter 2 is correct. But since Resident is liable to some defensive force, we must reject either the moral status account of liability or the view of moral rights defended in this chapter (or both).

I don't think this objection succeeds. To begin, we should interrogate more closely the premise that it is not reasonable to demand that Resident refrain from attacking the person at the door. Why is this demand not reasonable? It cannot be because Resident justifiably believes that if he refrains from acting he will die. Consider a different case: Albert justifiably believes that unless he eats a plump baby, he will die of starvation. Albert's justified belief does not show that it would be unreasonable to demand that Albert refrain from eating the baby, and this is true even when Albert's belief about starvation is true as a matter of fact. The proponent of the objection must therefore be making the following claim. What makes it unreasonable to demand that Resident refrain is not merely that he believes his life is at stake, but also that he justifiably believes that the person he confronts is liable to attack. The proposal must be that it is unreasonable to demand that people refrain from harming others when they have sufficient evidence to believe those others are liable to attack.

There are two questions here. The first is whether the arguments in this chapter commit me to this conclusion. They do not. I have argued that when a type of act—like the act of careful and conscientious driving—poses a sufficiently low *ex ante* chance of harming others, it may not be reasonable to demand that others refrain from performing the act. This is crucially different than claiming that when

---

[14] Cécile Fabre, Helen Frowe, and Mike Otsuka have each presented versions of this objection to me.

an act poses a sufficiently low *ex ante* chance of harming *non-liable persons*, it may not be reasonable to demand that others refrain from performing the act. So the proponent of the objection and I are using different tests to determine whether a demand is reasonable. The objector's test asks whether, given the agent's evidence, the agent's act poses an undue risk of harm to non-liable people. But the test I'm using asks whether an agent's act poses an undue risk of harm to others where the agent's evidence about who might be liable is bracketed. This is why my account distinguishes Resident from the conscientious driver. So the account in this chapter doesn't entail the conclusion that Resident is not liable to defensive force.

Now we can focus on a second question: Which test is a better interpretation of the general view of moral rights as reasonable demands? The objector may argue that his conception of the reasonableness test is more plausible—after all, how can it be reasonable to demand that Resident refrain from doing that which a reasonable assessment of the evidence implies to be necessary to save his own life from an attack by a culpable aggressor who has forfeited his immunity from defensive harm?[15] The suggestion is that if someone has a full epistemic excuse for φ-ing, it cannot be reasonable for others to demand that he refrain from φ-ing.

I think there are several reasons to resist this proposal. First, it yields counter-intuitive results in a range of cases such as Mistaken Attacker and Duped Soldiers. Second, as I argued earlier, there are powerful reasons why transfer, waiver, and forfeiture should depend on what the right-holder actually does rather than anyone's evidence about what she's done. Most importantly, this grants the right-holder a more effective degree of control over the right, something that is typically of central importance. But the same argument doesn't apply to the question of whether someone has a right in the first place. When we're deciding whether persons in general have a right that others refrain from φ-ing, it makes sense to focus on what we can reasonably demand of others. For example, can I reasonably demand that no one speak at a volume louder than a whisper on a busy city street? I don't have special interests in controlling the behaviour of others regardless of their evidence when I don't have a prior claim over their behaviour or over some part of the physical world. But once we decide that I do have a right that others refrain from doing something—for example the right that others refrain from throwing rocks through the window of my home—it makes sense to suppose my possession of this right should turn on my behaviour, rather than what other people may believe I have done.

Thus, when Resident is wondering whether he will contravene the rights of the person at the door, he should recognize that there are two distinct questions. One is whether the person at the door would have a right against being stabbed if he had done nothing wrong. The other question is whether the person at the door has

---

[15] Mike Otsuka formulates the question in this way in written comments on a draft of this manuscript.

in fact done anything that constitutes a forfeiture of his rights. I don't think it's odd to suppose that we apply different standards when addressing these different questions. I also don't think this poses undue burdens on duty bearers, such as Resident, since duty bearers can know that if they deliberately attack others, even when the evidence suggests they are justified, they take a gamble about the moral status of others.[16]

6.4 Frowe's Further Objections

I'll now turn to consider several objections pressed by Helen Frowe.[17] Frowe argues that the Revised Harm Thesis struggles to explain the difference between two cases:

> *Transplant*: A is in need of a kidney transplant or he will die. A does not receive the needed transplant and dies because B—who needs the same transplant— shows up at the hospital sooner and thus places himself ahead of A in the queue. Had B not acted in that way—had he shown up at the hospital slightly later—A would have survived.

> *Naughty Transplant*: B will die unless he receives a kidney transplant. The only available kidney is A's, so B lethally takes A's kidney.

As a reminder, I suggested that the following features can be relevant in deter-mining whether A can reasonably demand that B refrain from ϕ-ing (i) the importance of the activity B engages in by ϕ-ing, (ii) how costly it would be for B to refrain from ϕ-ing, (iii) whether B had sufficient opportunity to avoid finding himself in a situation where he faces the choice whether or not to ϕ, and (iv) whether A had sufficient opportunity to avoid finding himself in a situation where he might be harmed by B's ϕ-ing. The difficulty, Frowe argues, is that these features don't help us distinguish Transplant from Naughty Transplant. She claims that the importance of the activity—saving B's life—is the same in both cases, the cost to B is the same in both cases, and we can stipulate that B had no way of avoiding contracting the disease that threatens his kidney. She concludes that 'Quong's view fails to give us a way to distinguish between these cases.'[18]

---

[16] It's also worth noting that it is dialectically awkward for proponents of the moral responsibility account of liability to oppose requiring duty bearers to assume this sort of risk. On the moral responsibility account, duty bearers are exposed to *even greater risks* of bad moral luck than they are on my account, which restricts cases of bad moral luck to those instances where the agent gambles with the moral rights of others, as opposed to all cases where the agent performs a risk-imposing activity.

[17] Helen Frowe, 'Claim Rights, Duties, and Lesser-Evil Justifications', *Proceedings of the Aristotelian Society Supplementary Volume* 89, no. 1 (2015): 267–85.

[18] Ibid., 270.

There is, however, much more scope for the Revised Harm Thesis to distinguish between these cases than Frowe allows. The considerations listed as relevant in determining when a demand is reasonable weren't presented as exhaustive, and I think it's clear that other considerations will often be relevant. For instance, whether people have been given a fair opportunity to gain a scarce, non-private resource is another consideration that will sometimes be relevant, and this clearly bears on the distinction between Transplant and Naughty Transplant. This also affects the importance of the activity that B engages in. In one case the activity is partly constituted by a fair set of procedures for allocating a scarce good, whereas in Naughty Transplant the activity lacks this feature. The Revised Harm Thesis therefore can distinguish between the cases.

Setting this first disagreement aside, let's consider Frowe's alternative. She suggests that a narrower and more plausible interpretation of the Harm Thesis would restrict the thesis to claims against people harmfully interfering with our bodies or with things to which we are entitled.[19] She argues that this narrower view can easily distinguish between Transplant and Naughty Transplant, and that this version is compatible with the fact-relative view of moral rights.

I don't see, however, how this narrower account can avoid the moralized question of what we can reasonably demand of others. Consider one of the earlier examples, Too Noisy, where A suffers from an inner-ear condition causing extreme pain when anyone speaks louder than a whisper. Does B contravene a claim against interfering with A's body when he speaks at a volume louder than a whisper within fifty feet? Does it matter where A and B are standing when this occurs? I think plausible answers to these questions depend on asking what we can reasonably demand of others. And when we ask what we can reasonably demand of others, we cannot ignore the issue of what evidence we can reasonably expect others to possess.

The narrower version of the Harm Thesis that Frowe proposes can avoid relying on a moralized test only if we define interference with a person's body or other entitlements by reference to some nonmoralized standard, for instance, a purely causal account of what constitutes interference. But this would disable the thesis from reaching intuitively plausible results in a range of cases. To get intuitively plausibly results in cases like Too Noisy, we need more than a mere causal story about the interaction between A and B. But if a plausible version of the Harm Thesis must rely on some version of the moralized test, where we ask what we can reasonably demand of others, then we cannot ignore questions about what evidence others can be expected to possess.

Turning now to the issue of lesser evil justifications, Frowe thinks there's a problem with the caveat in the Revised Harm Thesis, one that allows that A can

---

[19] Ibid., 270.

have a claim that B refrain from φ-ing even when B has a lesser evil justification for φ-ing. For example, if B can save five people from a runaway trolley by redirecting the trolley towards innocent A, I am inclined to say that A has a claim that B refrain from doing so, but that the lesser evil justification provides B with a sufficiently weighty reason to *infringe* A's claim. Frowe argues that my position is puzzling for two reasons.[20] First, she says the presence of the lesser evil justification entails that it is not reasonable for A to demand that B refrain from turning the trolley. But if it's not reasonable for A to make this demand, then I should conclude that A does not have a claim against B turning the trolley.

In response, I think we should distinguish between two different parts of morality. One is the domain whereby we work out what we owe to others as a matter of justice. The Revised Harm Thesis belongs to this domain, and along with many others, I think that a person's rights against serious harm are not at the mercy of the aggregation of many other people's interests. Lesser evil justifications, however, require this kind of aggregative moral reasoning. Lesser evil justifications thus do not figure in what we can reasonably demand of each other in this sense. A person's demand can be reasonable despite the existence of a lesser evil justification—the latter justification simply has the capacity to outweigh a reasonable demand of justice. We unsurprisingly sometimes face situations where there's a conflict between what justice permits or requires, and averting some very harmful consequences.

Second, Frowe argues that *if* A has a claim in the trolley case, then surely we should reach a similar conclusion in Day's End, namely, that A has a claim not to be harmed by B's flipping of the switch. But there's an important difference between these cases. If we set lesser evil justifications aside—as not relevant to determining individual rights—A looks to have a reasonable claim in one case but not in the other. It's reasonable to demand someone refrain from knowingly sending a runaway trolley towards you, but it's not reasonable to demand others refrain from turning on any light switches given the miniscule chance that doing so might cause harm.

6.5 Wrong Question?

I have been focused on the question of whether moral rights against harm are fact relative. Some readers, however, may believe this question is of comparatively little interest. These readers may believe that the more fundamental question is the more familiar one, namely, whether moral obligation or permissibility is fact relative. Consider Day's End. If the permissibility of B flipping the

---

[20] Ibid., 275.

light switch is fact relative, then B must not flip the light switch regardless of whether A has a right against B performing this act. Of course, if the arguments in this chapter are sound, then the wrongness of B's flipping the switch will not be explained by appeal to A's right, and will have to be explained in some other way. But whether A possesses a claim right turns out to make no difference to what B ought to do. More generally, whether or not moral rights are fact relative makes no difference to what an agent ought to do, provided moral obligation is fact relative. Let's call this the *No Difference* objection to the main argument of this chapter.

This objection is mistaken. What one ought to do, in the fact-relative sense, depends on all the relevant reasons for action, including whether one's act constitutes a violation of anyone's moral rights. Rights are inputs into fact-relative conclusions regarding moral permissibility. Whether or not rights are fact relative thus changes what it is fact-relative permissible to do. Consider the following example:

> *Fireworks*: Albert is in a field setting off fireworks. He has taken all due precautions and has ascertained that no one is in nearby. Unbeknownst to Albert, a small child has wandered into the field and will be gravely harmed by one of the fireworks. If Albert knew all the facts, he could save the child from any harm by using his own body as a shield, though doing so would gravely harm Albert.

Whether Albert is morally obligated, in the fact-relative sense, to use his body as a shield and suffer grave harm depends on whether the child has a right not to be harmed by Albert's setting off the fireworks. If the child has this right, then Albert has stringent duties to do what he can to avoid violating his duty, and those stringent duties might include suffering significant harm to avert the harm to the child. On the other hand, if Albert's setting off the fireworks does not contravene the child's rights (because moral rights are not fact relative) this changes what costs Albert is fact-relative obligated to bear for the sake of the child.

This case is not unusual. As I've argued, many everyday acts impose very small risks of harm on others, yet these risks are sufficiently low that others cannot reasonably demand that we refrain from performing them, and thus we contravene no person's moral rights in performing these acts. In all these cases, if we perform the act and this results in a threat of harm to others, our fact-relative moral obligation to suffer costs to avert the harm, or to compensate the victim, are not as great as they would be if moral rights were fact relative. The No Difference objection is thus clearly false. The objection also fails to recognize the way in which judgements about fact-relative permissibility depend, in part, on who is liable to defensive force, which in turn depends on whether or not moral rights are fact relative. I'll return to this issue in the concluding section.

Before doing so, however, let's consider a modified version of the objection. Even if a sceptic concedes that the No Difference objection is mistaken, the sceptic might still insist that whether moral obligation is fact relative or evidence relative makes a large difference to the morality of defensive force—a much larger difference than the resolution of whether moral rights are fact relative. Moral rights are small potatoes compared to moral obligation. Call this the *Small Potatoes* objection.

I think this objection is misguided for two reasons. First, I'm not sure it is helpful or even meaningful to ask whether moral obligation is ultimately fact relative or evidence relative.[21] Instead I think there are different senses of wrongness or moral obligation that we can invoke.[22] Whether it's useful to invoke a particular sense depends on what further question we're addressing. If we want to know how blameworthy Albert is for φ-ing, it can be useful to consider whether φ-ing was wrong in the belief-relative sense. We are typically more culpable, other things being equal, when our act is wrong in this sense. For other questions, we may focus on the evidence-relative sense. I have argued, for example, that liability to defensive force depends in part on the agent's evidence. And the fact-relative sense may be most helpful for certain questions that arise after an act has been performed. For example, whether you have reason to regret the act may often depend on whether the act was wrong in the fact-relative sense. If someone insists that only one of these senses of wrongness is the 'true' or 'genuine' sense, I'm not sure what this claim amounts to.

Second, even if we assume for the sake of argument that only one of these senses of moral obligation or wrongness is genuine, this makes little practical difference when we consider various cases involving the use of defensive force where the facts and the evidence diverge. Consider Duped Soldiers. If moral obligation is fact relative, then the soldiers act impermissibly, whereas the soldiers act permissibly if moral obligation is evidence relative. But does this make much practical difference? For example, does it affect whether the soldiers are liable to defensive force? It does not. Even if permissibility is evidence relative, the soldiers are liable to defensive force. The moral status account declares that the soldiers are liable to defensive force in virtue of the way they treat the Gloops—they treat them as lacking basic moral rights—not in virtue of whether their act is permissible. Thus, from the point of view of the neutral peacekeeping force who must decide whether they may intervene, it makes no difference whether moral obligation is fact

---

[21] See Parfit, *On What Matters*, 149–62.

[22] That said, I share Tadros's worry that there is something 'fishy' about many attempts to invoke the fact-relative sense of moral obligation, since those who invoke this sense often fail to explicitly acknowledge the vast complexity of all the possible acts an agent might have reason to perform if the agent knew all the facts. As Tadros suggests, it may be more accurate to understand appeals to the fact-relative standard as appeals to a superior epistemic perspective, where that perspective still does not include *all* the facts. See Tadros, *The Ends of Harm*, 220–4.

relative or evidence relative. What matters is that the soldiers make a mistake about the moral rights of the Gloops.[23]

Consider a different case:

Unloaded: Albert intends to murder Betty. He points his gun at her and prepares to fire. Betty sees what Albert is about to do and reaches for her own gun to shoot Albert in self-defence. Albert's gun is in fact not loaded, though neither Albert nor Betty are aware of this fact. Carl is aware that the gun is unloaded, and he now has the chance to impose defensive harm on Betty to stop her from shooting Albert.

If Betty shoots Albert, this would be fact-relative impermissible, but evidence-relative permissible. If only one of these senses of permissibility is genuine, does this make any difference to what Carl should do? It does not. By threatening Betty with a gun and giving her every reason to believe he is about to murder her, Albert renders himself liable to lethal defensive force—he has no standing to complain if Betty shoots him.[24] Since Albert is liable to lethal defensive force, Betty is not liable to defensive force. Carl thus faces the following decision: How much harm can be imposed on a non-liable person (Betty) in order to avert the death of someone who is liable to lethal force? The answer, presumably, is: relatively little.[25] It seems permissible, for example, to sprain Betty's wrist if this could save Albert, but it seems clearly impermissible to paralyse Betty. None of this reasoning is affected by the question of whether Betty acts permissibly or impermissibly in shooting Albert. Judgements about Albert's and Betty's liability are central in determining how Carl should behave, and these judgements do not depend on whether Betty acts permissibly in shooting Albert.

In sum, the Small Potatoes objection gets things backward. Establishing whether or not moral rights are fact relative has important practical implications for the use of defensive force. Determining whether moral obligation is 'ultimately'

---

[23] A sceptic might protest that things aren't so simple. In Chapter 2 I argued that justification defeats liability. If so, then surely whether or not moral obligation is fact relative will play an important role in determining whether an agent is liable to defensive force. But this objection rests on a misunderstanding. As I explained in Chapter 2, on the moral status account, the type of justification that defeats liability is neither all-things-considered fact-relative justification, nor all-things-considered evidence-relative justification. Instead, what matters is whether the agent is evidence-relative justified in performing the act, where this justification does not depend on the assumption that any of the people who might be harmed by performing the act have forfeited, waived, or otherwise lost any rights that persons normally possess. This kind of justification is distinct from all-things-considered obligation or permissibility, and so there's no tension between the claim that justification defeats liability and the argument being advanced in this section.

[24] Recall the discussion of this issue in Chapter 2.

[25] As the arguments in Chapter 5 make clear, how much harm can be imposed on Betty in this case is calculated by asking what costs Betty is duty bound to bear to rescue Albert from death since Albert retains a right to be rescued by Betty when she can do so at reasonable cost.

fact relative or not, on the other hand, makes less practical difference to the morality of defensive force.

6.6 Conclusion

In closing, I want to say something further about the implications for the morality of defensive force. As we know from Chapter 2, there's a great deal of disagreement about the necessary and sufficient conditions for liability to defensive force. But despite these disagreements, most accounts of liability converge on one important point: threatening another person's moral rights, or acting as if one is going to do so, is a necessary condition for liability to defensive force. If B's φ-ing does not constitute at least an infringement of A's rights—if A is liable to the harm that will occur, or has consented to the harm, or in some other way lacks a claim against such harm—then most of the major accounts of liability to defensive harm agree that B does not render himself liable to defensive harm by φ-ing.[26]

This chapter's main thesis thus has major implications for liability to defensive force. If the fact-relative view of rights against harm (and also the foreseeable-harm view) is false, the class of people who are liable to defensive harm is much narrower than some have suggested. In particular, proponents of the *moral responsibility account* of liability claim that the typical criterion for liability to defensive harm is moral responsibility for posing a fact-relative wrongful threat of harm. In this formulation 'wrongful' means those who are harmed are not liable to this harm, implying that the victims retain claim rights against the harm.

But the arguments in this chapter suggest that there is a serious problem with this view. When a careful and conscientious driver gets behind the wheel of her car, she knows there is always a tiny chance something beyond her control will go awry, and her car may threaten to harm an innocent person. But this does not mean she threatens to violate anyone's rights when she gets behind the wheel of the car and drives carefully and conscientiously, and this is true even if the very unlikely but foreseeable threat of harm does eventuate. Why? Because her behaviour is justifiable or reasonable in light of the distribution of the burdens and benefits of the driving, the rules of the road, and the opportunity to avoid the practice.[27] It would not be reasonable for anyone to demand that she refrain from engaging in the act of careful and conscientious driving. Thus no one can have a claim against being harmed by this act.

---

[26] For an important exception to this consensus, see Gordon-Solmon, 'What Makes a Person Liable to Defensive Harm?'

[27] I'm assuming, as I did in Chapter 2, that the correct moral theory yields this conclusion about careful and conscientious driving. If you find this assumption implausible, many other examples can serve the same purpose.

To establish a person's liability to defensive force, we must ask whether that person threatens the moral rights of others by φ-ing. And the answer to that question cannot be determined by asking whether it would be wrong for the person to φ if she knew all the facts. Rather, it must be determined by asking, among other things, what it would be reasonable for others to demand of her given the importance of the affected activities, the costs involved, the options available, and the relative harms that others might suffer. For example, if you cast your ballot for a very good political party C in a general election, you can foresee that there's a very small chance your vote plays an important causal role in electing C and that C may go on to cause fact-relative impermissible harm to many persons domestically or internationally. Or consider the Red Cross doctor who saves the life of a soldier, and who can foresee that her doing so may causally contribute to that soldier posing an impermissible threat of harm to others in the future. For proponents of the moral responsibility account, such examples have proved very awkward; either they must counterintuitively admit that you make yourself liable to defensive harm by casting your ballot and the doctor makes herself liable by saving the soldier, or else they must appeal to implausible claims about the moral significance of causal remoteness and degrees of responsibility to explain why voters in democratic elections, doctors, cooks, computer service technicians, and many others are not liable to defensive harm.[28]

But these examples are only awkward if we endorse the fact-relative view of moral rights. What matters is whether voters, doctors, cooks, computer service technicians, and others are acting unjustly—whether they are contravening duties of justice they owe to others—when they perform their role-based obligations under normal conditions. I don't pretend that this is always an easy question to answer, but it's the right question to be asking if we want to know whether these people act in ways that make them liable to defensive harm. I also think that when we focus on this question, we get more plausible answers regarding who is liable to defensive harm. Voters in democratic elections do not have duties of justice to refrain from casting their ballots for candidates or political parties when they reasonably believe those candidates or parties meet certain moral conditions. Doctors do not, at least under most conditions, have duties of justice to refrain from healing wounded patients, even if there is a risk that those patients might later act impermissibly.

The arguments in this chapter thus provide an additional reason—one alluded to in Chapter 2—to reject the moral responsibility account of liability. In Chapter 2 I remained neutral on the question of whether moral rights are fact relative. I argued that regardless of whether moral rights are fact relative, we ought

---

[28] For McMahan's discussion of noncombatant immunity, see McMahan, *Killing in War*, chap. 5. For criticisms of McMahan on this issue, see for example, Frowe, *Defensive Killing*, chap. 6; and Lazar, 'The Responsibility Dilemma for Killing in War'.

to embrace the moral status account of liability, which focuses on the type of evidence-relative justification an agent has for acting in a way that threatens harm. But now we can see that the moral responsibility account faces a different objection, one that doesn't depend on a specific conception of liability:

P4   A necessary condition for A to be liable to defensive force is that A must threaten to contravene the moral rights of another person, or wrongly create the impression of doing so.

P5   Moral rights are not fact relative. It is possible to act in ways that pose fact-relative wrongful threats of harm without contravening anyone's moral rights.

P6   The moral responsibility account declares that A is, in principle, liable to defensive force whenever he acts in a way that he can foresee might pose a fact-relative wrongful threat of harm, and the fact-relative wrongful threat eventuates.

P7   The moral responsibility account therefore declares that A can be liable to defensive force in cases where A does not contravene anyone's moral rights (via P5 and P6).

Therefore,

C2   The moral responsibility account is false (via P4 and P7).

You don't need to accept the moral status account of liability to endorse this argument. You only need to accept the first three premises. The third premise is simply a description of the moral responsibility account. This chapter has offered arguments in support of the second premise, and many philosophers who work on the morality of defensive force already endorse the first premise.[29]

The normal way a person makes himself liable to defensive force is by threatening the rights of others. But moral rights are not determined by asking how we ought to act if we occupied some impossible, omniscient perspective. They are instead determined from the more ordinary interpersonal one—by asking what we can reasonably demand of each other given the evidence we have about how our actions and demands affect others.

---

[29] One person who explicitly rejects P4 is Kerah Gordon-Solmon. See her 'What Makes a Person Liable to Defensive Harm?' In brief, Gordon-Solmon argues that what matters is not whether A threatens to infringe B's moral rights, but rather whether A is morally responsible for the fact that a situation has arisen where someone must suffer harm. I won't offer a full response to this proposal here, but I do not believe it is one we should endorse. If moral responsibility is divorced from a threatened rights violation, this generates counterintuitive results such as those described in the preceding paragraph (e.g., doctors are liable to defensive force when they heal wounded patients). The only way to avoid counterintuitive results like this is to build a conception of moral rights into the account of moral responsibility.

7

The Means Principle

In the previous chapter, I argued that our moral rights against harm are sensitive to the evidence that others can be expected to have regarding the consequences of their acts. We cannot reasonably demand that others refrain from φ-ing when others lack any evidence that φ-ing might pose any significant risk of harming us. Our moral rights are thus not fact relative, but instead depend on the reasons and evidence that others can reasonably be expected to possess. This view of moral rights, in some sense, occupies a middle ground between two alternatives. On the one hand, there those who argue that moral rights are determined only by facts about the world, and not by anyone's beliefs or evidence. On the other hand, some argue that at least some of our moral rights against being harmed are sensitive to others' beliefs and intentions. In this chapter I argue that we should, at least in part, resist this latter suggestion. More precisely, I defend an account of the means principle that dispenses with any appeal to the acting agent's intentions. The means principle, recall, played a crucial role in my account, developed in Chapter 3, of why it is permissible, in certain circumstances, to defensively harm or kill justified attackers and non-responsible threats. In that chapter I offered only a brief account of the means principle, and I only gestured towards its rationale, promising to do more later in the book. This chapter aims to make good on that promise, and in doing so, further develops the account of moral rights that has emerged from the preceding chapters.

The chapter proceeds as follows. Section 7.1 introduces several pairs of puzzling cases involving harm. Section 7.2 introduces the means principle and argues that it is a more promising way to explain the puzzling cases than the leading alternatives. In section 7.3 I provide a rationale for the means principle, one grounded in a broader picture of distributive justice and the independence of persons. Section 7.4 confronts various objections to the means principle. Section 7.5 focuses on the implications for the morality of defensive force. In Section 7.6 I address a final worry that might be pressed by proponents of the doctrine of double effect and others who believe an agent's intentions can sometimes decisively affect whether a harmful act is morally permissible. Section 7.7 concludes by considering the wider implications for our understanding of moral rights.

The Morality of Defensive Force. Jonathan Quong, Oxford University Press (2020). © Jonathan Quong.
DOI: 10.1093/oso/9780198851103.001.0001

7.1 The Puzzling Cases

There are many pairs of cases where, although the consequences of acting are the same, many people believe what it is permissible to do differs. Recall the following well-known cases:

> *Switch*: There is a runaway trolley whose brakes have failed headed down a track where five people are trapped and will be killed unless the trolley is diverted. Fortunately there is a side track onto which the trolley can be diverted, but there is one person, Betty, trapped on this side track, and Betty will be killed if the trolley is diverted. Albert, an innocent passerby, has seen and understood the whole situation, and he uses a switch to redirect the trolley towards Betty.

> *Overpass*: There is a runaway trolley whose brakes have failed headed down a track where five people are trapped and will be killed unless the trolley is diverted. Fortunately, before the trolley will hit the five people it must pass under an overpass. Albert and Betty are standing on the overpass. Albert understands that Betty's weight, but not his own, will be sufficient to stop the trolley before it reaches the five people. By pushing a button, Albert topples Betty off the overpass and onto the tracks below, where she is killed, but her body stops the trolley and saves the five.

And the following cases:

> *Strategic Bomber*: A person who fights for a just cause in a just war drops a bomb on an unpopulated military target, the destruction of which is very important to the success of the war effort. The bomber foresees that dropping the bomb will kill several nearby innocent noncombatants, but killing those noncombatants is not his aim in dropping the bomb.

> *Terror Bomber*: A person who fights for a just cause in a just war plants a bomb that will kill several innocent noncombatants. The bomber's purpose in killing innocent noncombatants in this way is to terrorize the enemy population in a way that will be equivalently important to the success of the war effort as the bomber's action in Strategic Bomber.

Many people believe that killing in the first case in each pair is permissible, but impermissible in the second case. Let's call these (and similar pairs) the *puzzling cases*. A lot of philosophical energy has been devoted to explaining how the puzzling cases can differ with regard to what is permissible. What makes it true that Albert acts permissibly in Switch but not in Overpass, and what makes it true that the bomber acts permissibly in Strategic Bomber but not in Terror Bomber?

The most influential answer is the doctrine of double effect (DDE). In its canonical formulation, the DDE states that harming a person can be permissible when the harm is (a) only a foreseen but not intended consequence, (b) of an action whose intention is to produce a good outcome, (c) where the harm is not a means to produce the good outcome, and (d) where the good outcome is proportionately greater than the harm caused.

Much of the recent literature has focused on the first two features of the DDE. One group of philosophers defends the view that intentions can directly affect the permissibility of a harmful act, and that this fact is central in explaining the puzzling cases.[1] Another group insists that, at least for the most part, intentions do not bear directly on the permissibility of harm-imposing acts.[2]

My sympathies lie with the sceptics of the relevance of intentions to the permissibility of harm imposition. But I don't want to rehash this debate. Instead, I argue that we can explain the puzzling cases in a better way—by appeal to the constraint against harmfully using persons or their rightful property as a means. It is wrong, I argue, to harmfully use a person or her property as a means, but the wrongfulness of doing so is not explained by reference to the acting agent's intentions.

This might seem hard to understand. The special wrongfulness of harming others as a means might seem unavoidably tied to the intentions or attitudes of the harm-imposing agent. As Warren Quinn puts it (albeit in describing direct harmful agency generally):

Someone who harms by direct agency must therefore take up a distinctive attitude towards his victims. He must treat them as if they were then and there *for* his purposes. But indirect harming is different...those who will be incidentally rather than usefully affected—are not viewed strategically at all, and therefore not treated as for the agent's purposes rather than their own.[3]

If intentions or attitudes do not affect the moral permissibility of harm imposition, what can be salvaged of the idea that it is wrong to harm others as a means? One can point to the fact that the person who is harmed plays a causal role in the achievement of some outcome, but why attribute moral significance to particular causal patterns once those patterns have been disconnected from the intentions of the acting agent?[4] As Scanlon says, 'being a means in this sense—being causally

---

[1] See for example, Matthew Hanser, 'Permissibility and Practical Inference', *Ethics* 115, no. 3 (2005): 443–70; Matthew Liao, 'Intentions and Moral Permissibility: The Case of Acting Permissibly with Bad Intentions', *Law and Philosophy* 31, no. 6 (2012): 703–24; Jeff McMahan, 'Intention, Permissibility, Terrorism, and War', *Philosophical Perspectives* 23, no. 1 (2009): 345–72; Tadros, *The Ends of Harm*, 139–68; Ralph Wedgwood, 'Scanlon on Double Effect', *Philosophy and Phenomenological Research* 83, no. 2 (2011): 464–72.

[2] F. M. Kamm, *Intricate Ethics: Rights Responsibilities, and Permissible Harm* (Oxford: Oxford University Press, 2007), chap. 5, and 'Terrorism and Intending Evil', *Philosophy & Public Affairs* 36, no. 2 (2008): 157–86; T. M. Scanlon, *Moral Dimensions*, chap. 1–2; Thomson, 'Self-Defense'.

[3] Quinn, 'Actions, Intentions, and Consequences', 348.   [4] Tadros, *The Ends of Harm*, 149–55.

necessary—has no intrinsic moral significance, in my view. What matters is the cost to the person involved, and the claim that person has to be informed about the nature of his involvement.'[5] Since what happens from the victim's point of view is the same regardless of the causal structure, Scanlon concludes that the idea of harming someone as a means cannot do any explanatory work in the puzzling cases. My aim in the following sections is to show that this conclusion is mistaken.

7.2   Extensional Adequacy

Here, recall, is the *means principle*:[6]

It is morally wrong to harm Y in the pursuit of an objective if doing so involves using Y's body or other things over which Y has a rightful prior claim,[7] unless Y is duty bound to suffer this harm, or has consented to this harm.[8]

As I explained in Chapter 3, X uses Y's body or other property when the outcome that might justify X's act cannot be achieved without X's body or other property, or without access to some relevantly similar body or property. To test whether X's act violates the means principle, we can ask whether X's act could succeed in the absence of Y and Y's rightful property. If the answer is no, then X uses Y as a means.

The means principle can explain all the paradigmatic puzzling cases. It explains the difference, for example, between Switch and Overpass, and between Strategic Bomber and Terror Bomber. In Switch and Strategic Bomber, the harm-imposing agent does not use the victims to achieve the objective that ostensibly justifies the act, whereas he does use his victims to achieve this objective in Overpass and Terror Bomber. The means principle is also superior to competing principles in terms of extensional adequacy when we consider a wider range of cases.

Consider principles that attempt to explain the puzzling cases by reference to the acting agent's intentions. Proponents of such principles argue that, other things being equal, it is morally worse to intend harm than it is to merely foresee harm. These principles, however, face a serious problem when we consider cases where the acting agent is mistaken about certain key facts, and this mistake leads

---

[5] Scanlon, *Moral Dimensions*, 118.

[6] As I noted in Chapter 3, a number of other philosophers endorse a principle that is at least somewhat similar to the means principle. See Quinn, 'Actions, Intentions, and Consequences', 344; Alexander, 'The Means Principle', 251–64; Øverland, 'Moral Obstacles', 481–506; Ramakrishnan, 'Treating People as Tools', 133–65; Tadros, *The Ends of Harm*, chap. 6; Walen, 'Transcending the Means Principle', 427–64, and 'The Restricting Claims Principle Revisited', 211–47.

[7] Or at least a claim that is stronger than any claim of the agent who might harm Y.

[8] Your failure to save Y also counts as harming Y, in my view, when Y has a right to be saved by you. When Y lacks this right, your failure to save Y is not a case of you harming Y.

the acting agent to have apparently harmless intentions. Consider the following case:

> *Assumed Consent*: Albert wants to have sex with Betty. They are at a party and each has been drinking. Albert recklessly and unjustifiably believes Betty consents to have sex with him, even though she has not consented. Albert has sex with Betty believing he has her consent when he does not.

Albert does not intend to harm Betty as a means. He sincerely believes that he is having consensual sex with her, but it is in fact rape. This is a clear case of harmfully using a person as a means. Those who appeal to intentions cannot reply by saying that what matters in this case is the fact that Albert *ought to have known* Betty did not consent, or *ought to have taken* the appropriate steps to assure himself of Betty's consent. These claims about what Albert ought to have known and done are true, but they also illustrate that Albert's intentions are unnecessary to explain the particular wrongness of nonconsensually using someone in this way. What Albert ought to have believed or have done does not bear on the nature of his intentions in having sex with Betty.

The point can, of course, be applied to any case of harmful using (e.g., Overpass). Even if the agent who imposes the harm does not intend to harmfully use someone else as a means—if the agent unjustifiably believes that he has the victim's consent or has made some other unjustifiable mistake of fact—the agent's act remains an instance of harmful use that is intuitively wrongful for that reason. The particular nature of the wrongness is most obviously explained by the fact that we have powerful reasons not to appropriate or exploit other people's bodies without their consent. The appeal to intentions thus appears superfluous and renders such views unable to explain the full range of puzzling cases.

Now consider a starkly different moral principle: Kamm's Doctrine of Productive Purity (DPP), which purports to explain the puzzling cases without any appeal to the agent's intentions:[9]

> (1) If an evil* cannot be at least initially sufficiently justified, it cannot be justified by the greater good that it is necessary (given our act) to causally produce. However, such an evil* can be justified by the greater good whose component(s) cause it, even if the evil* is causally necessary to help sustain the greater good or its components. (2) In order for an act to be permissible, it should be possible for any evil* side effect (except possibly indirect side effects) of what we do, or evil* causal means that we must use (given our act) to bring about the greater good, to be at least the effect of a good greater than it is working itself out (or the effect of means that are noncausally related to that greater good that is working itself out).

---

[9] Kamm, *Intricate Ethics*, 164.

This principle is extremely complex, and I won't endeavour to explain all of its elements here. For our purposes, the principle is of interest since it makes no reference to the acting agent's intentions, and thus it cannot be vulnerable to the type of objection I pressed above. The principle instead makes reference only to the causal processes by which good consequences are created. Though the DPP explains many of the puzzling cases, it cannot distinguish between certain important cases.

A particular problem with the DPP is that it rests on a distinction between harms that are upstream from a good outcome and that help to produce the good outcome, as opposed to harms that are downstream of the good outcome or harms that are necessary to help sustain the good outcome. The former harms are condemned by the DPP in a way that the latter harms are not. To illustrate, in Overpass the harm to Betty is upstream from the good outcome (saving the five) and it also helps to produce the good outcome. But when the trolley is redirected in Switch, the harm to Betty is downstream from the good outcome. In Switch the good outcome is the five being saved, and the trolley being turned is, as Kamm puts it, the noncausal flip side of the five being saved.[10] Although this distinction may seem to explain our intuitions in the puzzling cases, it also generates clearly counterintuitive results. Here is a modified version of a case presented in Chapter 3:

> Large Alcove Crush: Five innocent people are in a tunnel. A villain has sent a runaway trolley towards them and it will kill them if they do not escape. They can only escape the trolley by jumping into an alcove in the tunnel. Unfortunately, there is already a large man in the alcove. The five could jump into the alcove, which would keep them safe from the oncoming trolley, but doing so would also crush and kill the large man since the alcove is too small to safely accommodate anyone apart from the large man.

According to the DPP, as I understand it, this case is morally analogous to Switch.[11] The good outcome is the five jumping out of the way of the trolley, and thus the large man being crushed is not upstream of the good outcome, nor does it produce the good outcome, though it may help sustain it. The DPP thus tells us that it's permissible for the five to jump into the alcove, but I believe it's clearly impermissible.

Now compare this with another case:

---

[10] Ibid., 141.

[11] Kamm presents a somewhat similar example, Tumble Case, and agrees that the act is not condemned by the DPP. See ibid., 139.

Bridge with Five Victims: A villainous aggressor is pursuing five innocent victims, and in order to escape to safety, they must run across a narrow and wobbly public bridge. Unfortunately, a bird watcher is currently standing on the bridge, oblivious to their plight. If they were to get onto the bridge they would wobble it such that the bird watcher would fall off into the ravine below and be killed. It is not possible to communicate with the bird watcher and get him to leave his location before the villainous aggressor kills his victims.

In this case the harm to the bird watcher is upstream of the five being safe: his death is not an aspect of the good being worked out; he dies right after the five step onto the bridge, but the five will not be safe until well after they have run across and reached some point on the other side.

Intuitively, this case is analogous to Large Alcove Crush; the harms should be equally difficult to justify. But the DPP tells us that it's permissible to act in the first case but impermissible to act in the latter. I believe this is a significant reason to be sceptical of the DPP.

Another important reason to reject the DPP is that it lacks a compelling rationale. There seems no reason why mere causal structures should have the sort of moral significance that the DPP accords to them.[12] I won't pursue this objection, however, since my aim here is simply to point out the extensional advantages of the means principle when compared to some alternatives.

Let's now compare the means principle to a closely related principle recently offered by Ketan H. Ramakrishnan. He defends the following principle:

Utility: It is especially difficult to justify infringing a person's rights on the basis of her usefulness to others.[13]

This principle can explain the intuitive difference between many of the puzzling cases. But unlike the means principle, Utility cannot explain the intuitive difference between all the cases. It cannot, for example, explain the difference between the following cases:

Driftwood: Albert and Betty are each at risk of drowning in the open ocean. There is a piece of driftwood floating nearby, but it is very small, and only one person can use it to remain afloat until help arrives. Albert swims more quickly than Betty, and gets to the driftwood first. As a result, he survives and Betty drowns.

Life Jacket: Albert and Betty are each in the open ocean. Betty is wearing her life jacket (purchased with her fair share of resources). Albert, however, has no life

---

[12] For a forceful version of this critique, see Tadros, *The Ends of Harm*, 152–4.
[13] Ramakrishnan, 'Treating People as Tools', 134.

jacket and will not survive without one. Albert swims over and steals Betty's life jacket. As a result, he survives and Betty drowns.

Intuitively, there is a clear difference between these cases. What Albert does in the former case seems permissible to me, whereas what he does in the latter case is clearly impermissible. Even if one is unsure that Albert acts permissibly in the first case, there is an obvious moral difference between the two cases: the latter act is worse than the former. But Utility cannot explain this difference since it focuses only on the utility of persons, and says nothing about the utility of persons' property. The means principle, by contrast, easily explains the difference between this pair of cases, since it condemns using anything over which a person has a rightful claim, unless the person is duty bound to permit such use or has consented to it.

A defender of Utility might protest that there is a morally significant difference between persons as opposed to property, and thus different moral principles govern the use of persons as opposed to property. On this view, what Albert does in Life Jacket may well be worse than what he does in Driftwood, but we shouldn't expect a principle like Utility to explain this difference—some other principle governing property rights will explain the difference. But this response seems inadequate. The wrongness of what Albert does in Life Jacket seems to be of the same type as other paradigmatic cases where someone is wrongfully harmed and used as a means. It would be a very strange coincidence if the moral principle that explains the difference between Driftwood and Life Jacket is entirely different than the principle that explains the difference between other puzzling cases like Switch and Overpass. It's much more plausible to suppose that the same moral principle can explain all these cases.

Unlike the principles canvassed in this section, the means principle accurately tracks the intuitive difference in all the relevant cases. It is the best candidate principle in terms of extensional adequacy. We can now consider its underlying rationale.

7.3 The Rationale

The means principle, recall, declares:

> It is morally wrong to harm Y in the pursuit of an objective if doing so involves using Y's body or other things over which Y has a rightful prior claim, unless Y is duty bound to suffer this harm, or has consented to this harm.

Although this principle coheres with most people's intuitions regarding the puzzling cases, some are sceptical that there is an independently plausible rationale for the principle. I believe this scepticism is misplaced. Once we think about the role that persons' rights over their bodies and other property play in securing a fair system of interaction between persons, we will see that rights against having one's body or other property harmfully exploited or appropriated are more stringent than rights against harm or destruction of property.

7.3.1 Mere Harm versus Harmful Use

It's instructive to begin with two potential rationales that do not succeed. First, consider the following explanation of the distinctive wrongness of harmful use: if Y is not duty bound to bear some cost, C, for the sake of goal, G, then it is wrong to impose C on Y for the sake of G. This rationale clearly fails since it gives us no reason to distinguish cases of harmful use from cases of mere harm. For example, it does not distinguish between Switch and Overpass. In both of these cases Betty is made to bear a cost that she is not duty bound to bear.

Now consider a rationale proposed by Tadros. He suggests that the distinctive problem with violating the means principle is that we 'compel [a victim] to act for the sake of some end that she is permitted to reject for herself'.[14] This rationale, however, confronts a dilemma when we try to give a more determinate account of what's involved in compelling someone to act for the sake of some end that she is permitted to reject. On the one hand, we could say that a person is compelled in this way whenever she is made to bear costs that she is not duty bound to bear. But this is simply the first answer, and we have already seen that this answer does not succeed. On the other hand, we could stipulate that a person is compelled in the relevant sense if and only if her body or other property is instrumental to achieve G, she is not duty bound to allow such use, and she does not consent to it. But this turns the explanation into a tautology. The notion of compelling a person to act for the sake of some end that she is permitted to reject for herself was supposed to be the independent explanation of why harmful use is distinctively wrong. Once we define the relevant sense of 'compelling' as harmful using, the explanation amounts to saying: harmful using is distinctively wrong because it involves harmful using. We're still missing the explanation of what's distinctively wrongful about harmful use as opposed to mere harm.

The best explanation, I believe, is grounded in a view about distributive justice and independence.[15] Principles of distributive justice allocate to each of us rights

---

[14] Tadros, *The Ends of Harm*, 127. The material in this paragraph summarizes an objection developed at greater length in Thomas Sinclair and Jonathan Quong, 'The Means Principle: Still in Need of a Rationale' (unpublished manuscript).

[15] Walen has recently developed a similar rationale that also places central emphasis on the independence of persons constituted by distributive principles. See Walen, 'The Restricting Claims Principle Revisited'. Although our accounts converge in several respects, they also diverge in a number of ways, some of which I note below.

to control our bodies and a fair share of other resources. These rights give us a significant degree of independence from others and reflect the fact that we each have our own plans and projects. They give each person exclusive normative authority over a fair share of the world's resources, as well as a fair share of the benefits and burdens arising from our social life. Of course justice also requires us to do our fair share, for example: pay some portion of our income in taxes for various public purposes; perform civic duties such as jury duty; and I believe it requires us to rescue others from serious harm when we can do so at reasonable cost to ourselves. But within the limits set out by the appropriate principles, we are free to use our body and other resources however we choose, and no one else can permissibly make use of our resources without our permission. This is constitutive of a fair system of interaction among free or independent persons.

Assume some part of the world, P, rightfully belongs to B according to the correct principles of distributive justice. To make use of P without B's consent is to appropriate some of B's fair share of control over the world, and is wrong for that reason. The fact that P would be useful to achieve some goal, G, simply cannot serve as a reason to use P without B's consent.[16] The very purpose of having rights to control a fair share of the world's resources is to block this fact from serving as a reason. To allow P's usefulness to serve as a reason to use P without B's consent is to give up on the idea that each person has a sphere of independence where her decisions are sovereign.

Compare this to cases of mere harming, that is, harming that does not violate the means principle. When A merely harms B, the justification for the act need not involve any assumption that B lacks authority to decide how her fair share of the world will be used. To be sure, B is harmed by A's act, and this fact is a reason for A to refrain. But claims against being harmed are defeasible—they must be weighed against other considerations. The fact that B will be harmed by A's act does not block or exclude the positive reasons in favour of the act. If claims not to be harmed played this role, we would all be hugely constrained in our ability to pursue many of our plans, since a vast array of acts incidentally cause some harm to others. But our rights to control our bodies and other resources are different. These rights block certain facts from serving as reasons for action. On my account, part of what it means for B to have a rightful claim over P is that the fact that P would be useful to achieve G cannot serve as a reason for others to use P without B's consent.

Let me dispel one possible misunderstanding. I'm not suggesting that claims of rightful ownership entail that one's body or property can never be used for the sake of rescuing others. As I made clear in Chapter 5, I believe there are duties to rescue others from serious harm when one can fulfil the duty at reasonable cost to

---

[16] Compare with Ramakrishnan's somewhat different formulation in 'Treating People as Tools', 148.

oneself. Suppose that B can rescue A at little cost to herself—she only needs to allow B the use of her spare life jacket. B is duty bound to allow A to use the life jacket, and so it is not true that B has rights to control the life jacket under these conditions. A full account of distributive or social justice includes the right to be rescued, and this right informs our account of when B has rights to control some part of the world, P. If B is duty bound to allow others to use P in conditions C, then B lacks the right to control P in conditions C. But if B has a prior claim to P and is not duty bound to allow others to use it in conditions C, then the fact that P would be useful to others cannot serve as a reason for others to use P without B's consent.

7.3.2 The Prohibition

Some favour a weak version of the means principle, one that does not prohibit harmful use but merely says that, other things being equal, it is more difficult to justify harmfully using a person than it is to merely harm a person.[17]

I believe, by contrast, that it is never permissible to violate the means principle. To see why, consider rights against being seriously harmed or killed in a way that doesn't violate the means principle. These rights are not sensitive to the aggregate or total costs that the duties may impose. The fact that many people might be harmed or killed if Albert doesn't kill Betty is irrelevant to the question of whether Betty has a right that Albert refrain from killing her. Because rights not to be seriously harmed or killed have this structure, these rights provide weighty pro tanto reasons for action, but they do not settle the question of what the duty bearer may permissibly do since the justification of these rights does not include the full range of moral considerations. In particular, these rights are justified without considering the reasons we have to rescue others from harm.

Rights to control our body and other resources, however, are different. The scope of these rights is sensitive to the total costs these rights can impose on others. In particular, the contours of these rights reflect the importance of saving others from harm. If Betty can use her body to save someone else from serious harm at relatively modest harm to herself, then she is duty bound to do so. Under these conditions, Betty lacks the right against her body being used in this way because this would impose too great a cost on another.

Our duties to use our bodies or resources to rescue others are also sensitive to the total number of others we can rescue. Suppose, for example, Betty is duty bound to use her body at some modest cost to herself, say 10 units of harm, to save

---

[17] Ramakrishnan and Walen, for example, each endorse a principle that has this feature, that is, the principle merely states that it is more difficult to justify using persons, but does not prohibit all harmful uses. See ibid., 134; and Walen, 'The Restricting Claims Principle Revisited', 212.

Albert from death. She is also duty bound to save Carl from death if she can do so at a cost of 10 units of harm, and the same is true of Debbie, and so on. Now suppose that Betty can use her body to save fifty people from death at a cost of 500 units of harm to herself. Betty may have a duty to bear this cost for the fifty others, since in doing so she only bears a small cost—one she is duty bound to bear—for the sake of each individual victim. Whether Betty is in fact duty bound to do so will depend on several further questions. One is how exactly the costs we can be duty bound to bear for the sake of others are aggregated. Another is whether there is some maximum amount of harm a person can be duty bound to suffer in a rescue, regardless of how much good can be achieved via the rescue. Some believe, for example, that no person can be duty bound to suffer death for the sake of others, no matter how many others might be saved. Others believe that there is, in principle, no upper limit to the sacrifices we can be required to make for others if the numbers are large enough. I take no position on this issue (or the preceding one) here. What matters is the structural point that the extent of our rights to control our bodies and other resources depends on the extent to which possessing these rights imposes costs on others.

With this picture in hand, we can now return to our original question: Why is it never permissible to violate the means principle? The answer is that the harms that others might suffer have been taken into account in determining the scope of our rights to control our bodies and other resources. Suppose Betty has the right to control P in circumstances C, even though this means five innocent people may suffer harm. If Betty has the right to control P, this means Betty is not duty bound to use P (or allow P to be used) to rescue the five. Now suppose Albert violates the means principle in C, and harmfully uses Betty's P to save the five. In doing so, Albert is necessarily mistaken about the balance of moral reasons. He acts as if saving the five is sufficiently important that it justifies Betty losing the right to control P in these circumstances. But this is false. If it were true, then Albert's act wouldn't be a violation of the means principle; Betty would be duty bound to permit others to use P in these conditions. Violations of the means principle necessarily involve making this sort of mistake about the balance of reasons, and this is why such violations cannot be permissible.

A sceptic might respond that the preceding argument depends on a mistake. According to the sceptic, Albert may have a *combined justification* for violating the means principle. Suppose Betty is duty bound to bear a maximum of 100 units of harm to use her body to save five people from 1,000 units of harm. But suppose Betty can only save the five at a cost of 200 units of harm, and this is why she is not duty bound to save them. On the sceptic's view, since Betty is duty bound to bear 100 units of harm, Betty can have no complaint against the imposition of this level of harm. Thus, the choice Albert faces is whether to impose 100 additional units of harm on Betty that she is not duty bound to bear, or else allow the five to suffer 1,000 units of harm. There is a lesser evil justification for imposing this additional

100 units on Betty, and so the combination of lesser evil and Betty's duty of rescue explains why Albert can permissibly act contrary to the means principle.

I think we should reject this proposal. Lesser evil justifications can be used to justify imposing harm on innocent people, but they cannot be deployed to justify using another person's body or resources for the reasons I've already outlined. If Betty has the right to control her body under these conditions, this precludes Albert from taking the fact that Betty's body would be useful in saving the five as a reason to use Betty's body. By hypothesis, no single member of the five can reasonably demand that Betty bear 40 units of harm to rescue him. In violating the means principle, Albert would thus be harmfully using Betty's body in a way that none of the people he rescues can reasonably demand of Betty. Every violation of the means principle has this feature, and that's why all such violations are wrong.[18]

7.3.3 The Irrelevance of Intentions

Before turning to consider some objections to the means principle, let me draw attention to one of its most important features. Whether an agent violates or complies with the means principle is not determined by the intentions or motives of the agent.[19] Unlike the DDE, we need not ask whether the agent intends or merely foresees harm, nor need we inquire whether the agent intends to use a person or her property. Instead, what matters is whether the outcome that ostensibly justifies the agent's act (e.g., saving the five in Overpass) requires using some person or her property. If it does, then the principle has been violated regardless of whether the agent intended either the harm or the use. Suppose, for example, that Albert does not intend to harm Betty in Overpass. Suppose he unjustifiably believes that Betty will be entirely unharmed when the trolley hits her. Albert's false and unjustified belief means he does not intend to harm Betty.

---

[18] The sceptic may protest that when we consider cases where the additional amount of harm imposed on Betty (i.e., the amount over and above what she is duty bound to bear) is trivial, it is even clearer that a combined justification can justify Albert's contravention of the means principle. For example, suppose Betty is duty bound to bear 100 units of harm to rescue the five, but the five can only be rescued if Albert uses Betty's body and in doing so imposes 101 units of harm on her. Surely, says the sceptic, the one additional unit over and above what Betty is duty bound to bear cannot render Albert's act impermissible—the additional unit imposed will avert 1,000 units of harm and thus there is an undeniable lesser evil justification. But I think the structure of this example is illusory. If the one additional unit Betty might bear is so trivial, and so obviously justified in light of the massive benefits to the five, then why assume Betty is not duty bound to bear it? For the sceptic's argument to succeed, there must be some amount of harm that could be imposed on Betty by using her body or property, which it's clear she is not duty bound to allow, and yet where it seems clear Albert has a lesser evil justification for harmfully using her. I deny such cases exist.

[19] In this respect I agree with Walen. See Walen, 'The Restricting Claims Principle Revisited', 218–19.

But he still violates the means principle; he harmfully uses Betty's body to save the five.

Some might find this conception of the means principle puzzling. Surely, a sceptic might say, whether you wrongfully treat someone as a means must depend on what you intend, or what your attitude is with regard to the person in question. The sceptic is mistaken, however, and we can see this by reflecting on other forms of treatment. Consider some questions we might ask about how you were treated: 'Did he treat you politely?' 'Did she treat you as her employee or as her boyfriend?' 'Were you treated as a patient or as a customer?' In all of these cases, I think it's clear that what is being asked is whether an agent's behaviour conformed to a standard of conduct that is independent of the agent's intentions. A person may treat you politely even if her actual intentions are malicious. A person can treat you as her boyfriend even if her intention was to treat you as an employee. And patients in hospitals can be treated as customers without any of the staff intending to do so. Whether our treatment of another person violates a particular moral standard often depends only on various objective facts. Did we raise our voices? Did we make a sexual comment in a workplace environment? Regardless of what we intend to do, we can violate moral standards and thereby treat others wrongfully when we fail to respond correctly to the reasons that apply to us.[20]

When an agent violates the means principle, he acts *as if* the victim was under a duty to allow her body or property to be used despite the harm she would suffer. Since the victim is not under such a duty, the agent wrongfully treats the victim as a means. He behaves as if her body or other property could rightly be used as an instrument in the service of some objective. Even if the agent did not have this intention or attitude, his act still has this moral feature since the permissibility of his act depends on the premise that the victim is under the relevant duty. In Overpass, for example, the only thing that could render toppling Betty in front of the oncoming trolley permissible would be if Betty is under a duty to have her body used in this way. Since Betty is not under such a duty, Albert wrongfully harms her as a means, regardless of his intention.

The conception of the means principle I am defending is, in this way, revisionary. But the revision brings important advantages. Most importantly, it more clearly identifies the distinct wrongfulness at issue in cases where the means principle is violated. When an agent violates the means principle, he behaves as if other people's fair share of the world is available to be used in the service of some

---

[20] This is not to deny that sometimes our attitudes and intentions also play a role in the moral assessment of our conduct. For example, sometimes we have role-based obligations, or relational obligations, to refrain from taking certain reasons into account when we act (e.g., it matters whether an employer was motivated by inappropriate racist reasons when choosing among applicants). It's also true that the expressive dimension of an act is sometimes partly determined by an agent's motivating reasons for action, for example, an insincere apology fails to express the appropriate attitude. For a more detailed discussion, see Scanlon, *Moral Dimensions*, chap. 2.

goal. Treating others in this way disregards the moral independence or freedom of persons. It disregards the fact that a just world is one where each person has a sphere of independence, where each can decide for themselves, within limits, how to use their fair share of the world's resources.

7.4 Objections

I now turn to consider some objections.

7.4.1 Why Should the Victim Care?

Recall Scanlon's scepticism about the means principle: 'being a means in this sense—being causally necessary—has no intrinsic moral significance, in my view. What matters is the cost to the person involved, and the claim that person has to be informed about the nature of his involvement.'[21] To put it more bluntly, why do you care if you are killed as a means or as a side effect of someone else's act? You're dead either way.

But the means principle that I've proposed can easily answer this worry. First, each of us has a greater degree of independence from others when our bodies and rightful property are immune from being used without our consent. Of course, this constraint does not protect us from being harmed by others, but that doesn't undermine the point. The means principle affords each of us a greater degree of independence relative to a world where others can appropriate our bodies and property whenever this would be widely proportionate. Second, the means principle is partly a reflection of what it is to live with others on fair terms. The principles of distributive justice allocate to each person control over a fair share of the world's resources. To live on fair terms with others is to respect the fact that other people's bodies and properties are not available to be used whenever it would be socially beneficial to do so. If someone else is not duty bound to use her body or resources to help others, then if we appropriate her body or resources regardless, we treat her unfairly: we seize more than our fair share of control over the world. Each person has a powerful interest in living with others on fair terms, and so this is another way in which the means principle matters to potential victims.

7.4.2 Counterfactual Concerns

In Chapter 3 I suggested that whether X's act of self-defence involves the wrongful use of Y's body or other resources can be determined by considering a

---

[21] Ibid., 118.

counterfactual: Would X be safe without Y and anything belonging to Y? If the act of self-defence that X performs cannot succeed without Y or other things over which Y has claims, then the act violates the means principle. This counterfactual test invites several objections.

First, consider a case where X makes use of Y's body; suppose he uses Y's body as a shield to stop a lethal projectile. Suppose that had Y not been on the scene that day, some other person, Z, would have been there instead, and X would have been able to make effective use of Z's body. If this is the case, then the success of X's act does not depend on Y's body or other property being available, and thus X apparently does not violate the means principle when he harmfully uses Y's body.[22] But this conclusion is clearly unacceptable.

This objection, however, depends on a misunderstanding. The counterfactual test is not one where we imagine all the various ways the world might be changed if Y is not present. There are several reasons to resist this way of understanding the counterfactual. First, this formulation of the counterfactual is indeterminate, and there is no nonarbitrary way of resolving the indeterminacy. When we imagine that Y is not present, how do we explain his absence? Did he make a decision to be elsewhere? If so, where is Y located in the counterfactual and how does this affect the rest of the world? Or do we more dramatically suppose that Y does not exist at all in the counterfactual world? There is no nonarbitrary way to resolve these questions, but which counterfactual world is selected may have a decisive effect on whether X's act would succeed without Y. Second, such a counterfactual test doesn't track the morally relevant feature that is central to the means principle. What matters is whether, in the current world, the success of X's act requires Y's body. Even if X could have performed a similar act in a close possible world without Y, this doesn't change the fact that, in this world, the success of the particular act X performs requires the use of Y's body.

The appropriate counterfactual test is thus one where everything is held constant except for the removal of Y and Y's property. We aren't asking what the world would really look like without Y and his property—undoubtedly removing Y and his property would cause further changes. We're rather interested in a very narrow question: Given the world as it currently is, does the particular act X performs require the instrumental use of Y's body or other resources? To answer this question we only need to make one change: remove Y and his property. Once the counterfactual test is understood in this way, the initial objection no longer applies.[23]

---

[22] For a case with this structure see Walen, 'Transcending the Means Principle', 224.

[23] Suppose X can achieve goal G by harmfully using any one of several innocent people who happen to be present, and he arbitrarily selects Y. It might seem the means principle cannot condemn his act since he could have achieved G just as easily by using Z instead. But cases like this also don't present a problem. The particular act X performs that involves Y cannot succeed without Y, and thus it's condemned by the means principle. The fact that he could have performed some other wrongful act

A different worry is that the counterfactual test lacks a principled way of handling cases where the harm-imposing agent needs to use physical space in a way that threatens a potential victim. In Chapter 3, recall, I argued that we typically have prior claims to the space our bodies occupy.[24] This explains why you violate the means principle if you remove the person from the alcove in Alcove. You need the alcove space to survive, but the person already in the alcove has a prior claim to the space. Taking the space is thus wrongfully using something that doesn't belong to you.

But sceptics argue that this proposal runs into difficulty when we consider other cases.[25] For example, in Switch, Albert redirects a runaway trolley away from five innocent people and onto a side track where it will kill only one innocent person, Betty. Everyone agrees that Albert does not violate the means principle in this case. But it might seem that my account struggles to reach this conclusion. After all, why not say that Betty has a prior claim to all the space on the side track, and thus Albert needs space that belongs to Betty to redirect the trolley? To explain the difference between cases like Switch and Alcove, we need a principled account of the extent of physical space over which a person can have a prior claim. The sceptic argues that there is no such principled account available.

I disagree. If another person or object could occupy some non-private space, S1, without causing harm to the potential victim, then the victim doesn't have a claim over S1. In Alcove (and variants like Alcove Crush), it's not possible for you to occupy the space in the alcove without harming the person already inside, hence the person has a prior claim to the whole space. In Switch, by contrast, it's clearly possible for the trolley to occupy part of the side track without harming Betty (e.g., if the trolley suddenly stopped once redirected, Betty would be fine), thus she doesn't have a prior claim over the entire side track. She only has a prior claim over the part of the track where the trolley cannot be located without causing her harm.

Frowe considers a version of this solution, but argues that it has an unacceptable implication: the permissibility of Albert's turning the trolley in Switch will depend on where Betty is located on the side track.[26] If Betty is far enough down the side track, then turning the trolley is permissible since there will be sufficient

---

using Z does not change the fact that the particular act he performed required the instrumental use of Y. The same point can be made with regard to alternative *permissible* acts X could have performed to achieve G. The fact that X had some alternative permissible way of achieving G does not alter the fact that the act he chose to perform required the use of Y to achieve G.

[24] I am setting aside, here, any independent claims over space (e.g., private property claims or promissory claims).

[25] For versions of this objection, see Kimberly Kessler Ferzan, 'Self-Defense, Permissions, and the Means Principle: A Reply to Quong', *Ohio State Journal of Criminal Law* 8, no. 2 (2011): 513; and Frowe, *Defensive Killing*, 58–62.

[26] Frowe, *Defensive Killing*, 61–2.

track for the trolley to occupy part of the track before it reaches Betty. But if Betty is located immediately after the junction, such that the trolley will hit her before it has been completely diverted onto the side track, then Albert does use space belonging to Betty and diverting the trolley is impermissible. Frowe denies that the permissibility of redirecting the trolley should depend on Betty's location in this way.

Unlike Frowe, however, I don't find this implication of the means principle to be problematic. Whether we impermissibly harm someone, or use that person as a means, often depends on where the person is located. All versions of the means principle, and all versions of the DDE, allow that the permissibility of our acts can depend on where a potential victim is located, since a person's location can determine whether their body or property is required in order for the action to succeed.[27]

Here is one further worry about the counterfactual test. In some cases, the threat a defensive agent faces may be overdetermined. Consider the following case:[28]

Overdetermined: Albert straps innocent Carl to a large boulder and launches them towards Betty who is trapped at the bottom of a well. Either the boulder or

---

[27] Partly as a result of some of the objections described in this subsection, Walen argues that we should reject any version of the means principle that relies on a counterfactual test where we ask what would happen if the victim and his property were absent. See Walen, 'The Restricting Claims Principle Revisited', 222–8. On Walen's view, what matters is not whether the success of the agent's act depends on the presence of the victim or the victim's property. Rather, what matters is whether the agent makes use only of those items that belong in her 'toolkit' (i.e., those things she is morally entitled to control given the circumstances). Victims have less stringent claims against being harmed by agents who use only items in their toolkit, as compared to agents who make use of items outside of their toolkit. To illustrate this difference between our views, consider the following case (Walen presents a somewhat similar case in ibid., 222):

> *Switch with Button*: There is a runaway trolley whose brakes have failed headed down a track where five people are trapped and will be killed unless the trolley is diverted. There is a side track onto which the trolley can be diverted, but there is one person, Betty, trapped on this side track, and she will be killed if the trolley is diverted. The switch that can divert the trolley onto the side track has an unusual failsafe mechanism: it only works if a button on the side track is being pressed down. Betty's body is currently serving to press down on the button and she is unable to move. Albert, an innocent passerby, has seen and understood the whole situation and he uses the switch to redirect the trolley.

On Walen's view, as I understand it, this case is roughly analogous to the standard Switch case. Albert does not make use of Betty's body to turn the trolley. Betty's death is thus, on his account, a mere side effect of an act where Albert uses only things in his toolkit. On my view, however, this case is relevantly analogous to Overpass, and thus a violation of the means principle. Just like in Overpass, Albert needs Betty's body to achieve the good outcome of saving the five: Betty's body is instrumental to the success of the act. I think this means that Albert does make harmful use of Betty in the morally relevant sense. Unlike Walen, I thus don't think we can dispense with a version of the counterfactual test. Whether an agent's act makes use of a victim depends on whether the good outcome that purportedly justifies the act can be achieved without the victim and her property.

[28] I am grateful to Jonathan Parry for pressing me to consider the objection that this case motivates.

Carl would, on their own, be sufficient to kill Betty. Betty will thus be killed unless she vaporizes Carl and the boulder with a ray gun she finds at the bottom of the well. The ray gun, however, belongs to Carl.

My formulation of the means principle apparently prohibits Betty from using the ray gun to save herself, since if Carl and his property were absent, she would still face the lethal threat posed by the boulder. Some may find this result counterintuitive.

I, however, accept this implication of my view. Betty faces a lethal threat (the boulder), and she cannot save herself from this threat without using something that belongs to Carl while also shifting the harm of death onto Carl. The fact that Carl also poses a threat to her is not of fundamental moral significance since he is not responsible for posing this threat. What matters is the fact that she cannot save herself without using things that do not belong to her. If Carl was, for example, a bystander who would somehow be killed by Betty's use of his ray gun to destroy the boulder, Betty's use of the ray gun would be a clear violation of the means principle. Shifting Carl's physical position so that he also poses a non-responsible threat makes no moral difference.

7.4.3 Too Restrictive

Some believe that the means principle is too restrictive. Consider the following case, offered by Ramakrishnan:

> *Room*: Five people and one other person, Archibald, are suffering from a deadly virus. Waldo has enough medicine to save the five or to save Archibald, but not both. For Archibald has an especially malicious strain of the virus, and curing him would thus require Waldo's entire stock of medicine. Archibald's legs are in the doorway to theroom that contains the five, keeping the door ajar; if Archibald's legs were not in the doorway, the five people would be inaccessible to Waldo, and Waldo would be unable to treat them. Waldo chooses to save the five instead of Archibald.[29]

It might appear that Waldo harmfully uses Archibald to secure a greater good that he could not secure without him. Moreover, it doesn't seem plausible to suppose that Archibald is under a duty to die for the sake of the five. The means principle

---

[29] Ramakrishnan, 'Treating People as Tools', 146. Ramakrishnan presents this case as a counter-example to a slightly different formulation of the means principle than the one defended here.

thus apparently prohibits what Waldo does in Room, but Ramakrishnan says that this is the wrong result: Waldo's act is permissible.

This objection, however, does not succeed. Waldo does not harm Archibald, he merely fails to save him, and thus his act is not prohibited by the means principle. The means principle does not prohibit failures to save a victim unless the victim has a right to be rescued or provided with resources. Thus, the means principle only prohibits Waldo's act in Room if Archibald has a right to the medicine or a right to be rescued by Archibald.

Ramakrishnan anticipates a version of this response, but denies that it succeeds, since he apparently believes that Waldo's act of saving the five would still be permissible even if Archibald has a prior right to the medicine.[30] But I disagree. If we imagine a variant where Archibald has a right to the medicine (e.g., imagine Waldo has sold the medicine to Archibald and arrives to deliver it, only to discover the five in the room also need it) then it's no longer intuitive to suppose Waldo acts permissibly in giving the medicine to the five—doing this would be no different than stealing another person's lifesaving medical equipment and giving it to others.

7.4.4 Too Permissive

Others object that the means principle is unduly permissive. Consider the following case:[31]

> *Sneeze*: Albert and Betty are hiding from a wrongful attacker. The attacker aims to kill Albert, but only aims to take Betty's wallet. Albert and Betty have found a perfectly safe hiding spot where the attacker will not find them unless they reveal their location. Unfortunately, Betty is about to involuntarily sneeze and reveal their location. Albert realizes that the only way to save his life is to use his silent weapon to kill Betty before she sneezes.

The critic claims that it is intuitively wrong for Albert to kill Betty but that his doing so is not condemned by the means principle. After all, if Betty were not present, Albert would be safe.

I think this is a case where our initial intuitive reactions can lead us astray. It's very difficult to be certain that we are reacting to the case as it is described—in particular, that Albert can be sure that he must kill Betty to avoid being detected. I suspect it may seem intuitively wrong for Albert to kill Betty because many of us find it difficult to imagine Albert can be so sure, and instead we react as if Albert

---

[30] See ibid., 146.
[31] Frowe presents a version of this objection. See Frowe, *Defensive Killing*, 63.

cannot have the requisite degree of confidence that killing Betty is necessary to avoid being killed himself. After all, in any realistic scenario, Albert cannot be sure that Betty will sneeze, he cannot be sure how loudly she will sneeze, and he cannot be sure that the sneeze will reveal their location.

If we are careful to imagine a version of the case where there is no doubt at all that Betty's involuntary act will cause Albert's death, I think it's no longer counter-intuitive to suppose that Albert may kill Betty. Consider the following case:

> *Blink*: A wrongful attacker has decided to threaten Albert's life in an unusual way. He has rigged a perfectly functioning bomb that will detonate and kill Albert, who is trapped and cannot move. But the bomb will only detonate if it is triggered, and the trigger is Betty's blinking, though Betty is unaware of any of this. Albert knows that it is impossible for a human being to refrain from blinking indefinitely. The only way for Albert to save himself is to vaporize Betty using his ray gun before she blinks.

I do not find it intuitively impermissible for Albert to kill Betty, but the case is relevantly analogous to the first case. The only difference is that the details have been altered to make it clearer that Betty's involuntary act will certainly cause Albert to be killed. In both cases Betty is a non-responsible threat, and I've already argued it is permissible to kill non-responsible threats for agent-relative reasons. Sneeze is thus not a troubling counterexample to the means principle.

7.4.5 Property Rights Are Different

Some may object that the means principle errs in treating claims over property in the same way as claims over the body. Even if it is wrong for Albert to use Betty's body as a means when she is not duty bound to allow this use, surely it is not always wrong for him to use her property as a means? There's a morally important difference, says the sceptic, between using a person and using some other part of the physical world over which the person has a claim.

This objection is not plausible. Rights over our bodies may seem to be different in kind when compared to rights over external resources because we tend to associate the most severe harms with violations of bodily integrity. But the connection is a contingent one. We can sometimes cause much graver harm by taking a person's property rather than violating the person's rights over her body. You can, for example, kill someone by stealing her medication, or stealing the money she needs to buy some lifesaving equipment. As I suggested in Chapter 4, the stringency of a moral right is determined by the severity of harm that would befall the right-holder in the event of an infringement and the way the right protects or reflects the status of the right-holder. When we focus on these variables we can see that rights over our bodies are not, in principle, more stringent than rights over property.

7.4.6 Intentions and Puzzling Cases

Consider the following pair of cases:

> *Intending to Save Five*: There is a runaway trolley headed towards five people who are trapped on the main track, and the trolley will kill these people unless it is stopped or diverted. Fortunately, there is a side track on to which the trolley can be diverted, though Betty is trapped on this side track and will be killed if the trolley is diverted. Albert is a bystander who has seen and understood everything, and stands next to the switch that can divert the trolley. Albert diverts the trolley onto the side track with the intention of saving the five people from being killed.

> *Intending to Kill One*: There is a runaway trolley headed towards five people who are trapped on the main track, and the trolley will kill these people unless it is stopped or diverted. Fortunately, there is a side track on to which the trolley can be diverted, though Betty is trapped on this side track and will be killed if the trolley is diverted. Albert is a bystander who has seen and understood everything, and stands next to the switch that can divert the trolley. Albert has always hated Betty, and so he diverts the trolley on to the side track with the intention of murdering Betty.

Most people believe that Albert acts permissibly in Intending to Save Five. But some are likely to hold that Albert acts impermissibly in Intending to Kill One.[32] My account of the means principle, however, does not distinguish between these cases since it eschews any appeal to the agent's intentions. My general position might thus seem doubly problematic. First, unlike the DDE, it cannot distinguish between the cases. Second, because I generally deny the relevance of the agent's intentions in determining permissibility in cases of harm imposition, I am committed to the apparently counterintuitive implication that Albert acts permissibly in Intending to Kill One.

My response to the first of these worries is to deny that pairs like this are good cases for evaluating competing principles that purport to explain the puzzling cases. As I noted at the outset, a number of non-consequentialists deny that intentions make a difference to permissibility in the way assumed by the DDE. We should thus avoid relying on intuitions about such disputed cases when evaluating alternative moral principles that purport to explain the puzzling

---

[32] See Tadros, *The Ends of Harm*, 156–7.

cases—doing so involves appealing to intuitions that may not be that widely shared among non-consequentialists. Instead we should appeal to judgements about pairs of cases that are widely endorsed by non-consequentialists, including both proponents and sceptics of the DDE. When we consider only *these* cases—for example, Switch and Overpass, or Strategic Bomber and Terror Bomber—the means principle can explain the intuitive differences.

This response, however, will not satisfy our sceptic. In particular, the sceptic is likely to insist that we cannot ignore how counterintuitive it is to say that Albert acts permissibly in Intending to Kill One. Commonsense morality tells us that if you kill an innocent person simply because you hate that person, you have murdered the person and acted wrongly. Since my general view cannot reach this conclusion in this case, my view must be rejected.

Although superficially powerful, I believe this objection should be resisted. In the vast majority of cases where one person kills another for bad reasons—hate or jealousy or greed—there is no lesser evil justification for the agent's act. When one gang member murders another for profit, or when a husband murders his wife in a jealous rage, or when someone is murdered as part of a racially motivated attack, there are typically no important good consequences brought about by the agent's act. It's thus understandable that we might adopt the general rule that killing someone for such bad reasons is always impermissible; we simply aren't accustomed to considering cases like Intending to Kill One. When we do consider such unusual cases, we may understandably have the same reaction that we have in 'standard' cases of wrongful murder: we identify the act of killing and the bad intention, and conclude that the act must be impermissible. But this may be the misapplication of an otherwise good rule of thumb.

Part of the difficulty may be that our judgements about cases like Intending to Save Five are already a bit uncertain; at least some people aren't sure that it really is permissible to turn the trolley even with the best of intentions. So let's consider a case where the act is more uncontroversially permissible, at least when performed with the correct intentions:

> *Murders Averted*: Betty is about to murder two innocent people for the sake of an inheritance. Albert is aware of all the facts, and he realizes that the only way to save the lives of the innocent people is if he shoots and kills Betty. He shoots and kills Betty.

I suspect, given the description of the case, most people will agree that Albert acts permissibly in killing Betty. After all, doing so is the only way to save two innocent people from being murdered, and Betty is liable to defensive killing. The important point for our purposes is that my description of the case made no mention of Albert's intentions in shooting Betty. Readers might naturally assume that Albert shoots Betty with the aim of saving the innocent people, but this information wasn't provided, and it doesn't seem necessary to provoke the intuition that Albert acts permissibly.

Now consider four variants of the case. In the first version, Albert's only aim is to save the innocent people. In the second version, Albert's intention is to impress a girl that he likes. This girl has previously expressed admiration for 'tough guys' who have used weapons and killed people. Albert's primary intention is thus to impress the girl—he uses this particular opportunity to do it because he believes the facts of the case provide him with an opportunity to kill someone without getting in moral or legal trouble. If killing Betty didn't impress the girl, Albert would do nothing. In the third version of the story, Albert kills Betty because he hates her. He believes this is his opportunity to kill her without getting in moral or legal trouble. He would not kill her if he thought doing so in the circumstances was morally or legally prohibited. To borrow a distinction from Kamm, he shoots *in order* to give violent expression to his hatred of Betty, but also only *because* doing so will avert the murders.[33] In the final version of the case, Albert shoots Betty because he hates her. He would have shot her even if she were not about to commit the murders. His averting the murders is a foreseen but unintended consequence of his act.

Everyone, bar pacifists, agrees that Albert acts permissibly in the first version of the case. I also suspect that almost everyone will agree he acts permissibly in the second version of the case. His motives aren't praiseworthy; indeed it might be that he shows a blameworthy indifference regarding the lives of others, but he still acts to avert two murders and he doesn't intend to harm anyone he believes to be non-liable. But if we agree that Albert acts permissibly in this version of the case, it's difficult to see why he doesn't act permissibly in the third version. After all, in this variant Albert shoots only on the condition that shooting will avert the murders and thus his act is (at least Albert believes) morally and legally permissible. It's true that his act is motivated by his hatred of Betty, and he clearly can be condemned for this fact. But the most natural thing to say in this version of the case is that he does the right thing for the wrong reasons. Moreover, since Albert shoots Betty only on the condition that this averts the murders, averting the murders is one of Albert's aims. To be clear, I don't believe that Albert's intention or aim does affect the permissibility of what he does in Murders Averted. But those who believe intentions do bear on permissibility should believe that Albert acts permissibly even in this variant of the case since one of his main aims in acting is the good aim of averting the murders. If intentions bear on permissibility, then an agent who aims at the outcome that would (intentions aside) be sufficient to justify a harmful act—call this the *justifying property*—must act permissibly. Some neo-Kantians might insist that this isn't enough, that we must aim only at

---

[33] Kamm, *Intricate Ethics*, 92.

the justifying properties of an act and never have any ulterior motives in order for our acts to be permissible, but this is an extreme and implausible view. A shopkeeper who aims to give her customer the correct change, but does so only because she calculates that this will be good for her reputation, does not act impermissibly despite the motive.

The final version of the case is the one where intuitions are most likely to diverge. In this case Albert does not have the good aim of saving the two innocent people—he merely foresees this consequence. For proponents of the DDE, this makes all the difference, whereas I believe, along with other sceptics of the DDE, that this makes no difference to the permissibility of what Albert does. I'm not sure that any decisive argument is capable of resolving this disagreement. I will instead make two more modest points.

First, as I've already suggested, there are many instances where our wrongful treatment of others is not necessarily determined by our aims or intentions. We can treat others rudely or disrespectfully without intending to do so. Indeed, we can do so even if we have the opposite intentions. Just as we can treat others badly despite the best of intentions, I think we can accord others the treatment they are owed despite having bad intentions. This is what happens in cases like the final variant of Murders Averted. Albert has sufficient reasons to justify killing Betty, and thus if he kills Betty, his behaviour conforms to the standard of morally permissible conduct.[34] The fact that these reasons aren't the ones that motivate Albert is irrelevant in much the same way that a person's intentions can be irrelevant in determining whether she was rude or made a racist remark. Those who hold that an agent's bad intentions can make otherwise permissible acts (like Albert's killing Betty in Murders Averted) impermissible must explain why they do not typically hold that good intentions can make otherwise impermissible acts (being rude or making a racist remark) morally permissible. I am sceptical that it's possible to provide a plausible explanation of this puzzling asymmetry in the way intentions are alleged to bear on the permissibility of acts.[35]

Second, my primary aim in discussing Murders Averted is simply to cast some doubt on the objection that the means principle yields unacceptably counter-intuitive results in cases like Intending to Kill One. That allegation, I speculate, might hinge on some uncertainty about the permissibility of killing an innocent person. When we reflect on a case like Murders Averted, where there is no doubt that Albert acts permissibly if he acts with an appropriate aim, it is also less counterintuitive to suppose that he acts permissibly when he has bad intentions.

---

[34] Compare the suggestion here to Kamm's principle of alternate reason. Kamm, *Intricate Ethics*, 135.

[35] I develop this objection at greater length in 'Intentions and Permissibility: A Puzzling Asymmetry' (unpublished manuscript).

7.4.7 Poisoned Pipe

But consider the following case, provided by Tadros:

> *Poisoned Pipe*: Boss offers a reward of £1,000 to anyone who kills Victim. If more
> than one person kills Victim, the reward will be divided between them. Two
> henchmen, A and B, independently find different points in the water pipe leading
> to Victim's home. A puts sufficient poison in the pipe to kill Victim. At the same
> time, B puts sufficient poison in the pipe to kill Victim. Each sees what the other
> is doing. A's poison alone or B's poison alone would lead to a very slow and
> painful death for Victim. Their poison together kills Victim swiftly.[36]

As Tadros says, the two henchmen are not acting in concert: they would each
prefer to be the sole poisoner and collect the entire reward. Tadros argues that this
case provides support for the relevance of intentions to permissibility. He says the
commonsense conclusion is that both henchmen act impermissibly. But we must
appeal to their intentions to reach this verdict. If we change the case and stipulate
that one person puts poison in the pipe purely to avert Victim's suffering, this
person is, presumably, doing something permissible.

This case does not, however, provide support for the relevance of intentions to
permissibility. Instead I think it provides support for a different thesis, namely,
that groups can act impermissibly even if each individual acts permissibly.[37] A's
act of putting poison in the pipe is permissible since B will put poison in the pipe
regardless of what A does. And B's act of putting poison in the pipe is permissible
since A will put poison in the pipe regardless of what B does. Of course they
together should agree not to put any poison in the pipe. Although they are not
coordinating, we can still say that collectively they act wrongly.

Poisoned Pipe thus belongs to a more general class of cases, such as the
Prisoner's Dilemma, where each individual has sufficient reason to φ (holding
constant the behaviour of others) even though this causes an outcome that is bad
and could be avoided if enough people acted differently. Following Alexander
Dietz, I think these cases show that there are reasons for action that apply to
groups of people and these reasons cannot be reduced to individual reasons for
action. When a morally bad outcome is overdetermined because of the actions of
many others, it may not be wrong for you, qua individual, to contribute to the
outcome, even though we together ought to have acted differently. For example,
suppose most other people aren't going to reduce their carbon footprint, and this
is sufficient to cause catastrophic global warming. Under these conditions, your

---

[36] Tadros, *The Ends of Harm*, 159.
[37] Here I draw on Alexander Dietz's work on collective reasons. See Dietz, 'What We Together
Ought to Do', *Ethics* 126, no. 4 (2016): 955–82.

failure to reduce your carbon footprint may not be wrong—doing so won't make a difference, but it will impose a cost on you. But it is impermissible for all of us qua collective to fail to reduce our carbon footprint. I thus do not believe that Poisoned Pipe shows that intentions must be relevant to permissibility in cases of this kind.

Moreover, if we increase the moral stakes in Poisoned Pipe, I doubt many people will share Tadros's view that the two henchmen each act impermissibly:

> *Poisoned Pipe and Fumes*: Boss offers a reward of £1,000 to anyone who kills Victim. If more than one person kills Victim, the reward will be divided between them. Two henchmen, A and B, independently find different points in the water pipe leading to Victim's home. A puts sufficient poison in the pipe to kill Victim. At the same time, B puts sufficient poison in the pipe to kill Victim. Each sees what the other is doing. A's poison alone or B's poison alone would be sufficient to kill Victim (Victim's degree of suffering is the same regardless of whether one or both put poison in the water). But the poison in the water also generates fumes with the following effects. If one dose of poison is put in the water, the resulting fumes will kill Neighbour. But if two doses of poison are put in the water, the resulting fumes are nontoxic and Neighbour will be fine. Both henchmen are aware of these further effects, but neither cares what happens to Neighbour.

Here is what we should say about this case. Each henchmen acts permissibly (indeed each is morally required to put poison in the water) given the other will put poison in the water regardless. A must put his poison in the water to save Neighbour, and the same is true of B. But of course what they together should do is not put any poison in the water, thereby killing no one. But if one is going to act regardless, the other must, and vice versa. But if you share Tadros's view that each henchmen acts impermissibly in the original Poisoned Pipe case, then you must hold that each henchmen acts impermissibly in this case as well. I do not find this at all plausible.

Although I don't think the intentions of the henchmen are relevant to assessing the permissibility of what they each do, qua individual, cases like this do show that our conception of liability to defensive force must extend to include groups or collectives.

7.5 Some Implications

What are the implications of the means principle for the morality of defensive force? One implication has already been discussed at length in Chapter 3. In that chapter I argued that it's sometimes permissible to use defensive force against justified attackers and non-responsible threats in part because this can typically be done without violating the means principle. We are not morally required to allow non-responsible threats to harm or kill us when we possess the means to save ourselves. But there are further implications.

The means principle not only prohibits the harmful use of other people's bodies when they aren't duty bound to permit this use; it also prohibits the harmful use of others' property, which includes the physical space that others permissibly occupy. In this respect, the means principle prohibits a wider range of acts than many competing principles. Recall a case introduced earlier:

> *Large Alcove Crush*: Five innocent people are in a tunnel. A villain has sent a runaway trolley towards them and it will kill them if they do not escape. They can only escape the trolley by jumping into an alcove in the tunnel. Unfortunately, there is already a large man in the alcove. The five could jump into the alcove, which would keep them safe from the oncoming trolley, but doing so would also crush and kill the large man since the alcove is too small to safely accommodate anyone apart from the large man.

In this case the five cannot save themselves without making use of physical space to which the large man has a prior claim, and he is not duty bound to allow this use at the cost of his life. The means principle thus prohibits the five from jumping into the alcove and crushing the man already inside. Alternative principles do not. Kamm's Doctrine of Productive Purity (DPP) does not prohibit this act since crushing the person is the noncausal flipside of the five being safe inside the alcove. Ramakrishnan's Utility principle does not prohibit jumping into the alcove, since his principle only restricts the use of persons' bodies: external resources are explicitly excluded from the principle's scope.[38] And the DDE also does not prohibit the five from jumping into the alcove, since the five need not intend to harm the large man inside: they merely intend to enter the alcove, though they foresee that doing so will crush the man inside.[39]

This implication of the means principle extends beyond stylized examples involving trolleys and alcoves. Consider the following somewhat more realistic case:

---

[38] Ramakrishnan, 'Treating People as Tools', 158.

[39] Some proponents of the DDE may protest that the large man being crushed is so close to the act of jumping into the alcove that it must form part of the five's intention in jumping, and thus the DDE can prohibit the five from jumping. But this response robs the DDE of its ability to distinguish between many of the paradigm puzzling cases, for example, Strategic Bomber and Terror Bomber. Killing the civilians might be similarly close to the act of bombing the military target in Strategic Bomber. More generally, this response simply illustrates one of the DDE's most well-known difficulties: the notorious problem of closeness. For illuminating discussions of this problem, see Jonathan Bennett, *The Act Itself* (Oxford: Oxford University Press, 1995), esp. 210–13; Nancy Davis, 'The Doctrine of Double Effect: Problems of Interpretation', *Pacific Philosophical Quarterly* 65, no. 2 (1984): 107–23; John Martin Fischer, Mark Ravizza, and David Copp, 'Quinn on Double Effect: The Problem of "Closeness"', *Ethics* 103, no. 4 (1993): 707–25; and Victor Tadros, 'Wrongful Intentions without Closeness', *Philosophy & Public Affairs* 43, no. 1 (2015): 52–74.

Decoy House: A group of ten innocent civilians in the midst of a civil war is fleeing some culpable soldiers who are trying to kill them. The civilians are at grave risk of being found and killed by the soldiers unless they can deceive them regarding their location. The civilians come across a farmhouse and realize that if they leave false evidence that they have entered the house and are hiding there, the soldiers will stop and search the house. This will give the civilians enough time to escape to safety. But the civilians correctly anticipate that the soldiers will, during the search, interrogate and kill the two innocent people who own and live in the farmhouse.

The means principle correctly prohibits the civilians from using the farmhouse in this way. Other moral principles, such as Utility and the DDE, cannot explain the intuitive wrongness of using the farmhouse as a decoy in this way.

The means principle, however, has more permissive implications regarding cases where one agent is duty bound to provide resources to another. Consider the following case:

Medication: Betty has a heart condition and is having a cardiac episode. There is a medication that can avert the worst effects of the episode and save her life, but Betty can't afford the medication. Albert has the relevant medication, and could give Betty what she needs at no great cost to himself. Albert, however, refuses. Carl is a bystander who can use force against Albert (e.g., painfully twisting his arm behind his back) to get him to give the medication to Betty.

Following the arguments in Chapter 5, I believe Albert has a duty of rescue to provide Betty with the medication. Because he is duty bound to provide this aid, Carl can harm him as a means of getting him to provide the medication to Betty. Not only is it permissible for Carl to do so, there is no special presumption against harmfully using him in this way: he is liable to be used in this way. The means principle is thus able to explain why it is not always wrong to harmfully use some people as a means, even when the people being used pose no direct threat to others. When we fail in our duties to provide others with aid, we make ourselves liable to proportionate forms of harmful use, and thus there is no special presumption against this harmful use. Alternative moral principles, such as the DDE, which focus on the pro tanto badness of intending harm or intending use, may find it more difficult to reach this verdict.

7.6 Intentions and Permissibility

I have argued for a version of the means principle where the acting agent's intentions are irrelevant to the question of whether the acting agent wrongfully harms someone as a means. Some might worry that this view will yield counter-intuitive results when we consider the use of defensive force against agents who act with bad intentions. If some competing principle, such as the DDE, had more intuitive implications regarding the use of defensive force against agents with bad intentions, that would be a reason to be sceptical of the means principle. In this section, I'll argue that this worry is misplaced.

Recall the following variant of Murders Averted:

> *Murders Averted (Worst Motive)*: Betty is about to murder two innocent people for the sake of an inheritance. Albert is aware of all the facts, and he realizes that the only way to save the lives of the innocent people is if he shoots and kills Betty immediately. He shoots and kills Betty because he hates Betty; saving the innocent people is a foreseen but unintended consequence of Albert's act.

Some believe that Albert acts impermissibly because of his bad intention. Others, including me, believe Albert acts permissibly despite his bad intention. Does this disagreement about the permissibility of Albert's act generate further disagreements about the morality of defensive force? Consider two important questions. The first is whether Betty can use lethal defensive force against Albert to save her life. The second is whether it is morally permissible for a third party to impose harm on Albert to prevent him from killing Betty. Perhaps surprisingly, whether Albert acts permissibly need not determine our answers to these questions. Those who believe that Albert acts permissibly will conclude that he is not liable to defensive force, and thus it cannot be permissible for either Betty, or a third party, to use defensive force on Albert. Those who believe that Albert acts impermissibly can reach the same conclusion via a slightly more complex route. They can say:

> By acting impermissibly in attempting to kill Betty, Albert renders himself potentially liable to defensive force. But although he is potentially liable to defensive force, it is not permissible for anyone to impose the force on him. It is not permissible for Betty to do so, since she forfeits her liberty right to use defensive force by virtue of her wrongful attack on the innocent people. And it is not permissible for a third party to kill Albert in defence of Betty because doing so is not widely proportionate. It would result in one liable person being killed (Albert) and two non-liable persons being killed (the two innocent people Betty murders), whereas doing nothing would result only in one liable person (Betty) being killed.

So even if we cannot agree on whether Albert acts permissibly, this turns out to have little practical relevance to the immediate question of whether defensive force can be permissibly imposed on Albert.

What about the following pair of cases:

Albert's Bluff: Albert maliciously decides to scare Betty. He points what he knows to be an unloaded gun at Betty's head and says, 'I'm going to blow your brains out.' Betty, believing Albert's threat to be real, pulls out her own gun and kills Albert in 'self-defence'.

Carl's Bluff: Carl maliciously decides to scare Betty. He points what he knows to be an unloaded gun at Betty's head and says, 'I'm going to blow your brains out.' Betty believes Carl's gun is unloaded, but she has always hated Carl, and so she takes this opportunity to pull out her own gun and kills Carl in 'self-defence'.

Proponents of the DDE might argue this pair of cases illustrates the salience of intentions to the permissible use of defensive force. Surely, the proponent might say, Betty acts permissibly in the first case but not in the second, and this fact is explained by what she intends in each case. And because she acts permissibly in the first case but not the second, this will have further implications for whether defensive force can be imposed on her. It would be wrong for a third party to seriously harm Betty in the first case to defend Albert, but it would not be wrong for a third party to seriously harm Betty in the second case to defend Carl.

But we don't need to appeal to intentions to reach these conclusions. If Betty knows the gun is unloaded in the second case but not the first, then she has different evidence in the two cases. In the second case, she has sufficient evidence that killing Carl is unnecessary. It's wrong to kill someone when you have sufficient evidence that doing so is unnecessary. Conversely, if the evidence gives her a justified reason to believe that the gun is loaded in the first case, then she acts permissibly in the evidence-relative sense. We thus don't need to appeal to Betty's intentions to distinguish the two cases: we only need to appeal to differences in Betty's evidence.

One might protest that this pair of cases is too easy. Suppose, in Carl's Bluff, that Betty *unjustifiably* believes the gun is not loaded, that is, the evidence ought to lead her to believe the gun is loaded, but she mistakenly forms the true belief that the gun is not loaded. And because she has always hated Carl, she takes this opportunity to pull out her own gun and kill Carl in 'self-defence'. If Betty acts impermissibly in this version of the example, this can only be explained by appeal to her intentions. This case is unusual because the belief-relative and fact-relative standards converge (Betty's act is impermissible), but diverge from the evidence-relative standard (Betty's act is permissible).

But, once again, any disagreement about the permissibility of Betty's act turns out to be irrelevant to the further question of whether defensive force can be permissibly imposed on her. As I argued in previous chapters, in cases like this one, Carl has made himself liable to lethal defensive force; he has given Betty sufficient evidence that he is about to murder her. Thus even if Betty unjustifiably but correctly believes that Carl's gun is unloaded, it would be wrong for a third party to kill Betty to save Carl. He is liable and she is not. In this version of the case, Betty is analogous to someone who crazily believes that she doesn't need to use defensive force against an aggressor because she can jump to safety off the roof of a skyscraper. Even if this crazy belief somehow turned out to be true, so long as the defensive agent has no evidence for the belief then the wrongful aggressor remains fully liable to defensive force. The necessity condition must be indexed to the evidence we can reasonably expect the defensive agent to possess with regard to the threat and her other options.[40]

Even when we disagree about whether a person's intentions render her act impermissible, we can often still agree about whether the person is liable to defensive force, and we can often agree about what harms that different people might be permitted to impose in self-defence or in defence of others. I have argued that the means principle can explain the puzzling cases without appealing to the agent's intentions. If intentions also make little difference to many judgements about the morality of using defensive force against someone who acts with bad intentions, this strengthens the case for the means principle.

7.7 Conclusion

The means principle that I have defended in this chapter is part of a broader rights-based account of the morality of defensive force. In closing, there are two main features of this account that I would like to highlight.

First, I have emphasized that rights are moral demands that we make of each other. More specifically, if Betty has a right that Albert refrain from φ-ing, this means that she can reasonably demand that Albert refrain from φ-ing. Conversely, if her demand is unreasonable, Albert is under no duty to Betty to refrain from φ-ing. Moral rights are, in this way, mid-level moral concepts embedded in a wider normative theory—a theory that provides a framework for determining when one person can reasonably make demands of another.

This fact about moral rights has important implications. One implication—the focus of Chapter 6—is that we do not possess general, fact-relative rights against harm. We cannot demand that others refrain from performing any act that might cause us harm, since others are often not in a position to realize that their act poses any undue risk of harm. Our rights against harm are indexed to the information that we can reasonably expect others to possess regarding the

---

[40] See Lazar, 'Necessity in Self-Defense and War'.

potential consequences of their acts. Another implication—the focus of the present chapter—is that our rights against harm are not usually indexed to the intentions of the duty bearer. It typically doesn't matter what a duty bearer intends to do; duty bearers can wrong us without intending to do so, and they can also fail to wrong us even if they intend to.

Although I think this is true of most moral rights, I've focused on a narrower thesis: that we each possess rights against being used as a means. These rights prohibit others—regardless of their intentions—from using our bodies and our other property in pursuit of valuable objectives, unless we are duty bound to allow such use or have consented to it. By focusing on rights-as-demands, we avoid two common misconceptions. First, a right not to be harmed is not a claim that a certain state of affairs obtains: a state of affairs where no person's act causes us harm. Second, a right not to be harmed is not a claim that others form particular attitudes or intentions. A right not to be harmed is rather a claim that others' behaviour conform to certain reasonable standards of conduct—standards that are, at least in principle, publicly verifiable. Omniscience isn't a requirement to successfully avoid violating the rights of others. Conversely, we needn't have access to the mental states of others to judge whether our rights against harm are being threatened.

Let's turn to a second issue. Non-consequentialist constraints can seem puzzling, since they are sometimes presented as having intrinsic and nonderivative ethical significance. Why should there be a moral difference between doing as opposed to allowing harm, if this distinction simply supervenes on some non-moralized account of causation? Why should it matter whether an agent intends harm as opposed to merely foresees harm, when all the consequences remain the same? How can the location of a person's body in the causal chain of events have intrinsic significance? When presented in this way—as independent from any more general moral or political theory—the constraints seem mysterious. They may cohere with our intuitions in various cases, but they don't appear to reflect anything else that we take ourselves to have good reason to care about.

The view of moral rights that I've defended in this chapter, and throughout the book, hopefully goes some way towards addressing this worry. I have presented a view of moral rights as mid-level moral concepts. They constrain our behaviour because they form part of a more general theory of how free and equal persons can interact with one another on fair terms. We cannot make sense of the means principle, for example, without this more general picture. Principles of distributive justice allocate to each person rights to control a fair share of the world. The special prohibition against harmfully using another person's body or property is a reflection of this more general ideal. If a person is not duty bound to use her body or resources to pursue some greater good, then others cannot use her body or resources to pursue that greater good. This is part and parcel of what it means to allocate to each person a fair share of independent control over the world.

Our rights thus depend on a more general set of principles that regulate how free and equal persons can interact on fair terms. The same is true of the moral principles regulating the use of defensive force. The use of defensive force is sometimes the best way to protect a person's sphere of freedom or independence. If Albert acts as if Betty lacks moral rights that persons normally possess, then if Betty has done nothing to waive or forfeit her rights, Albert treats Betty unjustly. He fails to respect her rightful claims over the world, and thus renders himself liable to defensive force. To know whether someone is liable to defensive force, we thus must already have in hand a rich picture of the sort of moral rights that individuals possess over their bodies and the external world. This is remains true even when we consider the use of defensive force against non-liable persons, since such force must still serve to protect a person's rightful share of the world. Similarly, we can't make sense of the constraints on the use of defensive force without a more general picture of the duties that we owe to each other. Whether a given use of defensive force against an attacker is proportionate depends on understanding the stringency of the moral rights being threatened by the attacker. Whether a given use of defensive force is necessary, by contrast, turns on whether the use of force is consistent with the duty of rescue that we owe to each person, a duty that we owe even to wrongful aggressors.

The morality of defensive force is sometimes presented as a distinct topic, one that can be studied in relative isolation from theories of justice. One of my aims in this book has been to reject this view. If we want to understand the principles that regulate the use of defensive force, we need to understand how these principles cohere with our broader views about rights and justice. Because the morality of defensive force is, in this way, integrated within a broader rights-based moral theory, studying defensive force can also be a vehicle for reaching new insights about the nature of moral rights and justice.

Bibliography

Alexander, Larry. 'The Means Principle.' In Kimberly Kessler Ferzan and Stephen J. Morse, eds, *Legal, Moral and Metaphysical Truths: The Philosophy of Michael Moore*, 251–64. Oxford: Oxford University Press, 2016.

Alexander, Larry, and Kimberly Kessler Ferzan with Stephen Morse. *Crime and Culpability: A Theory of Criminal Law*. Cambridge: Cambridge University Press, 2009.

Appiah, Kwame Anthony. *Experiments in Ethics*. Cambridge, MA: Harvard University Press, 2008.

Bazargan, Saba. 'Killing Minimally Responsible Threats.' *Ethics* 125 (2014): 114–36.

Bazargan, Saba. 'Defensive Liability Without Culpability.' In Christian Coons and Michael Weber, eds, *The Ethics of Self-Defense*, 69–85. New York: Oxford University Press, 2016.

Bazargan-Forward, Saba. 'Vesting Agent-Relative Permissions in a Proxy.' *Law and Philosophy* 37 (2018): 671–95.

Bennett, Jonathan. *The Act Itself*. Oxford: Oxford University Press, 1995.

Bolinger, Renée Jorgensen. 'Mistaken Defense and Normative Conventions.' PhD Dissertation, University of Southern California, 2017.

Bolinger, Renée Jorgensen. 'The Moral Grounds of Mistaken Self-Defense' (unpublished).

Brownlee, Kimberley and Zofia Stemplowska. 'Thought Experiments.' In Adrian Blau, ed., *Methods in Analytical Political Theory*, 21–45. Cambridge: Cambridge University Press, 2017.

Burri, Susanne. 'The Toss-Up Between a Profiting, Innocent Threat and His Victim.' *Journal of Political Philosophy* 23 (2015): 146–65.

Cohen, G. A. *Rescuing Justice and Equality*. Cambridge, MA: Harvard University Press, 2008.

Davis, Nancy. 'Abortion and Self-Defense.' *Philosophy & Public Affairs* 13 (1984): 175–207.

Davis, Nancy. 'The Doctrine of Double Effect: Problems of Interpretation.' *Pacific Philosophical Quarterly* 65 (1984): 107–23.

Dietz, Alexander. 'What We Together Ought to Do.' *Ethics* 126 (2016): 955–82.

Doggett, Tyler. 'Killing Innocent People.' *Nous* 52 (2018): 645–66.

Draper, Kaila. 'Fairness and Self-Defense.' *Social Theory and Practice* 19 (1993): 73–92.

Draper, Kaila. 'Defense.' *Philosophical Studies* 145 (2009): 69–88.

Draper, Kaila. *War and Individual Rights*. Oxford: Oxford University Press, 2016.

Dworkin, Ronald. *Sovereign Virtue: The Theory and Practice of Equality*. Cambridge, MA: Harvard University Press, 2000.

Estlund, David. 'On Following Orders in an Unjust War.' *Journal of Political Philosophy* 15 (2007): 213–34.

Fabre, Cécile. 'Permissible Rescue Killings.' *Proceeding of the Aristotelian Society* 109 (2009): 149–64.

Fabre, Cécile. *Cosmopolitan War*. Oxford: Oxford University Press, 2014.

Ferzan, Kimberly Kessler. 'Justifying Self-Defense.' *Law and Philosophy* 24 (2005): 711–49.

Ferzan, Kimberly Kessler. 'Self-Defense, Permissions, and the Means Principle: A Reply to Quong.' *Ohio State Journal of Criminal Law* 8 (2011): 503–13.

Ferzan, Kimberly Kessler. 'Culpable Aggression: The Basis for Moral Liability to Defensive Killing.' *Ohio State Journal of Criminal Law* 9 (2012): 669–97.

Ferzan, Kimberly Kessler. 'The Bluff: The Power of Insincere Actions.' *Legal Theory* 23 (2017): 168–202.

Finnis, John. 'The Rights and Wrongs of Abortion: A Reply to Judith Thomson.' *Philosophy & Public Affairs* 2 (1973): 117–45.

Firth, Joanna Mary, and Jonathan Quong. 'Necessity, Morality Liability, and Defensive Harm.' *Law and Philosophy* 31 (2012): 673–701.

Fischer, John Martin, Mark Ravizza, and David Copp. 'Quinn on Double Effect: The Problem of Closeness.' *Ethics* 103 (1993): 707–25.

Frick, Johann. 'What We Owe to Hypocrites: Contractualism and the Speaker-Relativity of Justification.' *Philosophy & Public Affairs* 44 (2016): 223–65.

Frowe, Helen. 'Equating Innocent Threats and Bystanders.' *Journal of Applied Philosophy* 25 (2008): 277–90.

Frowe, Helen. *Defensive Killing*. Oxford: Oxford University Press, 2014.

Frowe, Helen. 'Claim Rights, Duties, and Lesser Evil Justifications.' *Proceedings of the Aristotelian Society Supplementary Volume* LXXXIX (2015): 267–85.

Frowe, Helen. 'If You'll be My Bodyguard: Agreements to Save and the Duty to Minimize Harm.' *Ethics* 129 (2019): 204–29.

Gardner, John, and François Tanguay-Renaud. 'Desert and Avoidability in Self-Defense.' *Ethics* 122 (2011): 111–34.

Gordon-Solmon, Kerah. 'Self-Defence Against Multiple Threats,' *Journal of Moral Philosophy* 14 (2017): 125–33.

Gordon-Solmon, Kerah. 'What Makes a Person Liable to Defensive Harm?' *Philosophy and Phenomenological Research* 97 (2018): 543–67.

Graham, Peter. 'In Defense of Objectivism About Moral Obligation.' *Ethics* 121 (2010): 88–115.

Green, Joshua D. 'The Secret Joke of Kant's Soul.' In Walter Sinnott-Armstrong, ed., *Moral Psychology Vol. 3: The Neuroscience of Morality: Emotion, Brain Disorders, and Development*, 35–79. Cambridge, MA: MIT Press, 2008.

Hanser, Matthew. 'Permissibility and Practical Inference.' *Ethics* 115 (2005): 443–70.

Horton, Joe. 'Aggregation, Complaints, and Risk.' *Philosophy & Public Affairs* 45 (2017): 54–81.

Horton, Joe. 'Always Aggregate.' *Philosophy & Public Affairs* 46 (2018): 160–74.

Jackson, Frank. 'Decision-Theoretic Consequentialism and the Nearest and Dearest Objection.' *Ethics* 101 (1991): 461–82.

Kagan, Shelly. *The Limits of Morality*. Oxford: Clarendon Press, 1989.

Kamm, F. M. *Creation and Abortion: A Study in Moral and Legal Philosophy*. New York: Oxford University Press, 1992.

Kamm, F. M. *Intricate Ethics: Rights Responsibilities, and Permissible Harm*. Oxford: Oxford University Press, 2007.

Kamm, F. M. 'Terrorism and Intending Evil.' *Philosophy & Public Affairs* 36 (2008): 157–86.

Kasachkoff, Tziporah. 'Killing in Self-Defense: An Unquestionable or Problematic Defense?' *Law and Philosophy* 17 (1998): 509–31.

Lang, Gerald. 'Why Not Forfeiture?' In Helen Frowe and Gerald Land, eds, *How We Fight: Ethics in War*, 38–61. Oxford: Oxford University Press, 2014.

Lang, Gerald. 'What Follows from Non-Liability?' *Proceedings of the Aristotelian Society* 117 (2017): 231–52.

Lazar, Seth. 'Responsibility, Risk, and Killing in Self-Defense.' *Ethics* 119 (2009): 699–728.

Lazar, Seth. 'The Responsibility Dilemma for *Killing in War*: A Review Essay.' *Philosophy & Public Affairs* 38 (2010), 180–213.

Lazar, Seth. 'Necessity in Self-Defense and War.' *Philosophy & Public Affairs* 40 (2012): 3–44.

Lazar, Seth. 'Associative Duties and the Ethics of Killing in War.' *Journal of Practical Ethics* 1 (2013): 3–48.

Lazar, Seth. 'Authorization and the Morality of War.' *Australasian Journal of Philosophy* 94 (2016): 211–26.

Lazar, Seth. 'Limited Aggregation and Risk.' *Philosophy & Public Affairs* 46 (2018): 117–59.

Leverick, Fiona. *Killing in Self-Defence*. Oxford: Oxford University Press, 2006.

Levine, Susan. 'The Moral Permissibility of Killing a "Material Aggressor" in Self-Defense.' *Philosophical Studies* 45 (1984): 69–78.

Liao, Matthew. 'Intentions and Moral Permissibility: The Case of Acting Permissibly with Bad Intentions.' *Law and Philosophy* 31 (2012): 703–24.

McMahan, Jeff. 'Self-Defense and the Problem of the Innocent Attacker.' *Ethics* 104 (1994): 252–90.

McMahan, Jeff. *The Ethics of Killing: Problems at the Margins of Life*. New York: Oxford University Press, 2002.

McMahan, Jeff. 'The Basis of Moral Liability to Defensive Killing.' *Philosophical Issues* 15 (2005): 386–405.

McMahan, Jeff. 'Debate: Justification and Liability in War.' *Journal of Political Philosophy* 16 (2008), 227–44.

McMahan, Jeff. 'Intention, Permissibility, Terrorism, and War,' *Philosophical Perspectives* 23 (2009): 345–72.

McMahan, Jeff. *Killing in War*. Oxford: Clarendon Press, 2009.

McMahan, Jeff. 'Who is Morally Liable to be Killed in War.' *Analysis* 71 (2011): 544–59.

McMahan, Jeff. 'Duty, Obedience, Desert, and Proportionality in War: A Response.' *Ethics* 122 (2011): 135–67.

McMahan, Jeff. 'Moral Intuition.' In Hugh LaFollette and Ingmar Persson, eds, *Blackwell Guide to Ethical Theory, Second Edition*, 103–22. Oxford: Wiley-Blackwell, 2013.

McMahan, Jeff. 'What Rights May Be Defended by Means of War?' In Cécile Fabre and Seth Lazar, eds, *The Morality of Defensive War*, 115–58. Oxford: Oxford University Press, 2014.

McMahan, Jeff. 'Self-Defense Against Justified Threateners.' In Helen Frowe and Gerald Lang, eds, *How We Fight: Ethics in War*, 104–37. Oxford: Oxford University Press, 2014.

McMahan, Jeff. 'The Limits of Self-Defense.' In Christian Coons and Michael Weber, eds, *The Ethics of Self-Defense*, 185–210. New York: Oxford University Press, 2016.

Miller, David. 'Are Human Rights Conditional?' In Tetsu Sakurai and Makoto Usami, eds, *Human Rights and Global Justice: The 10th Kobe Lectures*, 17–35. Stuttgart: Franz Steiner Verlag, 2014.

Otsuka, Michael. 'Killing the Innocent in Self-Defense.' *Philosophy & Public Affairs* 23 (1994): 74–94.

Otsuka, Michael. 'Saving Lives, Moral Theory, and the Claims of Individuals.' *Philosophy & Public Affairs* 34 (2006): 109–35.

Otsuka, Michael. 'The Moral Responsibility-Account of Liability to Defensive Killing.' In Christian Coons and Michael Weber, eds, *The Ethics of Self-Defense*, 51–68. New York: Oxford University Press, 2016.

Øverland, Gerhard. 'Moral Obstacles: An Alternative to the Doctrine of Double Effect.' *Ethics* 124 (2014): 481–506.

Parfit, Derek. *On What Matters: Volume One*. Oxford: Oxford University Press, 2011.

Quinn, Warren. 'Actions, Intentions, and Consequences: The Doctrine of Double Effect.' *Philosophy & Public Affairs* 18 (1989): 334–51.

Quong, Jonathan. 'Liability to Defensive Harm.' *Philosophy & Public Affairs* 40 (2012): 45–77.

Quong, Jonathan. 'Rights.' In Gerald Gaus and Fred D'Agostino, eds, *The Routledge Companion to Social and Political Philosophy*, 618–28. New York: Routledge, 2014.

Quong, Jonathan. 'Contractualism.' In Adrian Blau, ed., *Methods in Analytical Political Theory*, 65–90. Cambridge: Cambridge University Press, 2017.

Quong, Jonathan. 'Miller's Crossing.' In Daniel Butt, Sarah Fine, and Zofia Stemplowska, eds, *Political Philosophy, Here and Now: Essays in Honour of David Miller*. Oxford: Oxford University Press, forthcoming.

Quong, Jonathan. 'Intentions and Permissibility: A Puzzling Asymmetry.' (unpublished).

Ramakrishnan, Ketan H. 'Treating People as Tools.' *Philosophy & Public Affairs* 44 (2016): 133–65.

Ramakrishnan, Ketan H. 'Quong on Defensive Harm.' (unpublished).

Restatement (Second) of Torts § 519 (1977).

Ripstein, Arthur. 'Self-Defense and Equal Protection.' *University of Pittsburgh Law Review* 57 (1996): 685–724.

Ripstein, Arthur. *Equality, Responsibility, and the Law*. Cambridge: Cambridge University Press, 1999.

Ripstein, Arthur. *Private Wrongs*. Cambridge, MA: Harvard University Press, 2016.

Rodin, David. *War and Self-Defense*. Oxford: Clarendon Press, 2002.

Rodin, David. 'Justifying Harm.' *Ethics* 122 (2011): 74–110.

Rodin, David. 'The Reciprocity Theory of Rights.' *Law and Philosophy* 33 (2014): 281–308.

Scanlon, T. M. *What We Owe to Each Other*. Cambridge, MA: Harvard University Press, 1998.

Scanlon, T. M. *Moral Dimensions: Permissibility, Meaning, Blame*. Cambridge, MA: Belknap Press of Harvard University Press, 2008.

Scheffler, Samuel. *The Rejection of Consequentialism: A Philosophical Investigation of the Considerations Underlying Rival Moral Conceptions*. Oxford: Clarendon Press, 1982.

Scheffler, Samuel. 'What is Egalitarianism?' *Philosophy & Public Affairs* 31 (2003): 5–39.

Sinclair, Thomas, and Jonathan Quong. 'The Means Principle: Still in Need of a Rationale.' (unpublished).

Singer, Peter. 'Ethics and Intuitions.' *Journal of Ethics* 9 (2005): 331–52.

Sinnott-Armstrong, Walter. 'Framing Moral Intuitions.' In Walter Sinnott-Armstrong, ed., *Moral Psychology, Vol. 2: The Cognitive Science of Morality: Intuition and Diversity*, 47–76. Cambridge, MA: MIT Press, 2008.

Steiner, Hillel. *An Essay on Rights*. Oxford: Blackwell, 1994.

Steinhoff, Uwe. 'Debate: Jeff McMahan on the Moral Inequality of Combatants.' *Journal of Political Philosophy* 16 (2008): 220–26.

Stone, Rebecca. 'Private Liability without Wrongdoing.' (unpublished manuscript).

Strawser, Bradley Jay. 'Walking the Tightrope of Just War.' *Analysis* 71 (2011): 533–44.

Tadros, Victor. *The Ends of Harm: The Moral Foundations of the Criminal Law*. Oxford: Oxford University Press, 2011.

Tadros, Victor. 'Duty and Liability.' *Utilitas* 24 (2012): 259–77.

Tadros, Victor. 'Resource Wars.' *Law and Philosophy* 33 (2014): 361–89.

Tadros, Victor. 'Orwell's Battle with Brittain: Vicarious Liability for Unjust Aggression.' *Philosophy & Public Affairs* 42 (2014): 42–77.

Tadros, Victor. 'Wrongful Intentions Without Closeness.' *Philosophy & Public Affairs* 43 (2015): 52–74.

Tadros, Victor. 'Causation, Culpability, and Liability.' In Christian Coons and Michael Weber, eds, *The Ethics of Self-Defense*, 110–30. New York: Oxford University Press, 2016.

Tadros, Victor. 'Localised Restricted Aggregation.' In David Sobel, Peter Vallentyne, and Steven Walls, eds, *Oxford Studies in Political Philosophy*, Vol. 5, 171–203. Oxford: Oxford University Press, 2019.

Thomson, Judith Jarvis. 'A Defense of Abortion.' *Philosophy & Public Affairs* 1 (1971): 47–66.

Thomson, Judith Jarvis. *Rights, Restitution, and Risk: Essays in Moral Theory.* William Parent, ed. Cambridge, MA: Harvard University Press, 1986.

Thomson, Judith Jarvis. *The Realm of Rights.* Cambridge, MA: Harvard University Press, 1990.

Thomson, Judith Jarvis. 'Self-Defense.' *Philosophy & Public Affairs* 20 (1991): 283–310.

Tomlin, Patrick. 'On Limited Aggregation.' *Philosophy & Public Affairs* 45 (2017): 232–60.

Uniacke, Suzanne. *Permissible Killing: The Self-Defence Justification of Homicide.* Cambridge: Cambridge University Press, 1994.

Uniacke, Suzanne. 'Proportionality and Self-Defense.' *Law and Philosophy* 30 (2011): 253–72.

Van der Vossen, Bas. 'Uncertain Rights Against Defense.' *Social Philosophy & Policy* 32 (2016): 129–45.

Viehoff, Daniel. 'Legitimately Arresting the Innocent, and Other Puzzles About Officially Inflicted Harm.' (unpublished).

Voorhoeve, Alex. 'How Should We Aggregate Competing Claims?' *Ethics* 125 (2014): 64–87.

Walen, Alec. 'Transcending the Means Principle.' *Law and Philosophy* 33 (2014): 427–64.

Walen, Alec. 'The Restricting Claims Principle Revisited: Grounding the Means Principle on the Agent–Patient Divide.' *Law and Philosophy* 35 (2016), 211–47.

Wedgwood, Ralph. 'Scanlon on Double Effect.' *Philosophy and Phenomenological Research* LXXXIII (2011): 464–72.

Zimmerman, Michael. 'Is Moral Obligation Objective or Subjective?' *Utilitas* 18 (2006): 329–61.

Zimmerman, Michael. *Living with Uncertainty: The Moral Significance of Ignorance.* Cambridge: Cambridge University Press, 2008.

Zimmerman, Michael. *Ignorance and Moral Obligation.* Oxford: Oxford University Press, 2014.

Zohar, Noam. 'Collective War and Individualistic Ethics: Against the Conscription of "Self-Defense".' *Political Theory* 21 (1993): 606–22.

Index

For the benefit of digital users, indexed terms that span two pages (e.g., 52–53) may, on occasion, appear on only one of those pages.

Printed and bound by CPI Group (UK) Ltd, Croydon, CR0 4YY